Movement in the Rights Direction

PENNSYLVANIA STUDIES IN HUMAN RIGHTS

Bert B. Lockwood, *Series Editor*

A complete list of books in the series
is available from the publisher.

MOVEMENT IN THE RIGHTS DIRECTION

An Ethnography of the UN Human Rights Committee

Miia Halme-Tuomisaari

PENN

UNIVERSITY OF PENNSYLVANIA PRESS

PHILADELPHIA

Publication of this book was supported by a grant from
Stiftelsen Landshövding Per Westlings minnesfond

Published by
University of Pennsylvania Press
Philadelphia, Pennsylvania 19104–4112 USA
www.pennpress.org

EU Authorized Representative: Easy Access
System Europe—Mustamäe tee 50, 10621 Tallinn,
Estonia, gpsr.requests@easproject.com

Printed in the United States of America on acid-free paper
10 9 8 7 6 5 4 3 2 1

A Cataloging-in-Publication Data record is
available from the Library of Congress

Hardcover ISBN 978-1-5128-3039-2
eBook ISBN 978-1-5128-3040-8

CONTENTS

ACKNOWLEDGMENTS

The idea for this book originated in March 2008 with the simple question: "Wouldn't it be interesting . . . ?" The question—uttered midway through the three-and-a-half-hour marathon defense of my doctoral dissertation—was posed by my external examiner, the late Sally Engle Merry, as we briefly discussed the practices of UN treaty bodies. I didn't make much of the question at the time, but it stuck with me. *Wouldn't it be interesting indeed* to study what transpires during these cycles: what visions of world improvement they uphold, which actors they engage, what knowledge practices accompany them, and what impact—construed in the broadest possible terms—they yield. Sadly, Sally Merry passed away before this book was completed, but my debt to her endures. I hope that my book, in a small way, contributes to her vast legacy in legal anthropology.

Simultaneously, the book's origins reach back further to the early new millennium, to another seemingly inconsequential moment of the Summer Seminar at the Erik Castrén Institute of International Law and Human Rights, University of Helsinki. As we prepared to welcome a new speaker to the podium, the student beside me gasped: "This is a very important person, a member of the UN Human Rights Committee!" An anthropology major with a keen interest in international law, I tried to keep cool and conceal that, in fact, I had neither the slightest idea what the UN Human Rights Committee was nor why its member was a *very important person*. Yet the remark stayed with me: there was evidently something special about the Committee, and I had to find out what.

That I eventually wrote an academic book on this—or any—topic owes an enormous debt to Martti Koskenniemi. He welcomed an anthropologist into a community of critical international lawyers, encouraging and challenging me at every turn as I moved from anthropology major to LLM student, PhD candidate, and professional academic. I would not be the scholar I am today without your guidance. My years spent at the Erik Castrén Institute

(2002–2012), including the Finnish Centre of Excellence in Global Governance Research (2008–2009), were instrumental in shaping my thinking. Pivotal were the Academy of Finland project "Human Rights: Law, Religion, Subjectivity" (2009–2012) and the Kone Foundation–funded project "Bodies of Evidence" (2014–2016). My warmest thanks to Jan Klabbers, Pamela Slotte, Tuomas Ojanen, Ilpo Helén, Jukka Siikala, Heikki Patomäki, Mari Tapaninen, Marie-Louise Karttunen, Kaius Tuori, Jarna Petman, Päivi Leino-Sandberg, Jasper Krommendijk, Freek van der Vet, and Monica Garcia-Salmones, as well as our wonderful administrators Åsa Wallendahl and Sanna Villikka.

The year I spent in 2013 at the Department of Law and Anthropology at the Max Planck Institute for Social Anthropology in Halle/Saale contributed significantly to the research. Warm thanks to Marie-Claire Foblets, Andrea Klein, Bertram Turner, Christoph Brumann, Katrin Seidel, and Maria Sapignoli. The Global Governance Centre of the Geneva Graduate Institute of International and Development Studies provided a source of inspiration during numerous years of affiliation and visiting research stays. Warm thanks to Thomas Biersteker, Isabelle Schulte-Tenkhoff, Cecilia Cannon, Velibor Jakolevski, Annabel Littoz-Monet, Niko Krisch, Alessandro Monsutti, Monique Beerli, Fuad Zarbiyev, Andrea Biachi, Andrew Clapham, Camila Morais Silva, and Sylvia Nissam, and to many of the institute's researchers and students for fruitful exchanges. Yet another formative context was the Geneva Academy's Academic Platform on UN Treaty Body Strengthening. Warm thanks to Felix Kirchmeier, Kamelia Kemileva, and Domenico Zipoli.

Special thanks to Joshua Clark, Ukri Soirila, and Walter Kälin for diligently reading and commenting on every chapter! Thanks to Greg Feldman, Carole McGranahan, Elif Babul, Tommaso Soave, Reetta Toivanen, and Jasper Krommedijk for commenting on individual chapters, and to the two anonymous reviewers for their generous and helpful reports. Particular thanks to Jane Cowan for comments, guidance, and mentorship. Warm thanks to the many colleagues who have engaged with my project in diverse ways, including as editors of papers that enabled me to develop different strands of arguments included here, and as panel chairs when I presented those papers: Sarah Green, Marie-Bénédicte Dembour, Annelise Riles, Galit Sarfati, Lieselotte Viane, Lene Pedersen, Lisa Cligget, Ronald Niezen, Julia Eckert, Samuel Moyn, Conor Gearty, Harri Englund, Theodoris Kyriakides, Mark Goodale, Outi Korhonen, Tobias Kelly, Cris Shore, Heath Cabot, Erica Weiss, Negar Mansouri, and Daniel Quiroga-Villamarin. Thanks to my colleagues at Allegra Lab, including Julie Billaud, Judith Beyer, Antonio De

Lauri, Luigi Achille, Felix Kirke, and Taina Tuori, Lotta Haikkola, Henrik Rydenfelt, Anna-Maija Castrén, Suvi Kansikas, Aino Kuusava, Ninnu Koskenalho, and Alina Rapin at our Helsinki headquarters.

The book would not have been possible without the open-mindedness and generosity of my interlocutors at the UN Human Rights Committee, the UN Office of the High Commissioner for Human Rights, numerous NGOs, and the Unit for Human Rights Courts and Conventions at the Finnish Ministry for Foreign Affairs, as well as other Finnish ministries involved in human rights reporting. Special thanks to the late Sir Nigel Rodley, Yuval Shany, Zonke Majodina, Margo Waterfal, Fabian Salvioli, Gerard Neuman, Cornelis Flinterman, Konstantine Vardzelashvili, Victor Rodriguez, Anja Seibert-Fort, Michael O'Flaherty, Eibe Riedel, Simon Walker, Kate Fox, Arto Kosonen, Krista Oinonen, Päivi Mattila, Niina Lavapuro, Aija Salo, Päivi Pietarinen, Viveca Arhenius, Heini Huotari, Maija Iles, and Patrick Mutzenberg. Thanks to the members of the UN conference services, interpreters, and press officers for giving me their precious time—and to the wonderful lady at the Palais Wilson cafeteria who never forgot my afternoon snack order of "une pomme."

That the manuscript grew from a series of sketches into a full-length monograph owes an enormous debt to the generosity of the Helsinki Collegium for Advanced Studies, which granted me a two-year Fellowship (2018–2020). Warmest thanks to the Collegium team: Tuomas Forsberg (also for supporting me when finishing felt difficult), Hanne Appelqvist, and Kaisa Kaakinen, as well as many colleagues for camaraderie and fruitful debates, including Karoliina Snell, Elina Hartikainen, Elisabeth Holmqvist-Sipilä, Kirsi Lonka, Silva Nurmio, Emilia Mataix Ferrantis, Visa Kurki, and Jaana Simola. Thanks to my superb research assistants Suvi Huotari and Adam Rodriguez. Warmest thanks for diligent commenting and wonderful copyediting to Helen Faller.

Thanks to my colleagues at the Unit of Human Rights Studies at Lund University for welcoming me so warmly and for providing a setting to revise the manuscript with inspiring exchanges: Lena Halldenius, Lina Sturfelt, Dan-Erik Andersson, Andreas Tullberg, Olof Beckman, Erik Brandstedt, Kristina Robertson, Henrik Rosengren, Malin Arvidsson, Karin Zacchari, and Elizabeth Rhoades. Warmest thanks to my students for stimulating exchanges during our classes and supervision. Particular thanks to my brilliant research interns Dana Hausman, Lena Fonteyne, and Marianna Cambaldini. Special thanks to editors Bert Lockwood and Walter Biggins at the University of Pennsylvania Press for believing in my project and bringing it to completion.

Parts of this book have been presented at international conferences, including the American Anthropological Association's Annual Meetings, the European Association for Social Anthropologists' Biennial Conferences, and the German Anthropological Association's Biennial Conference. Its development has also benefited from invited lectures at the London School of Economics, the Geneva Graduate Institute of International and Development Studies, and the Universities of Konstanz, Sussex, Turku, Lund, and Helsinki, among others. Sections of Chapter 2 have appeared in "Methodologically Blonde at the UN in a Tactical Quest for Inclusion," *Social Anthropology / Anthropologie Sociale* 26(4), 456–470 (2018); Chapter 4 in "Guarding Utopia: Law, Vulnerability and Frustration at the UN Human Rights Committee," *Social Anthropology / Anthropologie Sociale* 28(1), 35–49 (2020); Chapter 6 in "From the Periphery to the Center: Emergence of the Human Rights Phenomenon in Finland," in *Finnish Yearbook of International Law*, ed. J. Klabbers and T. Tuori (Leiden: Brill, 2016), 257–281; and Chapter 7 in "Meeting 'the World' at the Palais Wilson: Embodied Universalism at the UN Human Rights Committee," in *Palaces of Hope: Anthropology of the United Nations*, ed. R. Niezen and M. Sapignoli (Cambridge: Cambridge University Press, 2017), 127–151. I thank the editors and publishers for permission to reproduce content from those publications.

It takes a village to raise a child—and it certainly takes a village for a mom to write a book. When the idea for this book was born, I was pregnant with our first child, Julius. He has since been joined by his younger brother, Noel, and both have grown into teenagers. During the writing process, my family accompanied me from Helsinki to New York, Halle, Geneva, Johannesburg, and Lund. The book would not exist were it not for our committed support network, which, when need be, traveled with us. Warmest thanks to my parents, Hannele and Lasse, for modeling uncompromising creative and scholarly work, and for the many days and nights you have spent with our boys. Thanks to my in-laws, Marjatta and Timo, for the many times you dashed in to help. Thanks to our valiant nanny, Krista, who joined us in both Halle and Geneva, and to my godmother, Helinä, who did the same. Neither this book nor my academic career would be possible without my husband Sami. The book is dedicated to him and our boys. Thanks for sticking with me—this is what Mommy was working on all that time!

—Helsinki, November 1, 2025

CHAPTER 1

Introduction

What happens inside the monitoring cycles of UN treaty bodies, and what impact do these cycles have locally and globally? What visions for world improvement do treaty body operations enact, and how do these visions relate to the universalizing ethos of human rights ideology? This book explores these questions from the vantage point of the UN Human Rights Committee, the treaty body that monitors state compliance with the International Covenant on Civil and Political Rights (ICCPR).[1]

The Human Rights Committee is regarded by many human rights scholars, state actors, and civil society activists as the most authoritative of the ten UN human rights treaty bodies monitoring central UN human rights treaties, including the International Covenant on Economic, Social, and Cultural Rights (CESCR), the Convention on the Elimination of All Forms of Discrimination Against Women (CEDAW), and the Convention on the Rights of the Child (CRC).[2]

By extension, in the continued, and perhaps permanent, absence of a UN human rights court, many scholars and activists view the Human Rights Committee as the UN's most lawlike and courtlike monitoring mechanism.[3] Simultaneously, both state representatives and scholars have challenged the effectiveness of UN treaty bodies, denoting them as an "empty diplomatic ritual."[4] Some scholars have already decades ago reflected on whether the entire UN treaty body framework is "in crisis."[5]

This book builds on prolonged multisited ethnography combined with rigorous documentary analysis to examine what transpires during the Human Rights Committee's monitoring cycles. It explores how states parties submit reports to explain their adherence to Covenant obligations, and how the Committee challenges these views with the assistance of shadow reports that NGOs submit. It digs deep into the icelike UN human rights apparatus to track how key insiders, denoted as Guardians of Vision, maneuver within it to facilitate the Committee's operations and to increase the salience of human rights within the UN and the world. Ultimately, the book describes how these reporting cycles form ongoing human rights dialogue, which aims to create *movement in the rights direction.*

The project's focus on movement builds both on the UN's own description of treaty body work as forming a never-ending cycle[6] and on ethnographic observations that depict movement as constitutive of these operations. Each treaty body session—occurring two or three times a year for a period of three to five weeks—activates manifold movements: avalanches of documents are exchanged between states, NGOs, and UN offices. Documents are accompanied by cohorts of treaty body members, state delegates, and NGO representatives, who all travel between their points of origin to Geneva and back.

At a more detailed level, I explore the multifaceted movement patterns and maneuvering through which the Human Rights Committee and its devoted insiders continually negotiate the Committee's mandate. The movement is anchored in Articles 36, 39, and 40 of the ICCPR, which established the Committee, with Article 36 stating: "The Committee shall establish its own rules of procedure."[7] The Committee has done precisely that, effectively extending the scope of its activities beyond what many states parties may have expected when the ICCPR entered into force five decades ago, an outcome provoking consistent opposition from some.

Movement metaphors were frequently used by my interlocutors to describe these operations and their outcomes. The "human rights movement" is further a common expression to refer especially to the civil society mobilization that human rights inspire.[8] Building on research focusing on global flows and "friction,"[9] to use Tsing's term,[10] as well as movement as constitutive of "life," to quote Ingold,[11] I dissect the movement accompanying the Human Rights Committee's sessions to examine the visions of world progress it embodies. I connect this inquiry to Eriksen's work on the continued acceleration of global processes resulting in "overheating."[12] By contrast, I examine the elements that remain constant—forming, in Latour's terms, "immutable mobiles"[13]—and reflect on how they form "pathways that make motion easier and more efficient" while, at the same time, limiting "where we go."[14]

"Movement in the rights direction" plays on the phrase's dual meaning: the notion of "rights direction" suggests a world where human rights hold an increasingly salient role, whereas "right direction" implies a single path for the development of humankind, contrasted with its opposite—the wrong direction.

The rhetoric of "right" and "wrong" is familiar from political speeches that refer to groups as being "with us or with the terrorists," to quote former US President George W. Bush, who memorably used such polarizing language.[15]

Scholars may likewise speak of states being on the right or wrong side of history, as in debates over the International Criminal Court and states that have chosen not to join it.[16] Scholars advocating for the recognition of distinct rights—for example, those of intersex people—may likewise describe legislative developments as "the right direction."[17] The notion of movement in a distinct direction is also embodied in the drafting history of the ICCPR and the ICESCR: in 1955, John Humphrey—the longtime director of the UN Human Rights Division and one of the core drafters of the Universal Declaration of Human Rights (UDHR), who was tasked with overseeing the treaties' drafting—wrote that "there has been no progress on the covenants." Instead, he noted, "some people would say that *the movement has been in the other direction*."[18]

On these bases the book advances two arguments. First, whereas the meaning and justification for such documentary processes as UN human rights treaty body reports are usually approached from their endpoints—the impact that they ideally have—I connect the ultimate meaning of these cycles to the very fact that they exist; that they create movement ideally steering the world *in the right direction*. I connect this insight to the forward-looking, progressive ethos of much human rights work and scholarship[19] to develop a rigorous argument on the consequent relationship between the past, present, and future. In making the argument, I tap into the affective elements of the Committee's work, as well as the Committee's knowledge practice and legal aesthetics, arguing that ultimately movement is sustained by hope and belief in a better future.

The second argument addresses what "movement in the rights direction" means in the Committee's operations. As subsequent chapters detail, the world improvement that the Human Rights Committee seeks to promote by its activities and documents does not consist of a random selection of initiatives deemed beneficial to the world. Rather, in the Committee's definition, world improvement consists of specific actions seen to ensure the increased realization of the ICCPR. I show how a tangible outcome of this goal is, paradoxically, the increased salience of the state as the central political and legal reference point, both domestically and internationally.

I examine how state centrality—embedded in the Committee's mandated role to assess state compliance with the Covenant—becomes manifested in the Committee's reporting cycles as they translate "real reality" into "UN reality."[20] I discuss how the Committee attempts, or fails, to address the state's role as both the central human rights violator and protector. Here my findings challenge the ethos of dominant human rights scholarship, which is geared toward curbing the power of states over individuals.

My analysis shows, instead, that the emphasis on the state as the primary political institution is tied to the notion of unilinear human progress—from the "savage" anarchy and lawlessness described by Hobbes and Kant to the modern juridical state, conceived as the culmination of the social contract.[21] Further, it reflects the belief that the rule of (state) law constitutes the ideal path to human advancement, mirroring the earlier civilizing mission of international law.[22] Finally, I discuss how "movement in the *right* direction"—whatever that might mean in the abstract—becomes distinct from "movement in the *rights* direction" as part of the Human Rights Committee's operations.

"No Sex, Drugs, or Rock 'n' Roll": Introducing the UN Human Rights Committee

The Human Rights Committee was founded in 1976, when the ICCPR entered into force, and began operations in 1978.[23] The eighteen-member Committee convenes annually for three sessions, each lasting about four weeks, in Geneva at the Palais Wilson, the headquarters of the UN Office for the High Commissioner for Human Rights (OHCHR). Committee members are nominated and elected by states for renewable four-year terms, yet they are expected to act as independent experts once appointed.[24] The Committee's proceedings entail both public and private sessions, and participants—depending on the session—include Committee members, UN Secretariat staff, state delegates, NGO representatives, scholars, and occasional members of the press, along with other observers.[25]

During each session, in public hearings called Constructive Dialogues, the Committee examines between five and eight periodic reports submitted by states parties on their compliance with the ICCPR.[26] The Dialogues—which are at the core of this book—are organized one state at a time at the Palais Wilson's conference room, and consist of two three-hour sessions that are open to the general public and webcast.[27] In these sessions only members of the Committee and state delegates may make formal interventions—as only states are parties to the Covenant—whereas civil society delegates have informal opportunities for engagement.

The Constructive Dialogues commence with statements from state delegates, followed by questions from Committee members and answers from state delegates that complement the information the state has submitted prior to the sessions in writing. The Dialogues are based on two documents: the List of Issues that the Committee adopts in the preceding session, which forms the backbone of the Dialogue; and the state report, in which the state party addresses the List of Issues by detailing how it has complied with relevant Covenant obligations. At the end of each session, the Committee prepares—or, more precisely, relevant UN staff prepare—a draft for a document called Concluding Observations, which the Committee subsequently discusses and adopts.[28]

All Concluding Observations for states reviewed during a session are published at the end of each session. They stipulate how, in the Committee's view, the state has complied with its Covenant-bound obligations and, ideally, improved its conduct since the previous state report examined by the Committee. They include recommendations that the Committee urges the state to implement, such as ratifying specific legislation.[29] Finally, they specify when the Committee expects to receive the state's next report—usually in six to twelve years—thus instigating the sustained reporting cycles that I examine. Unlike the Universal Periodic Review (UPR) by the UN Human Rights Council, states do not have the option to decide which recommendations they will accept or reject.[30] This follows from the reporting cycles' legal basis: states parties to the ICCPR have a legal duty to submit reports to the Committee, as Article 40 of the Covenant stipulates.[31]

From states that have joined the Covenant's Optional Protocol—117 of the 173 states that have ratified the ICCPR in 2023[32]—the Committee receives individual communications submitted by nationals of states parties, in response to which it delivers authoritative, legally nonbinding Views.[33] Deliberations on these Views occur in closed sessions, whereas the Views the Committee ultimately adopts are published at the end of the sessions on the Committee's website. In addition, the Committee adopts documents called General Comments, elaborate statements intended to clarify the meaning of specific Covenant provisions in light of legislative and other developments, including those shaped by the Committee, since the ICCPR entered into force five decades ago.[34]

The Committee commonly refers to its work, together with Concluding Observations and Views, as *jurisprudence*, a characterization that emphasizes the legal nature of its activities.[35] It also aligns with the profiles of Committee members who, with few exceptions, have legal backgrounds, often as law professors or judges, as Chapter 3 shows. An emphasis on law is evident in the Committee's documents, which follow a distinct legal aesthetic, organized into paragraphs and subparagraphs that resemble treaties, as discussed in Chapter 5.

The Committee's authoritative nature is reflected in its engagement with civil and political rights in particular—rights which, according to an increasingly contested genealogy, belong to the first generation of rights, with economic, social, and cultural rights, and collective rights emerging in subsequent generations.[36] The first-generation character of civil and political rights is reflected in the Committee's title: the Human Rights Committee is simply that—an all-encompassing committee examining human rights without specifying economic, social, or cultural rights, or the rights of particular groups, such as women, children, or people with disabilities, as is the case with the other UN treaty bodies.

Generality is visible in the breadth with which the Committee interprets its mandate as extending to a wide range of societal concerns across both state reports and the individual communications it receives. Such an expansive approach does not please all states, some viewing it as extending the Committee's mandate excessively by progressive interpretations of the ICCPR. As later chapters illustrate, such challenges by states parties may surface during Constructive Dialogues, yet such instances are rare. For the most part, the Committee performs its tasks diligently and professionally in carefully choreographed sessions, aided by relevant UN staff, with "no sex, drugs, or rock 'n' roll," as one long-term UN insider phrased the matter.

The Human Rights Committee operates within the UN human rights framework—described in Chapter 2 as an apparatus—which comprises two fundamental branches: legal monitoring conducted by treaty bodies and political monitoring embodied in the Human Rights Council's UPR.[37] The UN's human rights activities are overseen by the OHCHR.[38]

Resource Scarcity

The reporting cycles of UN treaty bodies, in principle, follow the intervals specified by the bodies. In practice, they are often significantly longer, owing particularly to state delays in submitting reports and to delays in processing these reports caused by backlogs resulting from limited personnel resources for the bodies' operations. Shortage of resources is a severe concern for treaty bodies—as well as the entire UN—and subsequently a recurring theme of the book. The UN's human rights pillar receives 4 percent of the organization's budget. In 2020, UN Human Rights received only 75 percent of its allocation due to outstanding state payments to the UN.[39]

The OHCHR increasingly relies on voluntary contributions, 41 percent of which come from the UN category "Western European and Other" (WEO) states—"Other" referring to the US, Canada, Australia, and New Zealand.[40] Voluntary contributions now account for 62 percent of the OHCHR's overall budget and cover 20 percent of mandated activities that should be funded by the Office's regular budget.[41] Voluntary contributions increased in 2022 compared to 2021 and have become increasingly unearmarked, complicating the OHCHR's financial situation and reducing flexibility. In 2022, the Office reportedly needed $400.5 million in voluntary funding in addition to the fixed general budget to meet all assistance needs.[42]

Numerous initiatives have been introduced by states, the UN, and the OHCHR to tackle resource scarcity. Before 2025, the most dramatic proposal had emerged in spring 2019, when the UN announced that, due to financial shortfalls, the travel budget for external experts would be eliminated.[43] The decision would have effectively canceled all treaty body sessions for the remainder of the year,[44] a catastrophic blow to UN human rights monitoring, as emphasized in a plea launched by over three hundred NGOs.[45] Jens Modvig, chair of the Committee Against Torture (CAT), warned that "instead of *going in a direction* where we [the treaty bodies] become more regular and credible, we may be considered less regular, less stable, less credible."[46]

Eventually, the proposal was abandoned and treaty body proceedings in 2019 went ahead as usual. However, the following year sessions were canceled—not because of resource scarcity but due to the COVID-19 pandemic, which made international travel impossible. The outcome was dramatic: for the first time since the bodies' creation no international experts, state delegates, or NGO representatives flew to their sessions from around the world to "embody the universal."[47] It was an abrupt halt to documentary cycles that, until then, had rotated steadily for decades. In reality, the halt was only partial, as some documents continued to circulate to and from Geneva and national capitals, from government delegates and NGOs to the UN Secretariat and back. Eventually, some treaty bodies temporarily moved their sessions online. The drop in the number of reports processed was, nevertheless, dramatic: whereas, in 2019, the Human Rights Committee processed on average seven state reports in its sessions, in 2021, only two.[48]

In 2025, an even more dramatic standstill occurred: due to an acute budgetary, or liquidity, crisis, the UN canceled the third annual session of several treaty bodies, including the Human Rights Committee, for the first time since the bodies' inception.[49] The funding cuts to the UN that President Trump introduced soon after the start of his second term contributed directly to the crisis, together with unpaid dues from numerous states.[50]

The results of canceling physical movement indicate the essential fragility of the UN human rights framework: despite operating for decades, the treaty body framework's foundation may be shattered when circumstances change, leaving the bodies' future uncertain. Prolonged problems plaguing UN treaty bodies contribute to fragility. These problems include, on the one hand, serious backlogs with extended processing times, particularly for individual communications.[51] These backlogs prompt worries within the human rights community about the Committee's, as well as the entire treaty body framework's, continued relevance.

On the other hand, treaty bodies contend with significant underreporting: according to a UN estimate, in 2017 only one in three states parties fulfilled their reporting duties, either on time or at all.[52] Subsequently, both the Committee's and the UN treaty body framework's operations may be characterized as success-by-failure:[53] they manage to complete what is expected of them only because most states do not carry out their treaty-bound responsibilities. Were all states suddenly to submit their state reports by the set deadlines, the treaty body system would not remain operational with its current resources.

Mandated Opaque Transparency

As has already been noted, and as Chapter 4 elaborates, treaty bodies have a complex relationship to law. While their mandates are based on legal provisions, their operations are often characterized as "quasi-judicial" as the documents that they produce are legally nonbinding. With the exception of the Committee on Economic, Social, and Cultural Rights (ESCR), all treaty bodies were established by treaty provisions.[54] Their legal mandate sets the bodies apart from the UPR. Another core difference is that the UPR involves no expert assessments of treaty violations, building instead on self-reporting accompanied by recommendations from peer states, a political monitoring mechanism Cowan has described as an audit process.[55]

Since the treaty bodies' creation, they have faced regular proposals—both from states and UN insiders alike—to restructure their operations to make them more efficient.[56] The first initiative dates from the early 1980s, only a few years after the Human Rights Committee began operating.[57] In 2006, the UN Secretary-General proposed a single-report model, backed by UN High Commissioner for Human Rights Louise Arbour's proposal for a unified reporting procedure.[58] Recasting the UN Human Rights Commission into the Human Rights Council in the same year undoubtedly intensified pressures to reorganize treaty bodies' operations.

Nevertheless, revising the treaty body framework is difficult, for reasons that have roots in the law: the bodies' treaty-based mandates restrict how far restructuring can go. Consequently, to unify all ten UN treaty bodies, as is sometimes suggested, the treaty texts would have to be reopened. In the current political climate, with a number of states actively eschewing their human rights obligations, this would be risky—a definitive step backward rather than forward toward the vision of improving the world by advancing human rights and the rule of law. It further appears as a step that no one, including states, the UN, or the civil society, is willing to take.

In 2012, a report by former UN High Commissioner for Human Rights Navi Pillay outlined proposals for treaty body reform, which the UN General Assembly adopted in 2014.[59] One tangible consequence was the recommendation to adopt a simplified reporting procedure—shorter state reports based on a specific list of issues provided by the relevant treaty body, which the Human Rights Committee has since followed. It has also realized another new initiative with the CESCR Committee in spring 2021 by scheduling certain state reviews back to back, introducing synergy in preparation and presentation.

In 2022, the treaty bodies agreed to establish a predictable eight-year calendar of reviews covering all treaty body reporting procedures and all states parties.[60] Upholding and synchronizing the calendar nonetheless remains complicated due to numerous factors, including frequent state delays in submitting reports. At present, the future of UN treaty body reform remains open.[61] One outcome nevertheless appears undisputed: the future will likely be characterized by fewer, not more, resources.

From Triumph to "Endtimes"

The Human Rights Committee, as well as UN treaty bodies in general, continuously face some states' resistance to any outside interference in their internal affairs. Reluctance applies to establishing an international human rights court with universal jurisdiction—even though numerous international tribunals addressing human rights violations have been created, including the Inter-American Court of Human Rights (IACHR) in 1979, the International Criminal Tribunal for the Former Yugoslavia (ICTY) in 1993, the International Criminal Tribunal for Rwanda (ICTR) in 1994, the International Criminal Court (ICC) in 2002, and the African Court on Human and Peoples' Rights (AfCHPR) in 2004.

From the viewpoint of legal human rights monitoring, treaty bodies remain the UN's "next best thing," and many scholars strongly oppose the creation of an international human rights court.[62] Over the past decade, the prospect of such a court has grown increasingly improbable due to mounting challenges faced by the international human rights regime, including the rise of populist politics and authoritarian leadership that marginalizes human rights perspectives in political and legal decision-making in many parts of the world.

These challenges were preceded by a period of veritable human rights triumph at the end of the Cold War. For example, dozens of states, among them many post-socialist states, rushed to join international human rights treaties,[63] and in the first years of the new millennium, all things pertaining to human rights increased rapidly. These included mentions of human rights in political speeches, international agreements, academic publications, institutions, NGOs, and everyday use of human rights language.[64]

The past decade has witnessed a reverse trend, connected to broader developments in which a growing number of states—led by the Trump-era US—have turned their backs on the fundamental principles of multilateralism that have formed the backbone of the post–World War II order.[65] African states are withdrawing from the International Criminal Court, raising collective charges of institutional racism,[66] and the unified fabric of Europe is tearing, as Brexit epitomizes. As the world recovered from the COVID-19 pandemic, Russia's invasion of Ukraine and Israel's military operations in Gaza drew widespread condemnation for violations of human rights and the laws of warfare. Both laypeople and specialists have increasingly lost faith in international law as an effective tool of world improvement,[67] with some prophesying about the "endtimes of human rights."[68]

These prophecies are intensified by ongoing demands to decolonize human rights,[69] linked to broader attempts to decolonize international law.[70] Climate urgency, increasingly dominant in the global political arena, poses additional challenges, prompting questions about whether the anthropocentric ontology of human rights is practically and morally defensible.[71] Today, an increasing number of voices reflect on whether the international human rights regime is "enough."[72] Others worry about the suitability of the paper-pushing practices in which human rights bodies engage to address the concerns of our quickly changing world. In response, some international organizations (IOs) are revisiting their foundational visions by inviting external consultants to study their organizational cultures[73] and by revising their mandates to remain relevant.[74] These developments raise increasing questions on whether, rather than continuing to expand, the institutions and practices of multilateralism established after World War II may in fact be declining.

Toward a Non-Normative Analysis of Consequences

Relatively little is known of the Human Rights Committee's operations—or the treaty body framework more generally—outside the immediate confines of human rights diplomacy and law. The Committee's name rarely appears in frontline international media. Among the enormous number of UN committees, councils, conventions, and covenants, even UN staff may confuse its name with another UN body. Lack of broader knowledge is compounded by existing scholarship: to date, works on UN human rights treaty bodies have been written largely by legal scholars, many of them former treaty body members.[75] Legal emphasis means that whereas the Committee's jurisprudence has been studied extensively,[76] there is an absence of scholarship that reflects "on the role of international institutions in sustaining a particular vision of world order,"[77] or treats the UN Human Rights Committee as a utopian site.

Missing are insights into the UN Secretariat's background work on the Constructive Dialogues, and the multifaceted processes of inclusion and exclusion that characterize access to the Committee's sessions. There exists limited knowledge about how the vision for a world order structured around human rights and the law has been ingrained in the Committee's operations, and the techniques by which key insiders keep the vision moving *in the rights direction*. These issues connect with the question of impact, effects, or simply consequences that the Committee's operations have.[78] Impact remains an understandable concern for those associated with the UN human rights framework, including state actors, NGO activists, and scholars: if there is no impact, UN treaty body proceedings have no purpose or legitimacy.[79] Existing scholarship has found limited evidence that the Committee's work influences domestic policymaking or political discourse.[80] This echoes recent scholarship on IOs, in which one recurring criticism is how, instead of doing something for the world, IOs "generate documents that heighten obscurity, while producing ideas and policies behind closed doors,"[81] and thus lead a "life of their own, distinct from that of their member state."[82]

The following analysis focuses on the multifaceted consequences that ensue from the Human Rights Committee's elaborate proceedings, even if they do not always match the expectations of what consequences should look like—such as changes in legislation or policymaking. To appreciate the plenitude of outcomes, the analysis moves beyond a normative framework and the prism of whether treaty body proceedings realize the objectives that they ideally *should* realize under the utopian vision of world reform with human rights and law. Instead, I consider the multifaceted outcomes of the Committee's operations in light of empirical observations, including the consequences that diverge from normatively loaded expectations.

The analytical move to discard a normative framework is one of this study's most significant departures from earlier scholarship. Here I build on anthropology's disciplinary tradition as an inductive field of research characterized by "pre-theoretical commitments,"[83] which enables theorizing from the ground up—in stark contrast to law as a discipline, which is not only normative but deductive. In other words, this book begins with the Human Rights Committee's operations and their inner logic, as embodied in participants' actions, together with a formal description of the Committee's mandate.

The outcome portrays the Committee, to quote Niezen and Sapignoli, as a "social world with distinct characters, influenced by their connections with civil society, states, transnational corporations, and publics."[84] It reveals how the Human Rights Committee, in Müller's words, "involve[s] collective and individual actors in [its] policy-making, absorb[ing] critique, attempt[ing] to neutralise political conflict, and creat[ing] new political fields in competition and collusion with local actors and national government."[85] It highlights the affective lives of bureaucracies within the Committee and, to build on Billaud and Cowan, shows "how actors maintain a sense of purpose and agency in spite of the tedious and burdensome nature of the administrative procedures in which they take part."[86]

In analytical terms, I explore the Committee from a threefold perspective that resonates with Foucault's genealogical method:[87] first, as a formal legal entity defined by its mandated tasks; second, in terms of the influence of individuals who shape its actions; and third, as a part of a broader community of practice[88] comprising actors with tacit insider knowledge. This threefold analytical stance is embedded in theorizing the UN human rights monitoring framework as a monumental Foucauldian apparatus. Thus, my work makes an integral contribution to improving our understanding of contemporary bureaucracies.

To describe the core group of actors in the community of practice, I adopt the phrase Guardians of Vision—inspired by Lauren's book *The Evolution of International Human Rights: Visions Seen*—to refer to individuals with long-standing involvement in international human rights work and UN treaty bodies.[89] I consider the unifying element among the Guardians—sometimes called "human rights believers"[90]—a shared belief in the possibility of improving the world by expanding the role of human rights and the rule of law.

Scholarly context is offered particularly on the past two decades of anthropological work on international organizations and human rights,[91] which constitutes a rapidly growing body of research on different UN bodies,[92] international law,[93] and international justice.[94] It includes ethnographies of international courts,[95] among them the European Court of Human Rights[96] and the International Criminal Court.[97] It includes analyses of truth-and-reconciliation commissions[98] and the UPR.[99] Of particular importance is earlier, albeit limited, anthropological analysis on UN human rights treaty bodies, including the Committees on the Elimination of Discrimination against Women,[100] Torture,[101] and Racial Discrimination.[102]

Relevant scholarship is linked to studies of expert techniques,[103] bureaucracies, and documents,[104] to anthropological work on the state and global phenomena,[105] and to scholarship on international activist and expert networks.[106] Likewise relevant is recent work on the growing influence of independent experts,[107] transnational legislation,[108] EU policymaking,[109] and informal law-making.[110] I also shed light on debates about governance arrangements beyond the customary "soft" and "hard" law terminology, including debates on the shifting authority of states. Finally, I engage with recent work on reform processes in international organizations and conceptualizations of their effectiveness.

Many themes that I explore connect with recent work focusing on the subjectivities, values, virtues, and ethics of international lawyers,[111] as well as on the "sentiments" of international law.[112] Pertinent are ongoing queries into the future of international law, including its recent "material" turn that examines its tangible artefacts and manifestations,[113] as well as scholarship on international law's complex entanglements and chains of influence beyond the state.[114]

The Conspicuous Ethnographer

I have conducted multisited and partially deterritorialized ethnographic research that includes participant-observation, interviews, open-ended debates, and documentary analysis.[115] I conducted the bulk of my ethnographic observations during the 106th, 107th, and 108th sessions of the Human Rights Committee in 2013, with follow-up visits in 2014, 2017, 2018, and 2022–2024. The Committee that I depict in the ethnographic glimpses reflects its 2013 composition, embodied in the figure of the late Sir Nigel Rodley—one of the Committee's brightest "stars," as Chapter 3 discusses. He appears as a recurring protagonist across different sections, often referred to as "Sir Nigel," as he was commonly called in the Committee's sessions.

I have interviewed members of the Human Rights Committee, state and NGO delegates, and UN Secretariat staff—many interviews took the form of ongoing conversations over the years—as well as members of the UN conference services and interpreters. I have examined state and NGO reports submitted to the Committee and, to a limited extent, to other UN human rights monitoring bodies. I have moreover analyzed media coverage concerning the visibility of the Committee and other UN human rights monitoring bodies.

In terms of participant observation, significant were the many hours I spent in the Committee's public Constructive Dialogue sessions, complemented by lunchtime briefings between NGO delegates and Committee members. These experiences were facilitated by my status as an informal intern to a Committee member, which included examination and analysis of different documents. Also significant were informal conversations both in the Palais Wilson cafeteria and at NGO offices in Geneva. In addition, I participated in different human rights meetings in Finland and elsewhere, including the expert meetings in Berlin and Paris regarding UN treaty body revision. Ethnographic research provided me with a holistic view of the "iceberg" that UN treaty body operations form, only the tip of which is visible using narrow legal analysis.

My research derived a detailed level of analysis from observing the entire documentary cycle of Finland's sixth state report, submitted to the Human Rights Committee in 2011 and reviewed in the Committee's Constructive Dialogue in July 2013. Finland's sixth reporting cycle was completed when Finland presented its seventh report in spring 2021, online due to the COVID-19 pandemic. I participated in drafting documents produced by Finland and NGOs for the Constructive Dialogue with the help of a research assistant. I interviewed staff at the Finnish Ministry for Foreign Affairs, particularly the Unit for Human Rights Courts and Conventions that attends to Finland's reporting obligations both to UN treaty bodies and the Council of Europe. Furthermore, I conducted interviews with relevant staff at other Finnish ministries, as well as politicians who participated in the state delegation in 2013. Finally, I interviewed NGO delegates and representatives of the Sámi people who submitted shadow reports.

Finland is widely seen as a "model student" of human rights. For example, in recollecting her Human Rights Committee membership, Dame Rosalyn Higgins singled out Finland as a state that has a particularly high record of meeting its reporting obligations.[116] However, over the past few years many local activists and organizations have challenged such a status in response to Prime Minister Petteri Orpo's 2023 government program, which they argue results in human rights violations for vulnerable segments of the Finnish population.[117]

My ethnography included participant observation during the Constructive Dialogue between Finland's state delegation and the Human Rights Committee at the Palais Wilson in July 2013, as well as at the delegation's preparatory meetings. My interviewees included UN staff responsible for preparing background documents for the Dialogue. To broaden my understanding of the context, I followed the Constructive Dialogue on Finland's sixth report to the Committee on Economic, Social, and Cultural Rights in October 2014 and observed the Human Rights Committee's Constructive Dialogue on Finland's seventh report online in March 2021. Historical context was provided by analyzing documents related to all seven documentary cycles since Finland ratified the Covenant in 1975.

Focusing on Finland's reporting cycles may appear unexpected. Although all states are allotted equal time in UN treaty bodies, faithful to the UN's organizing principle of sovereign equality of all nations, some UN insiders and NGO delegates suggest that these cycles are not *really* intended for prosperous, stable social democracies in the Global North. Rather, even some Committee members view them as mechanisms meant primarily for developing democracies in the Global South facing poverty and development challenges. Yet Finland's report offers valuable insights into the Committee's operations precisely due to the country's model-student status: it provides an ideal vantage point for examining human rights reporting as it *should* be while revealing the limits of what it can achieve.[118]

A question may arise as to why the primary focus on state reports. For many lawyers these routine, repetitive processes appear less significant or effective than the "courtlike" work of processing individual communications or the "legislative-like" work of drafting General Comments. Still, processing state reports remains the bread and butter of the Committee's work, continuing from session to session, year to year, away from international spotlight. It forms the most tangible embodiment of the utopian vision to move world order further toward the direction of human rights and the law. Also, processing state reports is emblematic of countless reporting cycles that have emerged in the post–World War II era in the UN, the EU, and elsewhere, amounting to tens if not hundreds of thousands of pages generated and processed annually. Focus on the Human Rights Committee's reporting cycles offers insightful analytical horizons into broader contemporary bureaucratic trends.

I build on the notion of the "conspicuous ethnographer"[119]—the opposite of the "innocuous observer," which has long guided anthropological research. One central part of being conspicuous entailed exaggerated transparency regarding my research while conducting fieldwork. Another part concerned establishing direct personal connections and indirect relations, which I cover in Chapter 2 in my discussion of the book's methodological approaches. The research, furthermore, employs cyclical ethnography for two reasons. First, the book studies a documentary cycle, and second, I conducted much of my ethnography on a bicycle, both in Geneva and in Helsinki, where UN buildings, government offices, and NGO headquarters are located close to one another—a minute detail that underscores how small human rights circles sometimes are.

The insights of my study are, I argue, for the most part intimately known to international human rights monitoring insiders. More than anyone, they are able to distinguish between the visions governing their work and the sometimes-disappointing organizational realities where these visions come to life. International human rights monitoring insiders—including NGO delegates—are usually highly educated, occasionally with doctorates, thus occupying the same professional space as scholars. Conducting ethnographic research thus entails entering negotiations over co-constructed knowledge:[120] what one writes will likely be read by one's interlocutors, who, in turn, may advance their own interpretations and analyses—and these analyses will often be much more influential than those of the anthropologist. Thus fieldwork in a high-profile human rights monitoring mechanism is, by definition, "studying up,"[121] even when these mechanisms include actors in unstable professional circumstances, such as interns. Such asymmetry in power relations makes fieldwork particularly challenging, while offering the possibility for powerful new insights.

For my interlocutors, I only refer to individuals by name when they speak publicly in their official capacity.[122] In the human rights field, individuals often speak on behalf of the organizations and governments they represent, and thus they are expected to engage in impersonal representation. Further, interlocutors may have personal reasons to protect their anonymity, as speaking under their own name might place their careers in jeopardy.[123] Such concerns apply particularly for the UN, which is characterized by incessant staff rotation, as detailed in Chapter 2.

Organization of the Book

The book is organized in seven substantive chapters, each offering a different lens on the Human Rights Committee's operations as well as the notion of movement in the rights direction. Chapter 2, "Gaining Access to the Iceberg," lays the foundation for the book's ethnographic theorization by depicting UN human rights bureaucracies as an icelike apparatus characterized by opaque transparency and fuzzy logic. I detail the complex processes of inclusion and exclusion by which different actors—the anthropologist, as well as other members of the international human rights community—gain temporary, insecure access to the UN human rights apparatus. The chapter focuses in particular on the impact of constant staff rotation, including how it contributes to the UN operation's fuzzy logic, enabling key insiders to support the Committee's work.

Chapter 3, "Guardians of Vision," focuses on the key actors in UN human rights treaty bodies who form a community of practice and maneuver in the icelike UN human rights apparatus. The chapter examines how, from a practice perspective, the categories of "expert member" and "UN staff" become blurred, and how blurriness is integral to the impact of human rights monitoring. Further, the chapter discusses how expert members and relevant UN staff are connected to each other by indirect relations and direct social connections—connections facilitated by their shared belonging in the "invisible community" of lawyers predominantly from the Global North. The chapter reflects on internal tensions within this community, marked by gender hierarchies and occasional sentiments of underappreciation, and shows how these tensions are soothed by shared adherence to the vision of improving the world by advancing human rights and the rule of law.

Chapter 4, "What's Law Got to Do with It?," is anchored around ethnography of the Committee's Constructive Dialogues and public discussions on General Comments, and examines the Committee's complex relationship to law from the viewpoint of its open-ended mandate. Set against a historical overview of legalization within the contemporary human rights phenomenon, the chapter analyses how Committee members effectively expand the Committee's mandate by updating the ICCPR's interpretation in response to global changes by the General Comments they adopt. At the same time, the chapter shows how expansion continues the earlier civilizing mission of international law, evident in the Committee members' emphasis on modern states and the rule of law.

Further, I discuss the embodied techniques that Committee members activate as they form a human interface that "constructively" eases tensions with states averse to such broad interpretations, so as to defend the Committee's expansive mandate. Finally, I examine a discussion regarding transparency among Committee members to show how law appears as an end in the Committee's work—but, more importantly, as a means of securing increasing salience of human rights worldwide.

Chapter 5, "From 'Real Reality' to 'UN Reality,'" documents the tangible translation processes that shape the Committee's work—including linguistic and aesthetic ones—by which everyday events become cast as potential ICCPR violations that the Committee is mandated to review. The chapter offers a detailed analysis of the drafting process accompanying Finland's sixth state report, showing how such documents bring an "it-ness" to the state, creating the illusion of solidity, while simultaneously erasing local governance structures from view. State centrality is a direct outcome of the Human Rights Committee's mandate—it only examines state actions as only states are parties to the ICCPR. The analysis illustrates how the Committee's practices, paradoxically, strengthen rather than weaken the role of the state as a political and legal reference point, thus contributing to the Committee's civilizing mission of promoting modern statehood.

The chapter's second part focuses on outcomes and effects, placing Finland's sixth state report in both historical and holistic comparative frames. The analysis first contextualizes Finland's report against the volume of documents processed by the Committee to illustrate the scale of flows these reporting procedures generate. It then examines the thematic change across all seven reporting cycles on Finland, highlighting recurring themes. Ultimately, the analysis illustrates how tangible outcomes may be elusive and, when they occur, difficult to attribute to the Committee's operations, setting up the subsequent chapters' reflections on affect and the importance of ongoing movement.

Chapter 6, "The Feeling of Reporting," analyzes the Constructive Dialogue on Finland's report at the Palais Wilson, highlighting the emotions and subjectivities of civil servants as they prepare for the hearing. The chapter illustrates—challenging prevailing scholarship premised on the antagonism between states and UN human rights bodies—how many long-term state delegates are integral participants in the Guardian of Vision's community of practice, committed to advancing the treaty bodies' successful operations. Concurrently these civil servants navigate dual roles as both representatives of their states and human rights defenders.

The chapter contextualizes its inquiry on a historical overview of Finland's relationship to the international human rights system in the post–World War II era, shaped by its imposed proximity to the Soviet Union. It reflects on the role that Constructive Dialogue plays in reaffirming state delegates' commitment to and belief in both human rights and UN monitoring mechanisms. The chapter contrasts these sentiments with the tale of the "Burned-out Bureaucrat," capturing how the ever-accelerating pace of reporting alienates civil servants from the work, undermining commitment and belief in future improvements.

Chapter 7, "Moving in the Shadows," focuses on the multifaceted roles NGOs play in the Committee's operations. The chapter again frames its inquiry with a historical overview of NGOs' roles in UN operations, outlining how their involvement has increased over the past decades, aided by the Guardians of Vision's careful maneuvering under the UN human rights apparatus's opaque transparency. In addition, the chapter focuses on the techniques and tacit knowledge that NGO delegates need for successful lobbying, and showcases the role of Geneva-based intermediaries in facilitating the participation of NGOs from around the world, thus fostering a type of embodied universalism.

Chapter 8, “Movement in the Rights Direction,” brings the insights of the previous chapters together to examine the nonstop movement of documents, people, aesthetics, and knowledge practices as constituting the Committee’s “life.” It explores how belief in human rights, UN treaty bodies, and the UN Human Rights Committee in particular sustains movement despite uncertain outcomes, and how the Committee may unilaterally jump-start movement in the hopes of establishing ongoing dialogue. The chapter considers the pace of movement as well as the forms that it needs to adopt in order to become the “right kind,” discussing human rights documents as civilized standards for a better world.

Finally, the chapter connects its analysis to the current world order, illustrating how the movement instigated and sustained by the Committee’s operations strengthens the role of the state as a central political and legal reference point in international collaboration. The chapter reflects on the Human Rights Committee’s—and, by extension, the other UN treaty bodies’—inability to engage with cross-border rights violations, and on such root causes of ongoing violations as structural inequalities emanating from the colonial era. The chapter concludes by returning to the importance of the human interface in the Committee’s Constructive Dialogues in keeping the reporting cycles alive.

CHAPTER 2

Gaining Access to the "Iceberg"

This is finally it! I unlock my bike, hop on, and pedal downhill in the direction of the lake. Shivering slightly from the damp morning air, I pass Cornavin station and make sure I am not caught in the tram tracks that crisscross the road. For a moment, I hesitate. Am I heading the right way? Then I begin to recognize familiar places. Although it has been a few years since my last visit to Geneva, the city center is so small that it is easy enough to find one's way. In a few minutes, I reach Paquis, thinking how, despite liking the city a lot in other respects, the area remains something of a "dump," as I have heard locals describe it affectionately. I veer to the left and see the Palais Wilson on my right.

I chain my bike to the fence surrounding the Palais and pause for a moment to admire the building: it is every bit as beautiful as I remember. I proceed toward the security booth at the gate, holding my passport tightly in my hand, and hoping my badge has arrived there as promised, rather than at the Palais des Nations where badges are usually issued. It has not. Disappointed, for a moment I fear sorting the matter out will take too much time, causing me to miss the session's opening. I am not pleased by the prospect—I am here to follow everything from start to finish in order to absorb the full picture of the Human Rights Committee's session. Fortunately, the issue is resolved in just a few moments after the security guards make a couple of calls to someone inside the Palais. I never find out why my badge was not ready or how the matter is fixed, but that matters little: I am in.

I thank the guards warmly for going out of their way to accommodate my participation and—feeling a bit like an academic Cinderella—make my way to the inner yard. I cannot help but feel that there is something magical about the building in front of me: whereas the other houses on either side of the Palais Wilson contain merely "normal" activities, this is the place where the "international" meets. I pause at the thought for a moment, only to be jolted back into reality by the sound of rushed footsteps as people making up the "international" pass by me on all sides.

I glance quickly at their wardrobes, hoping I fit in: I have swapped out my characteristic writing sweats for a classic tailored jacket, smart pants, and heels, but I fear the academic may be peeking out. Differences in the dress standards of academics buried in their chambers and professionals working in high-profile international human rights monitoring are tangible. Cinderella alright—in my field site one undoubted element of "studying up," as Nader memorably phrased it,[1] certainly includes dressing up. I finally reach the front door, make my way up the short staircase, and find myself in the impressive front lobby with its equally striking view of Lac Léman. In just a few moments, another session of the Human Rights Committee will open.

In this chapter, I analyze what multilayered processes of access—together with unexpected moments of exclusion—reveal about the inner contours of UN human rights bureaucracies. The chapter tells its story from the viewpoint of an anthropologist, myself, asking how one may negotiate access to such high-profile bureaucratic bodies as the UN Human Rights Committee.[2] Building on ethnographic theorization of UN human rights bureaucracies as a monumental ice-like apparatus characterized by partial opacity and fuzzy logic, the chapter reflects on what a detailed account of negotiating access reveals about the UN's operational dynamics. It connects these negotiations to incessant staff rotation within the UN, further reflecting on what these insights tells about how the Human Rights Committee and the other UN treaty bodies move the world *in the rights direction*.

At the heart of the chapter is the ethnographer's (that is, my) attempt to transform from an inconspicuous, detached scholar—a nobody—into a *somebody* whose existence was not only noted by the insiders of the Human Rights Committee with mundane small talk, but with whom they would occasionally have lengthy conversations, and who even played fleeting roles of relevance in Committee proceedings. Central to my efforts was the opportunistic embrace of a pre-existing category in UN bureaucracy, namely, that of *the intern*.[3]

Getting to the Palais Wilson

The Palais Wilson—the headquarters of the OHCHR and the venue for UN human rights treaty body sessions—sits casually and inconspicuously on a quiet street in a Geneva quartier.[4] Built in 1875, the building was originally a luxury hotel, under the name Hôtel National. In 1920, the League of Nations purchased the building, making it the organization's headquarters until 1936; in 1924, the building was renamed the Palais Wilson to commemorate the late US President Woodrow Wilson.[5] Although it boasts imposing architecture, the Palais is in no way extraordinary by Geneva standards, as the headquarters of international organizations and embassies, as well as the posh offices of multinational corporations, are scattered all across the city. Were it not for the UN sign on the gate and the modest security booth, a casual observer might not even recognize the Palais Wilson as a UN office.

In its unassuming location, the Palais starkly contrasts with the Palais des Nations, first the League of Nations' and later the UN's Geneva headquarters, located some two kilometers uphill. The latter is a grandiose complex, by design detached and largely inaccessible from the city, yet highly visible as it hovers over Geneva's skyline.[6] The Palais Wilson, by comparison, appears more accessible and connected to everyday life. The main conference room—which accommodates the Human Rights Committee's and many other UN treaty bodies' sessions—has unshaded windows, making the proceedings directly visible from the street. One can see the interpreters in their booths and the faces of individual participants, all of which contribute to the air of bureaucratic transparency.

The swift processing of people at the security gates contributes to an impression of accessibility; one feels as if one could just walk right in. The impression, nevertheless, is deceptive, as multiple layers separate the casual observer on the street from an insider eligible to go through the gates and participate in the Committee's sessions. In practice, one needs appropriate accreditation accompanied by a badge, a tangible plastic artefact, in order to be admitted. The question thus becomes: How does one secure a badge—and to what exactly does one subsequently gain entrance?

In principle, retrieving a badge is easy, as the instructions on the Human Rights Committee's website state.[7] Parts of the Committee's sessions are open to the public, as are those of other UN treaty bodies. Thus, anybody from anywhere in the world should be able to receive accreditation, provided that they can offer appropriate affiliation and a motivation for their visit. The application process entails filling in a registration form with sufficient advance notice, emailing the form to the correct address, and waiting for email confirmation that accreditation has been approved. The final step is to collect one's badge from the accreditation office at the Pregny Gate, located at the back of the Palais des Nations, a somewhat arduous uphill climb from the Palais Wilson.

Once one becomes accustomed to the intricacies of UN bureaucracy, all these details become routine. With some luck, one learns who in the UN Secretariat processes accreditation forms and can thus email them directly, or even telephone, if accreditation forms are not ready on time or, for whatever reason, need to be processed unusually quickly. For the newcomer and genuine outsider, all these steps pose considerable challenges. How does one know, to begin with, that one needs accreditation?

Where, on the OHCHR´s elaborate website, does one find the accreditation form, or where to send it once filled out?[8] Where is the information on processing times—and how does one know where to collect the badge once it is ready? The last question, in particular, may sound like a trick question, but it is not: UN insiders often quickly and casually refer to names of buildings, places, and UN abbreviations with no additional clarification, leaving outsiders and newcomers feeling baffled. Even the location and exact street address of a building may be missing from the UN website, a tacit embodiment of the insider knowledge that functions as a practical prerequisite for access.[9]

The guidelines themselves for securing accreditation, though clear-cut in principle, leave plenty of room for error. Will one know to reserve enough time to fetch the badge from the Pregny Gate—the same entrance tourist groups use when visiting the Palais des Nations, which can result in long lines, especially in the afternoon? Will one know to check that the badge is, indeed, for the Human Rights Committee and not, for example, the Human Rights Council, both of them sharing the acronym HRC, which can on occasion confuse even seasoned UN staff?

More challenges emerge if one needs to apply for a travel visa: Will accreditation be secured early enough for the visa application to be processed on time, something the UN is unable to assist with? Especially for anyone not fluent in the practices of UN bureaucracy, these details constitute a potential border of exclusion, resulting in moments of frustration and helplessness, wasted time, and possibly wasted money.

Once one arrives at the Palais Wilson with one's badge and proceeds past security, these details seem utterly insignificant. Looking through the windows of the main conference room out onto the street and seeing children playing in the adjacent schoolyard, everyday life feels close again, and the bureaucratic layers separating the outside and the inside appear slightly surreal, even fabricated. Nevertheless, it quickly becomes evident that the border between inclusion and exclusion has by no means been left behind. Rather, it continues to be embodied in different guises inside the Palais.

At the UN, there exist different categories of badges depending on the access one has: UN staff will have one type of badge, state delegates another, NGOs with continued access still another.[10] Also, a UN badge can signify continued access or temporary admittance. In practice, the tangible plastic badge is often only the first step toward access, both insufficient in itself and, at times, futile. By contrast, real access emerges from indirect relations with people in the international human rights field, paired with direct personal connections within UN human rights bureaucracies.

Encountering the Fuzzy Iceberg

From an analytical point of view, human rights bureaucracies appear, somewhat paradoxically, to exist both nowhere and everywhere while possessing distinct centers and peripheries marked by either fixed locations or itinerant conglomerations of action and expertise.[11] The Human Rights Committee is an undoubted center: first, its sessions bring together leading human rights experts from around the world, accompanied by state representatives and NGO delegates; second, its sessions are held in Geneva, home of the UN OHCHR and one of the world's undoubted focal points for international diplomacy and human rights work.

The Human Rights Committee possesses distinct multilocal aspects: outside its three annual sessions, it exists physically in its expert members' multiple locations and in Geneva in ongoing background work by designated UN staff. Concurrently, it exists without territory, embodied in the extensive documents the Committee produces and the knowledge practices that accompany them. These knowledge practices are not restricted to the Committee's expert members or UN staff, but extend to the innumerable state and NGO delegates laboring on documents submitted to and processed by the Committee.

The dualism of localization and deterritorialization has important ramifications for conducting ethnographic research in and on the Committee, as it would be erroneous to treat the Committee's sessions as the mere targets of straightforward participant observation. Feldman notes, "The global is not just local writ large, . . . a web of direct connections multiplied for the world stage," but rather involves "qualitatively different forms of organizing society."[12] To theorize these forms, I conceptualize UN human rights bureaucracies as a monumental human rights apparatus characterized, to utilize Feldman's terms, by mediated *relations* and direct social *connections*.[13] I borrow apparatus from Foucault, who describes it, that is, the *dispositif*, as a "heterogenous ensemble consisting of discourses, institutions, architectural forms, regulatory decisions, laws, administrative measures, scientific statements, philosophical, moral, and philanthropic propositions—in short, the said and the unsaid."[14]

To elaborate on the idea, I describe the inner contours of the UN human rights apparatus using the metaphor of ice, casting the sessions of the Human Rights Committee as the tip of a formidable iceberg. From a distance, ice seems transparent and solid, with a clear-cut exterior that separates it from its surroundings. On closer inspection it appears as porous and characterized by opaque transparency, distorting and partially concealing what lies within and behind it. Within the UN human rights apparatus, ironically, policies implemented to ensure transparency often cloud it, despite stated ideals. These qualities apply to the question of access: although clear-cut guidelines exist, the reality of UN operations is more intricate. Importantly, opacity may appeal to many UN insiders as an essential tool to protect the fragile human rights apparatus and enhance its impact, as my analysis details.

The metaphor of ice furthermore captures the "fuzzy logic" of the UN human rights apparatus. I borrow the concept from Bourdieu, who uses it to bridge the exaggerated rigidity of "system" or "structure" by combining them with the indeterminacy of the rules that agents mobilize in practice.[15] Fuzzy logic highlights the ambiguous, fluid, and indeterminate boundaries that characterize social life, reminding us that social categories are continuous rather than fixed.

Fuzzy logic helps illuminate the Committee's operations as a "community of practice" attended to by the "Guardians of Vision," discussed in Chapter 3, rather than as a set of neatly distinct roles—Committee member, UN staff, state delegate, and civil society representative. It provides an analytical entry point into the tacit influence wielded by insiders as they labor to increase the prominence of human rights, and it captures how the Human Rights Committee does not simply follow set rules. Instead, rules are continually negotiated by key insiders contesting meaning within fields of power, forming what I describe as ongoing movement in the rights direction. As Chapter 3 shows, Guardians often hold competing views on the Committee's operations—such as whether the UN Secretariat merely supports or more actively shapes the

Committee's positions. These tensions extend to broader struggles over the treaty bodies' nature and purpose, including their relationship to law, as I discuss in Chapter 4.

Finally, Bourdieu's fuzzy logic refers to the practical, embodied judgements by which individuals navigate social life, and aptly describes the pragmatism of insiders within the UN human rights apparatus, where constant staff mobility and regular Committee member elections create a continuously shifting institutional landscape. Those who remain when others move on must navigate the shifting terrain with situated, embodied logic—one that acknowledges constraints such as limited resources while remaining committed to the vision of advancing human rights with the Committee's work.

Transparency as a New Core Value

Much of the analysis of subsequent chapters centers around the notion of transparency. In recent decades, transparency has become, as Bianchi summarizes, "one of the fundamentally distinctive traits of contemporary Western culture."[16] It has further assumed, in Hood's words, "quasi-religious significance in debate over governance and institutional design."[17] Recommended by "psychologists to recover trust after infidelity" and "increasingly imposed on banks and financial institutions,"[18] Berliner notes that transparency has been "hailed as the key to better governance."[19] Further, Garsten and Montoya add that it implies "visibility, openness and communication,"[20] while Peters reminds us how, increasingly, "demands for more transparency have . . . been voiced by civil-society actors, by states, and within the international institutions themselves."[21] Transparency appears thus as a core component of the rule of law ensuring both good governance and low levels of corruption in "attempts to organize and control beyond local and cultural particularities."[22]

Alloa and Thomä further note how, "as opposed to concepts like regulation or surveillance, transparency doesn't seem to have a negative counterpart that would counter its ambitions,"[23] whereas notions such as secrecy and confidentiality have acquired "a negative connotation."[24] Transparency is assumed to increase accountability, even if this assumption has its critics, Fox reminds us.[25] A central line of critique asks whether transparency can ever be complete or is always opaque—what Ballestro describes as in "constant tension with obscurity and secrecy."[26] Strathern argues that calls for transparency have their own power dynamics tied to the "tyrannous side" of benevolent or moral visibility, since there is, in her words, "nothing innocent about making the invisible visible."[27]

The origins of transparency are strongly linked to current audit cultures, characterized as a "technology of mistrust." Thus, transparency "becomes a symbol of organizational trust and health."[28] By contrast, transparency has traditionally not been "immediately associated with international law." Bianchi states that "the world of international diplomacy and high politics has long been depicted as secretive and enigmatic, far removed from the public's eye." Bianchi continues that "the shrewdness and reputation of politicians and diplomats was measured by their ability to act discretely, striking deals behind the scenes and avoiding public scrutiny."[29]

Over the past two decades, demands for transparency have increased in international law with what Peters denotes a genuine "transparency turn."[30] She adds that, in international law, one core function of transparency is to guarantee "good governance and the rule of law, including foreseeability, accessibility, and legal clarity." She further notes how transparency can "arguably alleviate the "democratic deficit" in global governance."[31] Bianchi summarizes that "these expectations for transparency are even more acute in light of the potential for epitomizing everyone's desire for a better world," particularly in "the human rights movement and . . . the expectations raised by the international criminal justice system."[32] In reality, transparency is seldom realized in absolute terms; as the different chapters illustrate, it often becomes partial or opaque, contributing to fuzzy logic and enabling continued negotiation and movement under its guise.

From a "Nobody" into a "Somebody"

It is the end of yet another Committee session in the Palais Wilson's main conference room. Those present have once again discussed an issue of paramount importance: whether one of the Covenant's states parties is meeting its obligations under the ICCPR. A charged atmosphere characterized the Constructive Dialogue, attended, at least in principle if not always in practice, by numerous civil society representatives, alongside state delegates and UN staff. The immense preparatory work in UN offices in Geneva and various national contexts around the world, as well as all the practical hassle of coordinating work, schedules, visas, and, of course, travel to Geneva, make the atmosphere especially heightened.

The release of tension is palpable when a session ends and people rush out of the room: NGO delegates discuss whether the issues they had labored to bring to the Committee members' attention were, in fact, raised, and whether state representatives addressed or sidelined them. Calls home are made. Press releases may be drafted. Committee members make it clear they need a coffee break.

I feel the tension myself, but for very different reasons. Will I finally manage to strike up a conversation with one of the Committee members? Perhaps I can speak with a UN Secretariat member before she rushes off to prepare for the next session, or with an NGO activist, or a member of a state delegation? With my "UN expression"—an earnest portrayal of interest and excitement—plastered on my face, exhausting my jaw muscles from overuse, I linger at the doorway. Most of the Committee members simply pass by, either indifferent to my presence or acknowledging me with a faint nod.

By now, most of them recognize me. I have spent a fair amount of time in the sessions, and the number of people who consistently attend is not large. Still, most of the other attendees have neither the slightest idea who I am nor any interest in finding out. They spend their days at the sessions, their nights in preparation, mornings in breakfast meetings, lunches at different hearings or informal meetings, and evenings at dinners and receptions. There is simply no room for random chats with an anthropologist. Aware of this, I try a different tactic: I share a passing comment to someone walking by, attempting to fall naturally into the flow of their movement to find an opening for continuing our discussion during the walk to the cafeteria located at the other end of the corridor.

It feels as if I am fishing, hoping for a few gentle nibbles that will allow me to hook them. I try using personal detail as a lure and experiment by volunteering something of shared expertise. My ability to build rapport likewise hinges on my broad network of indirect professional relations and direct personal connections.[33] Having worked as a researcher at an institute focused on human rights and international law as an anthropology PhD candidate, I knew many of the same people as the insiders at the Palais Wilson.

It allowed me to drop familiar names of people and places in our exchanges, thus confirming that I was a part of the community of practice of human rights experts who could, slowly, be granted increasing access to the UN human rights apparatus. The shift in status helped establish my rapport with interlocutors at the Finnish Ministry for Foreign Affairs: some key officials had been researchers or students at the same law faculty or research institute as I. Often, we shared mutual acquaintances—a situation that likewise proved true for NGO representatives.[34]

In these moments, flashing direct personal connections to established figures within international law often becomes pivotal. It assists in gradually transforming me from a *nobody*—a random, detached observer of no relevance, to paraphrase Shipton, a "stranger, an alien, possibly an enemy" who "in an important sense [does not] exist" before I "reveal my networks"[35]—into a *somebody* who not only is doing something potentially worthwhile, but who in her professional relations has a distinct connection to her interlocutors. I succeeded in creating a sticky surface on the seemingly impenetrable façade of UN bureaucratic sociality: a slight thawing of the smooth exterior of the iceberg that allows a creative friction to emerge.[36] Our exchanges become a space for shared reflections, potentially evolving into the co-construction of knowledge.[37]

The three sessions of the Human Rights Committee I attended in 2013 demonstrate how my access to insider status increased. In the first session, I had an observer badge that entitled me to follow the Committee's public hearings. These included Constructive Dialogues between the Committee and state delegates, the drafting of General Comments, and sessions where the Committee discussed its working methods. Over time, I was able to initiate a series of lunch and coffee meetings with Committee members, NGO delegates, and the occasional member of the UN Secretariat. Despite merely having an observer badge, by the end of the first session I was considered sufficiently an insider to be allowed to sit in on lunchtime NGO briefings that were closed to state representatives. Eventually, I stayed in touch with one Committee member between sessions, performing small assistant tasks to help prepare for the next session.

By the second session in 2013, I was sufficiently an insider to serve occasionally as an "intermediary,"[38] connecting first-time NGO delegates to the people they were seeking, or more pragmatically, directing them to the snack machine on the ground floor of the Palais Wilson—useful in late afternoon hours when sessions dragged on and the upstairs cafeteria had already closed. I was able to make connections with inconspicuous members of the UN Secretariat—the personnel preparing background documents, the security guards, and interpreters—and to continue engaging with Committee members in interviews and informal exchanges. The second session included processing Finland's state report, in which I played an impromptu role by assisting in the preparation of a background document and even acting as an NGO advocate presenting information to a Committee member.

The Opportunistic Intern

During the third session, the boundary of inclusion shifted even further as a Committee member agreed to take me on as an informal intern. My association with the category of intern had already commenced during the very first Committee session I attended. Interns are, of course, integral to international human rights work: the UN welcomes them, as do NGOs, and, occasionally, expert members of the Human Rights Committee and other UN treaty bodies.[39] Whereas the selection processes for UN and NGO interns are elaborate and detailed,[40] the selection process for Committee member interns appears rather informal and connected to both personal connections and indirect social relations. At the sessions I attended, there were between three and five Committee member interns. Most were former or current students of the members, studying at the master's or doctoral level at the universities where the Committee members taught, commonly as law professors.[41]

Soon after the sessions started, the interns formed a social group of their own. Association with the interns allowed for the opportunistic navigation of the border between inclusion and exclusion. It all began as innocent inquiries about why certain sessions were closed to general observers, such as the lunchtime hearings between Committee members and NGO delegates, which were closed to state representatives.

The interns were nevertheless allowed access—but why? In discussion, I learned that not even the interns themselves were always certain whether they were formally permitted to attend. They followed subtle clues from the Committee member for whom they interned, waiting for an indication that their presence was appropriate. These clues revealed that the border between inclusion and exclusion at the Committee's sessions did not depend solely on predetermined, written guidelines; rather, it was governed by fuzzy logic, embodied in subtle maneuvering and tactical navigation.

As the weeks wore on, some interns became bolder in their experiments: they would simply show up at a meeting and, if not told to leave, treat this as permission to stay. I soon began to follow their lead: where the interns went, I went too. By then—because of my exaggerated transparency regarding my research—everyone in a position of responsibility, both Committee members and UN staff attending the sessions, knew I was an anthropologist conducting an ethnographic study. I started to treat our shared knowledge as my ultimate badge for inclusion: if those responsible for managing the border between inclusion and exclusion did not actively exclude me, I took it as a sign that I was allowed access. Of course, it is likely that not everyone remembered I was not an intern—still, nobody ever questioned whether I had the right badge to attend or not.

In fact, as part of my fieldwork, I never wore my badge—the plastic artefact with my name and affiliation printed on it—despite the security guards always telling me to do so when I entered the Palais. Nobody ever asked to see it, either. I learned that the real badge for access was personal connections paired with a confident demeanor and, in particular, a casual nod and slight smile when encountering previously unknown people in the hallways. I thus gained firsthand experience of the fuzzy logic characterizing the porous border between inclusion and exclusion in the Committee's sessions. Additionally, I learned about the microdynamics of power—here, indicated by who received access to the Human Rights Committee's closed sessions—that strategically placed insiders can mobilize during Committee sessions.

Moments of Unexpected Exclusion

In all the time I spent at the Palais, I encountered only one instance where someone questioned whether the interns actually possessed the required clearance to participate in a given session. Eventually, the interns, myself included, succeeded in defending our entitlement to stay by highlighting our personal connections to individual Committee members. In doing so, the interns capitalized on their knowledge of the Committee's inner dynamics: its members—renowned international experts on human rights, commonly either university professors or diplomats by vocation—are the "Stars" of the sessions, as discussed in Chapter 3, whereas many members of UN conference services attending to practical matters are junior UN officials.

Committee members are, by definition, *independent* experts, meaning they are neither UN staff nor under the authority of the UN Secretariat. This reveals the intrinsically porous nature of the Human Rights Committee: if members wish to include interns at sessions closed to state delegates, the UN Secretariat staff lacks the structural authority to deny them. The interns themselves were active agents in the accompanying maneuvering. Having identified the differences in professional ranks between their Committee-member patrons and UN staff, they boldly and opportunistically pushed the boundaries of inclusion in their favor, gaining further exposure to the full range of the Committee's operations.

These findings resonate with Cowan's and Billaud's ethnographic research on the UPR. Their research likewise shows how, despite seemingly clear-cut guidelines, the quest for access is, in practice, the subject of ongoing negotiations. In the case of the UPR, negotiations over access manifested in questions about who was allowed to observe the proceedings in the large meeting room where the Human Rights Council convenes at the Palais des Nations, who was required to follow them from the observation room two floors up behind glass, and who—namely, the unengaged public—was excluded from the sessions altogether, despite the UN's claim that the UPR is a public monitoring mechanism intended to be open to the world.[42]

My access to the Human Rights Committee as a whole was both temporary and vicarious: my informal internship lasted only for that one session. As soon as the session ended, I was an outsider again, with no access even to the Palais Wilson unless I renewed my accreditation—just like everyone else who had gained access to the UN bureaucratic apparatus for the session. Since my internship was merely the result of a verbal agreement, I had no paperwork to attest to my status, had someone requested proof at any point, which did not happen.

Elusive Borders of Inclusion Among the Never-Ending Movement of Staff

My experiences of achieving inclusion reveal how contingent the borders of inclusion and exclusion can be inside the UN human rights apparatus, and how temporary even the most careful plans to confirm access may become. What remains to be discussed is the tangible, overarching reason behind elusiveness: the continual movement of people within the Human Rights Committee, treaty bodies, and the UN. The eighteen expert members are elected to the Committee for four-year terms, with elections taking place every two years.[43] Thus the Committee's composition is in constant flux.

Also, the support staff at the UN OHCHR who attend to the Committee's documentation and pragmatics change regularly. Staff mobility, or "rotation," in UN parlance, is an established practice within the organization, discussed by the General Assembly since the 1980s.[44] Various UN offices present staff mobility from individual- and staff-centered approaches, describing it as an asset—part "of an integrated talent management system"[45] that supports career development and sustained engagement in rewarding tasks.[46] UN guidelines emphasize equity: staff members are not stationed in distant or difficult field locations for excessively long periods of time, and positions are to be filled equitably to avoid unwelcome vacancies.[47] Staff mobility is officially incentivized, as with the staff rules for the UN Human Rights Portal,[48] and, in some cases, expected, as for the UN Development Program.[49]

My writing process is a testament to rotation: by the time I finished my manuscript, the composition of the Human Rights Committee had entirely changed from that of the 2013 sessions, with even the longest-serving members having departed.[50] The key personnel in the UN Secretariat, all of whom have moved to new positions in the OHCHR, other UN bodies, or elsewhere, had changed, as had most NGO delegates submitting shadow reports to the Committee. Thus, the personal connections I established to conduct my research have become severed and replaced by indirect, mediated relations—alongside new personal connections I have managed to forge during subsequent fieldwork visits.

Staff attitudes toward professional movement appear mixed. A 2010 UN Staff Union survey found that many staff felt the UN did not sufficiently support them in cases of mobility. Almost a third of respondents were unaware of the expectation that they would change their post after a maximum tenure of five years. Staff expressed concern about the time and labor required to learn new positions and worried whether the UN was making the best use of existing expertise. Staff was divided on the social effects of movement, highlighting difficulties for mothers and single parents in particular.[51] Reservations about the expectation of ongoing mobility surfaced during discussions with UN personnel; they expressed anxiety and disappointment over delayed staffing decisions.

Ongoing staff movement has pivotal—and, so far, understudied—consequences for the inner dynamics of the UN human rights apparatus, including how the border between inclusion and exclusion is defined. Since all UN personnel occupy their positions for fixed periods, only a few people are genuine insiders in any given monitoring mechanism or expert body—individuals whom I term the Guardians of Vision. Most remain partial insiders and partial outsiders. Those staff members who have held their positions longer by serving numerous consecutive terms, or who have rotated across more UN positions, possess tacit insider knowledge and influence not held by their colleagues just starting their positions. It is often difficult, even impossible, to identify these influential insiders immediately—a finding that contributes to the fuzzy logic of the UN human rights apparatus.

At the minute level of UN operations, the nonstop movement of staff likewise contributes to fuzzy logic: it affects which interpreters or press secretaries are present week by week at treaty body sessions, or which UN conference service staff manage the conference room to maintain order and discipline when Committee members attempt to smuggle in food and drink. One week, an observer may know all of these individuals and their working habits personally, and the following week the personnel may have changed entirely. The outcome increases the influence of the select few who stay put. It further means that, instead of direct social contacts, many people, not just the ethnographer, are connected to the UN human rights apparatus by mediated indirect relations.

One might expect nonstop rotation to result in the dominance of the apparatus's operational logic—for example, diligent fulfillment of specific bureaucratic responsibilities rather than broad adherence to human rights. Nevertheless, that appears not to be the case in the Human Rights Committee's operations. Instead, the UN Human Rights Division staff appear to continuously have an affinity for the core values of their work. This observation stems partly from processes of social initiation: when observing the Human Rights Committee's sessions, it becomes clear that virtually no true outsiders are present. Rather, everyone—including interns and students—appears to belong, or aspires to belong, to the same Guardian of Vision community of practice, sharing the view that human rights and the rule of law are key to improving the world, as Chapter 3 elaborates.

Fuzzy Logic as Impact

These observations bring us back to the metaphor of ice. They demonstrate the opaque transparency of the UN human rights apparatus and the fuzzy logic of ongoing negotiations between the rigid "system" or "structure" of UN treaty bodies' legal mandates and the indeterminacy of the rules agents use in practice.[52] Just as one cannot fully deduce the detailed microstructure of ice from the outside, one cannot pinpoint exactly where the passageways of inclusion lie within the UN's bureaucratic contours. Just as ice melts and solidifies again, forever sealing the small cracks and toeholds that once existed on its surface, so do passages of access, for both an anthropologist studying UN bureaucracies and UN staff members who have moved to other positions. These passages may open, only to close again quite unexpectedly, without a trace.

Thus, like ice, the transparency of UN operations is always partial, distorted, and at times opaque, despite stated ideals or expectations. These ethnographic findings stand in stark contrast to the prevailing belief that contemporary bureaucratic practices are transparent—an ideal that also many anthropologists of bureaucracy have challenged, showing instead that transparency is an abstract ideal made impossible by bureaucratic intricacies.[53]

Simultaneously fuzzy logic is undoubtedly a source of frustration for UN human rights insiders, as was evident when the Human Rights Committee's membership changed drastically in 2014, following elections taking place in New York—even if the outcome was in no way new or unexpected to UN insiders. "No matter how things appear beforehand and who appear to be the top candidates, one will never know what the outcome will be before things are finalized," a seasoned UN insider explained. "That is how UN personnel selections always go," the insider continued, denoting it as the reason why many long-term UN staff are noticeably disinterested in UN electoral processes.

UN insiders are well aware of opportunities for informal influence that fuzzy logic offers, as a session on UN treaty body reform, which included high-profile UN staff, illustrated. In a roundtable discussion about the wording of the document to be submitted to the OHCHR as a platform for action, a senior UN official remarked that it was unwise to develop formulations that were too specific. After all, many elements of treaty body operations are at the discretion of the bodies themselves due to their open-ended mandates, the official reminded the participants. Committing different issues in writing would only complicate matters by bringing them to the attention of states reluctant to accept the treaty bodies' broad scope of operations.[54] Any written codification, the official emphasized, would thus only offer concrete grounds for formal state opposition.

In international diplomacy and realpolitik, the prevalence of fuzzy logic raises concerns about dubious actions carried out under its guise, including attempts by powerful states to block the advancement of human rights. As Chapter 4 elaborates, such attempts and motivations are doubtlessly part of UN human rights bureaucracies. However—as one of my primary arguments goes—ethnographic research on the UN human rights apparatus tells how fuzzy logic serves as an important tool for human rights insiders to work for their advancement while resisting efforts to sideline human rights in the face of realpolitik. It protects the ice-like fragility that generally characterizes the work of the Human Rights Committee and UN human rights monitoring.

And the Movement Continues

The first few days of a new Committee session are marked by a sense of enthusiasm and concentration: people arrive punctually, few leave the conference room for impromptu coffee breaks or personal chats, and most maintain their focus on the events at hand. The only distraction is the occasional UN staff touring the room to check on practical matters, such as whether the microphones of the interpreters are working or the informal NGO meeting schedules are continually current. During these days, the facial expressions of those in the meeting room are somber and attentive, with every participatory detail highlighting the importance of the ceremony we are all jointly bringing to life. In these fleeting few days, it is possible to observe and meet the archetype of the international human rights community in action: a group of concerned world citizens who have traveled great distances to participate in a shared ritual to improve the world.

By day three, the presence of this archetype begins to fade as the community becomes increasingly transformed into real people—people for whom, like all other people, it is simply impossible to remain solely focused on the ceremony. Instead, audience members seated at the back of the Palais Wilson seek occasional retreat to their "real reality" outside in modern technologies—replying to emails, checking newspaper websites for world events, updating their social media statuses. Some use the rare opportunity of sitting still to work on outstanding publishing commitments, editing texts and drafting new ones. Some appear visibly bored, twitching in their seats; a few relish the opportunity for a short nap.

In the weeks that follow, a more relaxed atmosphere slowly begins to characterize the sessions. Since the number of participants in the Committee's sessions is relatively small—at the lowest, they may include fewer than forty people—security guards at the gate recognize most regulars and sometimes ease up on the formalities of presenting a badge or passport, waving select people straight through the metal detector. By week two, people start slipping into the conference room late. One can overhear newly acquainted audience members sharing their experiences of the previous night in Geneva, and the occasional Committee member may sneak in a formally forbidden snack or a soda.

At the podium, the liturgy continues while state delegations change: the endless litany of legislative reforms, policy initiatives, committees, communications, plans, and follow-ups. All continue their work to construct a seamless tale of progress. The "international" is in action and full swing.

CHAPTER 3

Guardians of Vision

Existing scholarship on the Human Rights Committee and other UN treaty bodies tends to examine their operations solely from the viewpoint of their expert members. I complement those depictions by offering a holistic view of the Committee as a *community of practice* that includes its eighteen expert members and the UN Secretariat staff. Furthermore, this chapter paves the way for a broader discussion continued in Chapter 6 on how the community at times extends to state representatives—contrary to portrayals of states as adversaries in treaty body proceedings—illustrated below with a vignette from the Committee's 3,000th session.

I call the participants of this community *Guardians of Vision*: professionals who subscribe to human rights values and devote their careers to advancing them. Amid constant staff rotation, Guardians are professionals linked to UN treaty bodies and the Human Rights Committee for notably lengthy periods, sometimes decades. Whether they serve as the Committee's expert members, UN staff, or NGO delegates, Guardians share tacit insider knowledge of the UN human rights apparatus's fuzzy logic. In addition, they have extensive networks of indirect relations as well as direct personal connections that confer informal power. This chapter showcases the subtle techniques Guardians of Vision use to navigate the UN human rights apparatus to hold so-called political influences at bay while sustaining movement in the rights direction. In addition, it reflects on the impact and consequences of the bureaucratic infrastructures that accompany international human rights monitoring.

3,000th Session: Breaking Ice

"Does someone want to break more ice?" The 3,000th session of the UN Human Rights Committee had been underway for a good hour when the chair, Sir Nigel Rodley, looked around the room inquisitively. To mark the occasion, the meeting was held, contrary to the usual venue at the Palais Wilson, in one of the large conference rooms at the UN headquarters, the Palais des Nations.[1] Outside, the July heat was scorching, making the metaphor of breaking ice feel like wishful thinking. The session had drawn an unusually large number of state delegates, reflecting its purpose: to meet with states as the Committee's primary stakeholders. The aim was to celebrate the Committee's work while discussing the key perils facing both the Committee and the UN treaty body framework as a whole.

Although Sir Nigel's invitation to "break more ice" carried a characteristic lightness reflecting his chairing style, it masked somber undertones. The exchange between the Committee and states experienced a rocky start when the Belarus delegate seized the floor to address the contested requirement of exhausting all domestic remedies before sending an individual communication to the Committee.[2] At the heart of the contestation was what constitutes effective remedies and who has the final authority to determine exhaustion—the Committee or the state?

This dispute ties into long-running controversies regarding UN treaty bodies' operations, anchored in their open-ended treaty-based mandates: exactly what is the scope of their work, and to what extent may treaty bodies define the details and scope independently of states parties? Only a year earlier, these tensions crystallized in a proposal advanced by an "intergovernmental" coalition to steer treaty body reform toward notably narrower discretion and greater state control.[3] Metaphorically, the proposal sought to freeze the ongoing movement generated by the Guardians of Vision under the UN human rights apparatus's fuzzy logic—momentum that had increasingly enabled international oversight to promote human rights and the rule of law inside states' internal affairs. Furthermore, the proposal laid bare geopolitical fault lines: it was presented by Russia and supported by eighty-five states, mostly from Africa and Asia, including China and Belarus, while sixty-six states, including many from Western Europe, North America, and Latin America abstained.[4]

While the proposal was ultimately sidelined in the treaty body reform process, so too was the intervention by Belarus in a persuasive demonstration of human rights diplomacy in action. Under Sir Nigel's chairmanship, the Committee addressed Belarus's questions only a quarter hour after the delegate raised them. By then, the debate had coalesced around a different theme introduced by state delegates from Ireland, Costa Rica, Uruguay, Chad, the UK, Paraguay, and the US.

Their interventions shifted focus on the Committee's continued effectiveness, in particular the backlog the Committee's insufficient resources caused.[5] Both the majority of state delegates and Committee members responding to them highlighted resource scarcity as the chief threat to the Committee's ongoing work. Some commentators even warned that resource scarcity jeopardized the Committee's legitimacy—a diagnosis notably at odds with Belarus's portrayal of excessive Committee discretion as the central problem.

When the members finally turned to Belarus's intervention, their tactic recalled an efficient hockey team. One member addressed the exhaustion of domestic remedies from the viewpoint of prior case law and jurisprudence. Another underscored the broad consensus concerning the Committee's discretion, calling Belarus's approach "not convincing to the Committee." A third emphasized the Committee's Covenant-bound mandate to interpret the ICCPR and its optional protocol. A fourth aligned the Committee's practice with "every other judicial body of international law," arguing that the Committee's interpretative discretion was beyond question. Confirming the points scored in defense of the Committee's broad discretion, Sir Nigel concluded by suggesting that there may have been a "problem of translation" in Belarus's remarks, subtly portraying the intervention as lacking a full grasp of the Committee's jurisprudence and the nuances of human rights diplomacy.

During the debate, the issue of resource scarcity centered on one overarching theme in particular: a shortage of personnel resources, meaning insufficient UN staff to assist the Committee in its work—or perhaps more accurately, to *realize* the Committee's operations. Since the Committee's eighteen members are not UN staff but independent experts receiving per diems, they cannot themselves meet the UN bureaucracy's formal requirements: the intricate processes for submitting and registering documents in the UN system as well as preparing them for the sessions.

At the 3,000th session, Committee members highlighted the practical consequences that staff shortages had for preparing background documents. They noted that although the Committee's expert members would have time during the Committee's sessions to process additional individual communications—work that would help reduce the consistent backlog plaguing the Committee—the secretariat lacked sufficient personnel to assign to the task. Several members pointed to their repeated unsuccessful appeals to the General Assembly for additional staff to work on the high number of pending cases.

Throughout the exchange, UN Secretariat staff remained in their assigned seats, as an embodied reminder of the session's special character. By contrast, during ordinary sessions the staff is conspicuous in their nonstop movement: entering and exiting the Palais Wilson conference room with stacks of papers; moving from the front of the room to the back while distributing documents; circulating around to deliver remarks to individual Committee members or state delegates; and intermittently engaging with press secretaries, members of the UN conference services, interpreters, and NGO delegates.

The Community of Practice of the Guardians of Vision

Recent research on international collaboration and human rights that focuses on actors emphasizes, on one hand, the centrality of experts[6] and, on the other, the network-like character of activist and expert communities.[7] Also relevant is a recently revived discussion about epistemic communities, initially begun by soft constructivist scholars of international relations concerned with agency,[8] and recently embraced by international lawyers.[9] This discussion focuses on diverse values, principled and causal beliefs, and how discourses connect different actors: in other words, "the identities, interests, and practices that shape the identification of actors in international relations and law, subsequently shaping policies and legislation."[10]

The language of epistemic communities is illuminating but insufficient for my analysis. We can easily state that Human Rights Committee expert members form an epistemic community of their own, characterized by a commitment to shared human rights values and what Cowan characterizes "modes of acting virtuously."[11] They further deploy a shared human rights discourse to address the societal ills the Committee tackles as it examines state reports and individual communications.

Yet from an ethnographic viewpoint, the Committee's operations are not simply contiguous with its expert members. To achieve a holistic view, I therefore turn to the notion of a *community of practice*. The concept was initially developed by social learning theorists[12] and recently adopted by international lawyers to foreground the plurality of actors.[13] The term highlights multiple groups who participate in shared operations within their field, resonating with anthropology's long-term emphasis on practice.[14]

For the present analysis, the concept of the community of practice shows how, empirically, the Committee's work blurs the boundaries among "expert," "bureaucrat," "the UN," "the state," and the "NGO," while conflating the categories of "international" and "local." "Community," rather than "network," better captures the multifaceted, substantive, and enduring ways in which members of international human rights bureaucracies connect to each other.[15] To employ the language of "practice" instead of "episteme" highlights how, when examined empirically, the Human Rights Committee's work is only partially dominated by its core epistemic community of expert members. Moreover, the sense of community and shared aptitudes that span different formal roles involve more than "knowledge" per se, including also shared beliefs *and* practices.

"To Me, Human Rights Are Law"

Focusing on practice offers a perspective for considering the international, even *universal* character of human rights monitoring. Here Riles's observation is instructive: "What makes law global is the technical, in other words, the fact that a lawyer in Dubai or London will approach a legal document from a largely similar set of routinized pathways of thought."[16] This insight resonates with the Committee's legally oriented community of practice. The vast majority of Committee members have a legal background, and—even though all UN treaty bodies essentially perform the same legally grounded task of examining how states comply with their Covenant obligation—the Committee consistently has the highest percentage of legally trained members.[17]

Legal emphasis further appears in how Committee members describe their involvement: in interviews, some said that the Human Rights Committee was "the only treaty body that attracted them," while others emphasized their professional profile as black-letter lawyers. One Committee member summarized the relationship between human rights and the law succinctly, stating "to me, human rights are law." Legal emphasis impacts further how some Committee insiders view the UPR. One member called it "a detriment to the treaty bodies, taking up both serious resources as well as attention." The Committee member further noted the UPR's "superficial" nature, as well as the fact that it is "purely political," as opposed to the Committee's more legal character.

The UN Secretariat staff who prepare the Committee's background documents—who administratively belong to the Human Rights Treaties Division, one of the OHCHR's three divisions[18]—likewise predominantly have a legal background. In discussions, UN staff working with the Committee often underscore its legal nature, again by comparison with the UPR. Others take a more conciliatory view, acknowledging that the UPR has increased the treaty bodies' visibility and prompted states to be more attentive to their reporting obligations. As Chapter 6 elaborates, the profiles of state delegates who prepare documents for the Committee and attend Constructive Dialogues also highlight legal backgrounds.

The Invisible College of Northern Lawyers

The community of practice surrounding the Committee's operations thus echoes the "invisible college" of international lawyers.[19] Often the Guardians of Vision share similar training in human rights and the law, such as master's degrees or study exchanges in universities in Western and Northern Europe or the United States. Shared education backgrounds are particularly common among younger professional generations, echoing the timescale during which the contemporary human rights phenomenon has expanded: whereas foreign affairs officials in the 1960s and the 1970s were unlikely to have formal training in human rights—such educational programs did not exist as, for instance, LLM degrees in human rights law have proliferated only since the mid-1990s[20]—today such education is commonplace.

In addition to sharing a legal background, many core actors share similar geographic origins. The UN OHCHR's staff predominantly originate from the Global North: statistics from 2014 showed how, of slightly over five hundred permanent staff, half were from the UN category "Western Europe and Others" (WEO), which includes the US, Canada, Australia, and New Zealand.[21] For comparison, slightly over 10 percent of the world's population falls into the same category.[22]

Eight countries are particularly prominent among OHCHR staff: one in eight originate from the UK, the US, or Canada, and one in four from France, Germany, Italy, Spain, or Switzerland.[23] In light of these figures, "the international'" that the OHCHR staff encompasses aligns heavily with the Global North. Geographic overrepresentation is a concern for the UN, as states parties expect it to ensure equitable geographic representation. One response has been to introduce action plans to increase diversity. These initiatives, nevertheless, have not altered staff composition: by 2020 the number of permanent staff had grown to more than seven hundred while the geographic distribution remained essentially unchanged.[24]

These statistics reflect the composition of the Human Rights Committee, as most of its members, since the Committee's inception, have come from the

Global North.[25] Over a third of all current and former members are from the "Western European and Others" category. Further, more than one-quarter of all Human Rights Committee members originate from Western European states, whereas these states account for 16 percent of UN human rights treaty ratifications and only 6 percent of the world's population.

By contrast, only 13 percent of the members of the Human Rights Committee come from Asian-Pacific countries, whereas these countries account for 60 percent of the world's population.[26] Since the Committee's founding, Asia-Pacific representation has steadily declined: between 1977 and 2000, the region averaged three members per Committee; between 2010 and 2022, the number fell to one. Despite continual rotation of both individual Committee members and relevant Secretariat staff, their legal backgrounds as well as their predominantly geographic origins have remained constant features of the Committee's operations, forming parts of the "pathways"[27] that guide those operations' ongoing movement, as Chapter 4 elaborates.

The Stars

The Human Rights Committee's principal actors—whom I call the Stars—are its eighteen expert members, who fulfill the Committee's raison d'être by assessing states' compliance with the ICCPR and conducting court-like evaluations of individual communications. Members often embrace—and are expected by the international human rights community to embrace—a proactive role in developing the ICCPR's meaning, including drafting General Comments, which sustains the forward-looking momentum of progressive human rights work.[28]

The members' Star status is manifested by their physical movement both before and during the Committee's sessions. The "International" truly comes to life when the Stars arrive at the Palais Wilson from across the globe, bringing expertise, charisma, and suitcases. During the sessions, those suitcases keep moving: many Stars bring their luggage into the Committee's sessions to accommodate the voluminous paper stacks that the Committee's work entails.

Inside the sessions, members' relative immobility underlines their star status, setting them apart from others present. UN staff shift seats at the podium; state delegates come and go; outside observers move within the audience as seats free up. By contrast, the Committee members occupy fixed U-shaped seating around the room's perimeter, each place clearly marked with a nameplate. These plates display the only personal names in the conference room, whereas all other seats are labeled generically as "state delegation," "NGO representative," or "UN Secretariat." Committee members' Star status is further marked by broad access. Aside from designated UN staff, they alone may access all Committee sessions: in the mornings, members pass through security with a certain VIP ease; inside the Palais, they walk along the corridors with a distinct Star aura, since many people know who they are while they themselves recognize only a few observers.

What does it take to become a Star? First, it requires a huge amount of work, both before and during Committee membership. Committee members sit in up to fifteen weeks of intensive sessions per year in Geneva, in addition to the required advance preparation for those meetings. New members sometimes express surprise at how much work is involved; as one remarked to me, "If there was a handbook on what it means to be a treaty body member, there should be a warning."[29] For those members assuming such additional responsibilities as drafting a General Comment—a task that requires tremendous work due to the extensive scope of background material one must consult, including the Committee's "jurisprudence"—work commonly extends between sessions. As one member stated, one is "lucky to go two days without having some communication from the Secretariat." Many note that the pace has intensified because the Committee processes increasing numbers of state reports during each session.

Experiences with preparations differ somewhat between new and more seasoned members: whereas everyone emphasizes that the Geneva sessions are intense, descriptions of advance preparations vary. Some say preparations often happen "at the last minute" to balance other responsibilities as university professors, sitting judges, or consultants; one particularly seasoned member even shared that preparations "do not take me long at all." Such experiences, however, appear to be an exception. Some Committee members use assistants, whereas long-serving members may choose to prepare alone—one member explained that assistants would "only get in the way at this point."

Workload and preparation time vary depending on the sub-committees known as tasks forces in which members participate. Task Forces are responsible—with the support of UN staff—for preparing the draft list of issues and the draft Concluding Observations to be discussed and adopted by the Committee. Members commonly join between one to three Task Forces per session, though some may not join any, perhaps owing to other obligations. Additional work falls to Committee members who serve as rapporteurs for state reports, holding the primary responsibility for organizing the Committee's background preparations and opening the Constructive Dialogue with state delegations. Significantly more work, and influence, falls on Committee members who become part of the Committee's bureau, comprising the Committee's chair, three vice chairs, and a rapporteur responsible for preparing the Committee's annual report.[30]

An indication of the importance of the Committee's community of practice is that many nominees for the Committee have often already engaged with the Committee's work, sometimes extensively. Numerous candidates have centered their academic endeavors on it, including possible doctoral dissertations, and many have attended the Committee's sessions in other capacities such as junior NGO delegates or observers. In terms of age, numerous Human Rights Committee members are elected in their fifties or sixties, while some are significantly younger, in their mid-forties or even late thirties.[31]

Seniority within the Committee shifts quickly because membership rotates every two years when half of the members are elected to four-year terms by states parties at the UN General Assembly. Thus a member who began two years earlier as the "baby of the group," as one described, may find themselves an experienced senior a mere two years later. Turnover appears faster on the Human Rights Committee than on many other treaty bodies, where members may serve several terms spanning decades. By contrast, after the 2014 elections, for example, one-third of the Committee's members changed.

Expertise Fitting for a Star

Even though new members are continuously elected, the sense of the community of practice remains strong. When candidates are proposed for the Committee, the primary formal selection criterion is recognized competence in the field of human rights.[32] Emphasis on independent expertise emerges in how Committee members describe their role. As one member put it: "As an expert, I did not represent my government or check my views from any domain. The views I put forth were my own and based on my academic and other experience."

In concrete terms, competence, or expertise, often means substantial prior experience with the UN, such as drafting expert statements for treaty bodies or advising state delegations.[33] Many have backgrounds in NGOs such as Amnesty International, as well as experience as judges, or have served as experts in domestic human rights–related proceedings, such as asylum cases. Many are associated with national human rights institutes (NHRIs). Another key element of recognized expertise is academic standing: statistically most Committee members are professors of either international or human rights law.

Upon describing how they were elected, most members state that they were asked to join. One recalled receiving "the most unexpected call" from the Ministry for Foreign Affairs as "nobody even knew that they were looking to nominate someone." The call came as a surprise because the candidate was quite young and Committee membership had been a "professional dream one day," a culmination of a career and "certainly not something that would arrive right in the middle of things." Nevertheless, saying no was not an option, the member shared. If they had refused, another person would be nominated and, if elected, might serve two four-year terms. After such outcomes, the foreign ministry "most certainly would not have called again." Thus, it was "either this moment or never."

By contrast, some members explained that they campaigned actively—even "aggressively," as one phrased it—for their election. Concurrently, no one said that they had initially volunteered for the position. Rather, someone in a relevant government position must have been aware of their qualifications in order to consider them.[34] Awareness of individual expertise links back to the idea of human rights work as rooted in a distinct community of practice—the Guardians of Vision—built on both mediated, indirect relations and direct, personal connections.

Some Stars Shine Brighter Than Others: Sir Nigel Rodley

Whereas all Committee members enjoy Star status to some degree, as elsewhere, some Stars shine brighter than others. Within each Committee, a few members—consistently singled out by fellow members, UN staff, state representatives, and NGO delegates—stand out in the Guardians of Vision community for their international reputation, legal skill, or eloquence—or, ideally, all three. These bright Stars often author leading texts on treaty bodies' work and may move on to serve as UN special rapporteur or take on other high-profile UN tasks.[35] Insiders of the UN human rights apparatus often describe such figures as "stellar legal minds" or even "geniuses," to whom the more technical parts of the Committee's work fall, such as drafting the first versions of General Comments.[36] In the Committee's sessions, their impact is visible in sustained, active engagement—including, at times, joining the Constructive Dialogues on states for which they were not on the task force. After the Dialogues, state delegates describe these members as "having done their homework," enabling the Committee to craft sharp, on-point recommendations for the Concluding Observations.

Stars will commonly have native-level English proficiency, which matters for the Committee's work: although the operational languages are English, French, and Spanish, English predominates in practice. Language skills are especially significant when drafting General Comments, where preparatory work is done in English and often turns on the nuances and connotations of individual words.

The late Sir Nigel Rodley was undoubtedly among the Committee's brightest Stars. His profile shows how, for Guardians of Vision, the categories of advocate, expert, and bureaucrat—and treaty body, UN staff, and NGO—intersect. Simultaneously it illustrates how influential distinct individuals within the community of practice can be, both for the functioning of UN treaty bodies and for the broader expansion of the contemporary human rights phenomenon. A lawyer by training, Sir Nigel moved from the UK to Canada for his first academic post as an assistant professor of law at Dalhousie University in 1965.[37] He then moved to New York to serve as associate economic affairs officer at the UN Department of Economic and Social Affairs. In 1972, he joined Amnesty International's New York office, founding and leading the organization's legal office, which soon became central to the organization's operations.[38]

In 1990, Rodley re-entered academia at the University of Essex, becoming first reader and later professor of international human rights law. He co-founded the university's human rights LLM (master of laws) program, recognized as both the UK's and the world's first such program. It has since trained thousands of students, who have become integral participants in the Guardians of Vision community of practice around the world.[39] Rodley lectured at numerous institutions around the globe and was described as an energetic teacher and devoted mentor.[40] He maintained strong ties to human rights NGOs, serving on the boards of Justice, Freedom from Torture, Penal Reform International, REDRESS, and the Universal Rights Group.[41] He was president of the International Commission of Jurists[42] and was said to have "never lost his attachment to Amnesty."[43] In recognition of his work for human rights and international law, he was knighted in 1988.

Concurrently Rodley was deeply engaged in human rights work at the UN. He contributed to drafting the UN Convention Against Torture and Other Cruel, Inhuman, or Degrading Treatment or Punishment (CAT).[44] From 1993 to 2000, he served as special rapporteur on torture.[45] In 2000, he was appointed to the Human Rights Committee and served for fifteen years, which made him one of its longest-serving members. In 2013–2014, he chaired the Committee. Upon his passing in 2017, the breadth of his mediated relations and personal connections was reflected in tributes from former colleagues and students from around the world, including former US President Jimmy Carter.[46]

His vast personal connections were visible during the Human Rights Committee sessions in subtle and conspicuous ways. These included shared lunch and coffee breaks with UN insiders, informal chats and shared jokes with state delegates and NGO representatives, and people "coming over to him and greeting him with a warm hug."[47] They included such public displays as welcoming Jane Connors, director of the OHCHR's Research and Right to Development Division, who was speaking on behalf of the UN high commissioner for human rights, to a Committee session by noting how they "have been working together in more ways than either one of us cares to remember."[48] His former students appeared at Committee sessions, not only as part of the UN Secretariat and NGOs but in state delegations.[49] Rodley was described as "particularly delighted" by a session in which alumni argued both sides of an individual communication before the Committee.[50]

The International Diplomat

Due to the treaty bodies' complex electoral process, even the brightest Stars are not guaranteed election, as the selection processes are embedded in broader UN dynamics characterized by Bourdieusian fuzzy logic of politics, negotiations, and deal-making.[51] This observation returns to members' duality regarding states: although, once elected, members are expected to act as autonomous human rights experts, they are nominated for candidacy by their home states. Thus, during the electoral process they are seen as state representatives[52]—which, in turn, invites political bargaining: states may form alliances to support each other's candidates in exchange for favors, such as supporting a state's candidacy for a UN Security Council seat.[53]

As an outcome of the UN's electoral logic, alongside "Stars," each Committee includes individuals whom members of the Guardians of Vision community might call "International Diplomats." These are individuals whom UN staff and state delegates see as having secured their positions not because of expertise but because of other considerations connected to state politics. The Achilles' heel created by electoral bargaining is a common complaint among human rights insiders: as one UN staff member put it, excellent candidates can be overlooked, while "less than ideal" candidates are elected. UN insiders sometimes note, with a sneer, that retired diplomats may be presented candidacies as a reward for long careers.[54] State delegates may likewise criticize particular members as falling short of the ideal they should meet.[55]

Once elected, UN staff may view them as lacking substantive expertise in human rights law. Further, their engagement may be seen as echoing state concerns, including pointed views on state sovereignty, rather than human rights concerns. UN insiders sometimes characterize International Diplomats as disappointing in their work ethics for failing to prepare for sessions with the expected diligence. As one Committee member candidly noted, "some members take the work more seriously than others, or more specifically, some take it less seriously than others." Simultaneously these examples reveal the significance of the UN Secretariat's subtle maneuvering under the icelike, partially opaque UN human rights apparatus to keep the Committee running smoothly—both by balancing views that represent state interests and by subtly marginalizing views that indicate a lack of advance preparation.

The Bureaucrat

"It's the UN Human Rights Committee!" Maria's eyes glimmer as she talks about the Committee's work. Her tone communicates that, to her, we are not talking of just any Committee, but rather the most important component of the UN's human rights framework—and by extension, one of the most important human rights bodies in the world. We are enjoying a coffee break a short walk from the Palais Wilson in the middle of yet another long day of sessions. The week has been packed with reports from numerous high-profile states as well as a few first-time reports, always a noteworthy occasion.

After several intense days, a collective exhaustion has settled over the Palais. It shows in the stressed pace of UN staff dashing in and out of meetings to ensure that every detail is handled and background papers are distributed on time. Committee members, too, display signs of fatigue after workdays stretching from morning into evening, with few breaks beyond lunch. During sessions, a few close their eyes in quieter moments; others extend the occasional coffee break well into session time.

Simultaneously, the pervasive sense of collective commitment to, and appreciation for, the work at hand remains unchanged, emerging in discussions with UN staff, NGOs, and states, as well as with Committee members. For this community of practice, to serve on the Human Rights Committee is to be "a very important person" who performs a function of utmost significance for the realization of international human rights. Many Committee members may characterize the role as among the most fulfilling positions a human rights expert and a lawyer can hold—a position that may crown a career. Likewise, staff who work with the Committee often view their role as one of the most meaningful positions within the UN for advancing human rights—and for the interns aspiring to become human rights experts themselves, "It's the dream!," as one put it excitedly.

Whereas in the Committee's operations, the Stars shine brightly at center stage, staff of the UN Human Rights Treaties Division operate inconspicuously in the margins.[56] UN staff's frequent movement around the Palais Wilson's conference room—described at the opening segment—represent only a fraction of the behind-the-scenes work that they perform in a role akin to infrastructure: when everything flows as expected, the infrastructure is near invisible; when disruptions occur, it becomes exposed.[57] Below, I discuss the Secretariat's role in the Human Rights Committee's sessions and the treaty body framework more broadly, showing how staff balance the identities of detached bureaucrats and passionately engaged activists.[58]

To preserve interlocutor anonymity, I tell the story with two pseudonyms, each an amalgamation of interviewed UN staff.[59] "Maria" represents lower-level staff who handle practical matters, such as drafting texts and other support work for the Committee. "Taylor" represents senior-level staff who have long experience in treaty body operations but are no longer engaged in nuts-and-bolts tasks. To reflect gender patterns of UN staffing, Maria is referred to as "she" in recognition of women forming the majority in lower-ranking UN staff positions, whereas Taylor is referred to as "he" because men predominate in higher-level positions.[60]

The UN Secretariat's work for the Committee's sessions spans numerous integral tasks: with the exception of General Comments, every document processed by the Committee is first worked on by a staff member. Before each session, Secretariat staff prepare draft documents known as Lists of issues under the guidance of the Committee member serving as rapporteur, these draft documents forming the basis of the Committee's Constructive Dialogue with states.

During these sessions, staff take notes of the proceedings and use the material to write the first drafts of Concluding Observations, the legally non-binding assessments of how states have, or have not, met their obligations under the ICCPR. The Committee then discusses the drafts, and the staff take notes, editing the drafts as needed before the Committee adopts the finalized document. After a session concludes, Secretariat staff draft follow-up documentation aimed at increasing compliance with the Committee's recommendations.

The Secretariat's role is also significant when it comes to drafting General Comments. The Secretariat posts the Comment's first draft on the UN website, solicits feedback, then collects and summarizes it. The volume of documents is often significant; as Maria noted, "last time, we had over one hundred submissions of five pages on average, together amounting to circa five hundred pages." Secretariat staff summarize NGO submissions accompanying state reports—discussed in Chapter 7—for Committee members. Here, too, volume is often high: many state reports are accompanied by several dozen NGO reports, together amounting to several hundreds of pages.

The importance of their work is recognized in the Committee's thank-yous that consistently accompany its sessions. Such expressions of appreciation are particularly warranted when sessions run past schedule, requiring the staff, as well as the interpreters and the UN conference service staff, to work overtime. The Secretariat's centrality is evident in repeated pleas for greater personnel resources by both Committee members and state delegates.

Members' views, nevertheless, differ on the Secretariat's substantive importance. Whereas some characterize it as having "minor, non-existent input," as one member responsible for drafting the first version of a General Comment put it, others see its role as integral. Many Secretariat staff share the latter view. As Maria noted, since Committee members are not paid for their work, "they do not have enough time to get into the nitty gritty of [document] drafting." Instead, such detailed work falls to the Secretariat.

The ethnographers of documents have over the past decade made evident how significantly the processes surrounding a document's drafting affect its content, as is elaborated in Chapter 5. These insights are central for the

Committee's work: in condensing background information from a wide array of NGO submissions, Secretariat members unavoidably make choices as to the information they consider relevant. Rather than merely and mechanically summarizing background material, they become active agents in constructing "truthful documents."[61]

Sir Nigel echoed this in discussion of the Committee's 2012 annual report. He stated that the Committee is grateful for the Secretariat's input, as "a lot of thought goes into thinking what are the relevant parts of our jurisprudence."[62] In discussion, Secretariat staff were likewise candid about their influence. Some even saw themselves as doing the "real work," whereas they described the Committee's engagement as essentially "a branding exercise": the Committee members' Star status bestows the Committee's documents prestige and legitimacy as expert knowledge. The characterization captures a key difference between the work of Committee members and Secretariat staff. Whereas the Stars' contributions are personalized and identifiable, Secretariat work is depersonalized and anonymous, with their names appearing on none of the documents they craft. Anonymity masks the Secretariat's input and influence, making it difficult for outsiders to detect.

The Secretariat's prominent role stems in part from the Covenant provisions that created the UN treaty bodies, which left broad discretion to the bodies themselves to arrange their work.[63] In practice, it means broad discretion for those staff members who oversee Human Rights Committee sessions under the UN human rights apparatus's "fuzzy logic"—for example, in drawing the line between who is included, and who is excluded from, the Committee's sessions. Over the decades, the discretion has resulted, among other changes, in a continuously expanded role for NGOs, as elaborated in Chapter 7.

The continual rotation of Committee members intensifies the Secretariat's influence, particularly for staff who have worked with treaty bodies in various roles for a great number of years. As much is apparent when a newly elected cohort of members arrives at the Palais Wilson, jetlagged from transatlantic flights, disoriented by the intensity of the sessions, and unprepared for the level of detail in the Constructive Dialogues. Under such circumstances, UN Secretariat staff members need to be prepared to both support and guide members who are not up to speed, while keeping the sessions running smoothly.

Secretariat staff need to balance out the uneven contributions of Committee members stemming from differing work ethics. In conversation, staff were candid. As Maria summarized, some are "clearly not up to par with the responsibilities that are expected of members." Such statements reflect the high performance expectations Secretariat staff set—standards that not all members reach. Reservations furthermore arise when members present "potentially biased assessments." In such instances, the Secretariat may discreetly intervene, for example, by approaching the Committee chair.[64] Together these instances illustrate that the Secretariat's ultimate allegiance, particularly among experienced staff, lies with the Committee's integrity.

Discretion is likewise required when even the brightest Stars "simply make mistakes," such as asserting on record that the Committee has previously said X or Y "when that is simply not true," Maria recalled. Having the Committee contradict itself on paper is the worst outcome of the sessions and something experienced staff seek to avoid at all cost. In such moments, the Secretariat walks a tightrope, since Stars are not always receptive to having their views questioned; after all, they are supposed to be the ultimate experts on the ICCPR's interpretation and the Committee's jurisprudence.

These examples show that, in practice, Secretariat staff—far from being mere bureaucrats providing "minor assistance"—serve as the Committee's Guardians, safeguarding the vision of a world order with continuously greater prominence for human rights and the rule of law. As true insiders of UN bureaucracies, they know the small, porous openings and cracks in the UN human rights apparatus's icelike inner contours that, to an outsider's gaze, appear nonexistent. The staff's maneuvering is embedded in the UN's fuzzy logic and partial opacity, making it difficult for outsiders to perceive. It is, nonetheless, precisely by such maneuvering that the Guardians arrange practical solutions that they understand to secure greater realization of the ICCPR's provisions, and of human rights in general.

Long-term members of the Secretariat and the Committee, in particular, often maintain direct personal connections. When the Committee is in session, these connections are visible in shared lunches or coffee breaks in the Palais Wilson cafeteria. During the sessions themselves, they surface in direct exchanges between members and staff, accompanied by shared smiles and laughter.

Sometimes the Secretariat staff's intense engagement raises questions—as Taylor noted—over "who has ownership of this process." Committee members have their own views on how treaty body work should evolve—for example, whether the Committee should focus more closely on its mandated functions, that is, processing state reports and individual communications, and prioritize accordingly,[65] while Secretariat staff may have different ideas. Furthermore, the OHCHR has its own mandate to propose developments to the UN human rights machinery, adding complexity. The UN monitoring framework's users—states as well as stakeholders such as NGOs and individuals—may additionally have their own ideas.

As a result of the UN treaty body framework's continued expansion, it has become difficult, if not impossible, for any one person to maintain a comprehensive overview of all the bodies and their operations. "When we started," Taylor recalls, "we had six bodies and we at the Secretariat took care of five bodies. Every staff member knew exactly what the work entailed, and how to react with NGOs." Today, such oversight has become increasingly difficult. As Taylor notes, "Nobody knows all the treaty bodies." The situation has intensified in recent years with the creation of four new treaty bodies and three additional procedures for individual complaints. New states parties to the treaties also intensify the treaty bodies' work. For example, in 2017, the number of state ratifications and accessions for UN human rights treaties, in total, grew by forty-two, significantly increasing the volume of state reports UN treaty bodies process annually.[66]

To accommodate the steadily growing workload, the joint annual meeting time for treaty bodies has continually increased: in 2000, treaty bodies were in session for fifty-six weeks, in 2010, that number was seventy-two weeks, and, in 2017, it had grown to ninety-three weeks. Treaty bodies have developed into "a big machinery," as Taylor put it, marked by "linear growth" that the UN has publicly described as "unsustainable."[67] Combined with constant personnel rotation, the current situation may appear a "little schizophrenic," Taylor noted.

Crossroads Between Commitment and Professionalism

The "schizophrenic" reality around treaty bodies has consequences for Secretariat staff, who find themselves juggling commitment to human rights with professional standards and an ever-growing volume of work. It applies particularly to those who handle the practical drafting: many share that they are chronically overworked. Upon describing her role, Maria observed that "everyone is overwhelmed." The intensity spikes further when something must be completed urgently, for example, when the Committee members request last-minute changes to documents during a session, or a document must be finalized against a hard deadline.

Another example of stressful moments arises when the Secretariat needs to draft follow-up questions to states, or when it receives written responses from states parties with a short turnaround time. Workload intensifies particularly for long-term Secretariat staff when new personnel draft Concluding Observations for the first time, or when the Committee includes several new members. In addition, particularly taxing periods occur during examinations of large states, which may be accompanied by dozens of NGO shadow reports, leading staff to work, as Maria said, "for twenty-four hours, also during the weekends."

Under such circumstances, staff may feel pressured to manage the consequences of personnel shortages on their own. As Maria summarized, "It does not reflect well on your performance if you are not able to meet the expectations of your position and complete assigned tasks." A grave failure, she noted, would be the discovery that staff had not been available to assign to specific country reports, resulting in delays in processing state reports—something, Maria adds, almost happened once.

Such a postponement would halt the Committee's nonstop movement and undermine the monitoring mechanism's overall viability. On a personal level, shortcomings in performance can trigger negative assessments, jeopardizing staff members' future appointments in the UN rotation when their current contract ends. The costs to staff members' health, well-being, and family life are similarly immense.

Working conditions—and workers' rights—in international organizations and INGOs have recently become a topic of concern, after decades of neglect.[68] An important development was Amnesty International's 2019 study of its organizational culture, prompted by the deaths of two staff members, one of whom directly cited work-related stress as a contributing factor to their suicide. The study's findings were stark: a large proportion of workers described experiencing acute stress leading to mental or physical health issues, directly attributable to their work at Amnesty. Many placed significant blame on excessive workload compounded by poor management culture, with numerous employees describing the atmosphere as "toxic."[69]

Calling attention to such experiences can be difficult for workers at human rights organizations, including the UN. Most people in the field are deeply devoted to human rights, and thus their employment often amounts to more than just a job—it is akin to a vocation or life cause that provides a compelling sense of purpose and meaning. In practice, such sentiments can translate into excessively long working hours or readiness to relocate.

High degree of commitment is commonly expected of the OHCHR staff, as the Office is seen to mark the departure from the earlier "bureaucratically inclined Human Rights Division"[70] toward an era driven by devotion and activism. As a result, the increasing professionalization of the human rights field awakens occasional concern among long-term insiders that human rights may become "simply like any other job—and moreover a source of comparatively lucrative employment," instead of something sustained by, as O'Flaherty and Ulrich describe, "passionate personal commitments and some element of personal sacrifice,"[71] long characteristic of the community of practice of the Guardians of Vision.

During the Committee's sessions, Secretariat staff—the only paid workers attending to the documents that the Committee produces—are expected to combine commitment to human rights values with high professional standards. These expectations occasionally generate tensions between Committee members and the Secretariat. Staff may express disappointment at the invisibility of their work in both the Committee's practical operations and existing scholarship. As Maria stated frankly, some feel that "the Committee assumes the glory, not the responsibility." Concretely, it means that when everything during the sessions, including the provision of correct background documents, goes according to plan, the Committee receives credit. When something goes wrong, the blame falls on the Secretariat—an outcome that underscores the Secretariat's role as the integral infrastructure of UN human rights monitoring.[72]

The privileged status of Committee members vis-à-vis Secretariat staff may likewise generate tension. Many members emphasize that they are unpaid experts serving the Committee on a voluntary basis. By contrast, Maria points to the "hefty per diems" members receive, referring to the $640 to $890 members receive per session day, annually amounting to over $50,000 tax free.[73] Such criticism is often directed particularly at Committee members "who have been in the Committees for twenty years without any limitation," whom some staff view as not investing adequate work. Sometimes staff express that professional standards for treaty body work are not set high enough within the professional UN hierarchy. Much of the workload falls on relatively junior UN staff, and especially the treaty bodies' Secretaries—who bear major responsibility for their operations and are "key to making the sessions run or not," as one UN insider noted. Yet they are placed at P4 level, a lower mid-level professional grade that some UN staff see as too low.[74]

These complaints have a gender dimension: while the Human Rights Committee members are predominantly male, lower-level OHCHR staff are predominantly female. Gender discrepancy has characterized the Committee since its inception. Before 1987, the Committee had no female members, and, until 1997, it never had more than three female members out of eighteen members in total, two of whom remained consistently the same: Rosalyn Higgins of the UK and Christine Chanet of France. Since then, the share of female members has increased to around one-third.

OHCHR staff shows a similar pattern of male dominance at higher professional grades: roughly three-fourths of upper-level positions from P4 and upward are held by men. At entry-level positions in the professional grades of P1 to P3, the scales are reversed: about 60 percent of staff is female.[75] The outcome is a professional reality where the Human Rights Committee's male Stars are supported in the "nitty-gritty of drafting" by overworked, anonymous female bureaucrats who diligently maneuver under the opaque transparency of the UN human rights apparatus to safeguard the integrity of the monitoring mechanism. Simultaneously this contradicts the egalitarian human rights ideology and the provisions of the ICCPR. OHCHR protocols stress that "a gender perspective is effectively integrated into all OHCHR policies, programs, and relevant processes.[76] In practice, the Office falls short of gender equality among its staff,[77] and, by extension, so does the community of practice of the Guardians of Vision.[78]

Realistically, there is nothing Committee members can do about gender disparity. They have no control over who is nominated or elected, and upon being nominated, they do not know who else is up for election. Simultaneously the Committee routinely comments on gender asymmetry in state delegations, and especially gender equality in states under state examination. In my observations, there were no instances of the Committee reflecting on its own gender imbalance or on the contradiction it creates with its mandate to oversee a Covenant that includes the equal treatment of men and women.

Conclusions

This chapter provides an ethnographic entry point into the Human Rights Committee's operations. It illustrates how, from an empirical viewpoint, the Committee not only comprises its eighteen expert members who form their own epistemic community, but rather includes a broad community of practice. Members of this community, whom I call the Guardians of Vision, additionally include relevant UN Secretariat staff, and as later chapters illustrate, NGO and state delegates. Together, the members maneuver within the ice-like inner contours of UN human rights bureaucracies characterized by fuzzy logic and partial opacity to advance the increased global prominence of human rights and the rule of law.

In addition, Guardians maneuver strategically to promote and curtail the initiatives of "international diplomats" operating in state delegations, the Secretariat, and even within the Committee. In these efforts, both the interventions of individuals and orchestrated collective engagement have significance. For state civil servants, as Chapter 6 elaborates, it amounts, for example, to forwarding and supporting requests for extra resources for UN treaty bodies to ensure they can maintain their operations. It may mean informing NGO delegates of sessions or facilitating their participation to bolster treaty bodies' legitimacy as incorporating views from civil society and, by extension, "the world."[79] Finally, it may entail defending the UN treaty bodies' autonomy and discretion in different UN contexts, such as the Committee's 3,000th session—thus strengthening the vision of a world order structured around human rights and the rule of law and bringing that vision closer to realization.

The community of practice of the Guardians of Vision within the Human Rights Committee is a transnational, English-speaking community of international lawyers who stem primarily from the Global North. In light of these findings, the Committee's practices reproduce the historic Northern dominance of human rights practice, sustaining rather than challenging long-standing North-South hierarchies. Furthermore, the community remains characterized by gender asymmetry, precisely the kind the Committee reproaches in the states under review. Taken together, these findings highlight a gap between human rights ideals of equal geographic, cultural, and gender representation and the Human Rights Committee's operations.

Although a large number of individuals attend the Committee's sessions, far fewer are long-term insiders. I have shown how Secretariat staff play an integral role in the Committee's smooth operations. From an empirical viewpoint, a shared vision for advancing human rights as well as shared practices connect the formal categories that structure the Committee's sessions. The Secretariat's largely invisible maneuvering within the UN Human Rights apparatus's opaque transparency helps ensure that the Committee's operations continue to prioritize law over political considerations. Secretariat staff safeguard the integrity of the treaty body framework by compensating for occasional lapses by the expert members, such as failing to prepare appropriately for a session. Ideally, as is the case with well-functioning infrastructure, the maneuvering remains invisible, only becoming apparent when there is a disruption. Visible or invisible, these insights show that the Human Rights Committee—like other UN treaty bodies—would be incapacitated without the Secretariat, thereby undermining the notion of the Committee consisting solely of its eighteen expert members.

CHAPTER 4

What's Law Got to Do With It?

"I have operated on the notion that the word 'include' is not exclusionary."[1] It had been almost an hour since the Committee members began discussing a General Comment—or more specifically, the draft text of a single three-sentence paragraph.[2] During the session open to the public, members had taken turns to share their understandings of the exact meaning of the word "everyone": Does it self-evidently include all persons with no exceptions, or should further elaboration be added? A staple in human rights language since the UDHR, the term proves linguistically complex when applied to cross-cultural contexts in practice.[3]

One member flagged the familiar problem of translation: lacking a gender-neutral equivalent of "everyone," the proposed French version used "les hommes et les femmes." Another highlighted the need to specify those groups who are "particularly vulnerable to restrictions." A third suggested complementing the paragraph with the phrase, "and everyone else." The mood of the debate was engaged, even passionate. Many members took the floor repeatedly to clarify and emphasize earlier points. Although the exchange remained courteous, differences in views, and flashes of frustration, were visible. A few jokes lightened the atmosphere; once again, the Committee's days had run long.

As the discussion continued, its core question became clear: Should the Committee, in light of its jurisprudence, highlight vulnerable groups particularly at risk of rights violations with an explanatory list, thereby making it evident that "everyone means everyone"? Or should it rather emphasize the Covenant's universality by avoiding additional categories? After all, "anyone can have their rights violated," as one member noted. Yet another member argued that an elaborated list would provide "one way we can overcome the tendency of states to interpret Article 9 very narrowly." Here, the reference was to the treatment of terrorism suspects detained at Guantanamo Bay and elsewhere, following the "War on Terror" the US launched, and several Western European states joined, after the 9/11 attack on the World Trade Center's Twin Towers in 2001. After a final round of comments, Sir Nigel, who chaired the session, concluded the paragraph's "first reading."[4]

Existing scholarship on the Human Rights Committee and the UN treaty bodies focuses primarily on their output, the voluminous documents that these bodies produce while fulfilling their mandated tasks. To foreground the documentary analysis of Chapter 5, I focus on the Committee's operations, turning my ethnographic gaze to the practices, techniques, and affects that its expert members mobilize while participating in the Committee's work. The chapter shows how members balance aspirations for the Committee's robust impact with state interests to restrain the Committee's influence by providing a "constructive" human interface in the proceedings. It details how they engage in the painstaking drafting work for General Comments, proactively updating the Committee's interpretation of distinct Covenant provisions. Further, it traces how members weigh in on the role of transparency in the Committee's operations, embodying both a means and an end.

Via these angles I continue the overall analysis of movement, focusing here on the maneuvering by Committee members to continually safeguard and expand the Committee's work. This maneuvering foregrounds Bourdieusian fuzzy logic in two ways. First, fuzzy logic characterizes how the Committee members navigate legal indeterminacy—norms that in themselves are abstract, open-ended, or unclear[5]—to expand the Committee's interpretative scope as well as its activities. Second, it shows how the Committee members balance the Committee's operations in regards to its legal mandate, and how they subsequently negotiate the Committee's relations with states to soothe possible contestations.

The examined sessions—discussions for General Comments and Working Methods—differ from the Committee's other sessions in that they do not usually rely on documentation prepared by the Secretariat. Instead, the drafting of General Comments is handled by an assigned Committee member, and discussions on working methods place a strong emphasis on verbal exchanges between Committee members. Thus here, unlike in the previous chapters, I emphasize the Committee as its eighteen expert members. Simultaneously, I continually anchor the analysis on the notion of the community of practice to capture how the Committee members mobilize a range of interventions, including embodied presence, as they contribute to the Committee's work.

The subsequent ethnographic glimpses are anchored in the broader exploration of the Human Rights Committee's relationship to law. Rather than taking a legalistic approach to assessing impact—for example, how courts employ the Committee's "jurisprudence" or how the Committee interprets the ICCPR[6]—I begin by reviewing how its expert members' engagement reflects broader efforts to advance the legalization of human rights, a central dynamic in the post–World War II human rights phenomenon, thereby moving the world in the rights direction. I discuss how the dynamic is embedded in the notion of universalizing a modern state-centric model of the law, and how the Committee's operations thus continue the earlier civilizing mission of international law.

The Human Rights Committee and Law

As previous chapters have discussed, treaty bodies, the Human Rights Committee included, face recurring challenges from states adverse to international human rights oversight. These challenges were reflected in the intervention of the delegate from Belarus at the outset of Chapter 3, which illustrated how state resistance may be linked to the legal nature of treaty body monitoring. Treaty bodies do not negotiate such issues as whether domestic remedies have been exhausted, nor do they ask if states will accept the recommendations they issue on the basis of periodic reports and Constructive Dialogues. Rather, the bodies' expert members identify violations of relevant treaty obligations in the Concluding Observations and Views—much as a judge would in a court of law—here standing in marked contradistinction to the UPR.

In legal scholarship, the Human Rights Committee, and treaty bodies more generally, are commonly called soft law actors. More precisely, whereas the Committee's operations have a "hard law" basis in the ICCPR—and, for Individual Communications, in the First Optional Protocol—the output of the Committee's work, including Concluding Observations, General Comments, and Views on Individual Communications, are legally non-binding and can be characterized as "soft law." Despite voluminous writing on the topic, there exists no consensus on the meaning of soft law.[7] Some scholars contend that "it is not law at all,"[8] treating the concept as undesirable and redundant.[9] Others aspire to rigorous theorization by proposing that soft law is "international common law" (ICL), defined, in Guzman's and Meyer's words, as a "nonbinding gloss that international institutions, such as international tribunals, put on binding legal rules."[10] Such approaches see soft law as central to the continued legitimacy of international law.[11]

A doctrinal approach defines soft law as "something [that] looks like a legal obligation in some ways (e.g., it is a written exchange of promises between states)," but which "nevertheless falls short of what is required to formally bind states."[12] To explain the use of "soft law" jurisprudence on UN treaty bodies, some scholars call it "liquid" law."[13] The argument is that the legally nonbinding documents the Committee issues would, in McCall-Smith's words, "in the domestic context . . . aid in filling the gaps in and among the hard law that governs rights assessment." Further, "the legal opinion of a treaty body can be validated by the court and can lend legitimacy to existing and future treaty body opinions."[14]

An anthropologist might characterize the Committee's relationship to law, like that of the other treaty bodies, as ambiguous—an endless straddling of the border of the law[15] as these bodies navigate the fine line between aspirations for robust influence and the need to appear constructive and non-threatening so as not to alienate states wary of external oversight. Simultaneously, the Committee's operations constitute a legal professional space, as was discussed in Chapter 3, and in ethnographic terms, its sessions are distinctly "court-like" in their references to the ICCPR's provisions, domestic law, and court cases.

The Committee's operations emphasize legal technicalities, as is apparent in the language of "jurisprudence" commonly used to refer to the Committee's earlier practice and documents, including Individual Communications.[16] Legal technicalities comprise what Brown, Reed, and Yarrow characterize as the "mundane forms through which [IOs] work"—the "boringly, even achingly, familiar routines."[17] Riles, in turn, describes technicalities as "those aspects of legal practice that cannot be reduced to norms, trust or other sociological concepts," framing law as "a profoundly aesthetic practice."[18]

The emphasis on legal technicalities acquires meaning from their intrinsic connection to a broader vision of world improvement through the ever-expanding role of human rights and law. Legal technicalities enhance the legitimacy of such "lawlike" organs as UN treaty bodies to work toward improving the world by ameliorating the realization of human rights, notwithstanding lack of binding force. Scholars often highlight that the Human Rights Committee is the "most legal" of the UN human rights monitoring mechanisms, with some seeing it as the "closest thing" to a UN tribunal.[19] By contrast, in discussion, most Committee members emphasize they do not see the Committee as a court and do not want it to be perceived as one.

Analytically, a more apt reference is an advisory body with features of an audit mechanism.[20] At the same time, legalistic aesthetics and technicalities characterize the documents that the Committee processes, commonly arranged in paragraphs and subparagraphs that echo treaty formats. Likewise, the precision and technicality with which the Committee works entail a distinct emphasis on legality, which undoubtedly contributes to its authoritative standing in the eyes of states parties, relevant UN staff, and NGOs.[21]

Additionally, ambiguity characterizes how states may view the Committee's work: whereas it and the other treaty bodies are recognized as "authoritative," states may argue that they need not comply with their recommendations due to their operations' legally non-binding nature. Such claims, nonetheless, are exceptional as most states instead emphasize the Committee's work as the practical realization of the states' Covenant-bound obligations, for example, during their Constructive Dialogues.

Toward Legal Human Rights

Ever since the UDHR was adopted in 1948, legalization has been central to the contemporary human rights phenomenon: from the adoption of new binding human rights instruments to their ratifications by an increasing number of states, legalization has been an explicit goal of countless human rights actors.[22] Donnelly notes that the "virtues of legalization" allow human rights to act as trumps, not reducible to mere value judgments.[23] Mazower states that efforts to upgrade legality are visible in narratives by human rights scholars that focus on the origins of human rights. He writes, "Looking forward rather than back, these compendia of texts, with their scholarly apparatuses, commentaries, and bibliographies, are not neutral; they themselves form a part of the ongoing effort to assert the power of the law over politics."[24]

Likewise, the human rights community of practice, along with the fields of diplomacy and the media, have commonly celebrated advances in legalization. For example, in 2002, when the Rome Statute of the International Criminal Court entered into force, many commentators characterized the outcome as "a great victory for justice, and for world order."[25] The 2006 adoption of the Convention on the Rights of Persons with Disabilities likewise awakened great satisfaction in numerous scholars and advocates. In these celebrations, lawyers are often at the helm, as illustrated by the adoption of the UK's Human Rights Act in 1998.[26] Alston noted these same sentiments a decade earlier when he described lawyers as operating on the front line to transform human rights from the exclusive realm of philosophy and moral reasoning into the domain of law.[27]

Celebrations by lawyers connect to broader attempts to legalize human rights via constitutionalization, an attempt to respond to the empirical fragmentation of the international legal order by reunifying different parts under certain shared principles.[28] The larger goal is to replicate elements of the domestic legal order at the international level, including a set of norms, a judiciary, and appropriate enforcement mechanisms.

Legalization also attracts criticism. Already two decades ago, Meckled-Garcia and Çali noted that human rights originate from moral ideals, emphasizing that nothing dictates they should primarily be realized through law. Furthermore, they argued, efforts to legalize human rights expand the importance of law as a means of social control.[29] A second criticism is that legalized human rights become entangled with the law's instrumental rationalities. As a consequence, searching for the absolute "truth" regarding a given situation becomes secondary to how the judicial process depicts it.[30] Simultaneously, over the past decade, the collective mood toward legalization has shifted. Instead of optimism, an ongoing debate has been increasingly marked by talk of "loss of faith,"[31] challenge and decline,[32] and scholarly apathy[33] toward international law both as a progressive tool for world improvement and an intellectual project.

These developments echo the Human Rights Committee's operations, which since its inception can be characterized as integrally engaged in the legalization of human rights. These efforts are visible during Constructive Dialogues in the satisfaction that Committee members express when new states accede to the Covenant as well as the Committee's frequent urging in its Concluding Observations that states become parties to the Covenant's Optional Protocols, which increase the salience of human rights in domestic legal systems. The Committee members encourage states to withdraw reservations that they entered to international treaties, and to greet all such developments with unfailing contentment.

In addition, Committee members prompt states to educate judges and other legal professionals about the ICCPR's provisions, hence seeking to increase the Covenant's influence on domestic legal systems.[34] They urge changes to bring domestic legislation into complete accordance with treaty provisions, as well as emphasize the importance of implementation mechanisms that increase the Covenant's application. In Committee sessions, increasing legalization of human rights appears to be, to cite Fidler, the new "general standard of civilization,"[35] which, in the Committee's view, limits the scope of acceptable state sovereignty.

Realistically, the new standard builds strongly on a Western-modeled, state-based legal order. By contrast, institutions such as customary courts or religious and traditional leadership structures are seen as challenging the ICCPR's application and as falling short of the vision of human rights legalization envisaged by the Committee.[36] Whereas the Committee occasionally discusses the compatibility of different legal traditions, such debates usually involve comparing a common law system with the continental civil law system. Thus, these discussions do not treat all the world's different legal traditions as equals, but instead reveal the Committee members' affinity for modern, state-based visions of the rule of law—an affinity that forms a constant in the continued flows in the Committee's operations. This focus correlates with the educational and geographic backgrounds of Committee members, most of whom have degrees in Western law, as Chapter 3 discussed, from this angle continuing international law's civilizing mission.[37]

In contrast to much ongoing discussion within international law, during my ethnographic research I encountered few sentiments of "loss of faith" either in transnational dialogue or the law. By contrast, while many human rights professionals criticize scarce resources and the flawed operations of many IOs and INGOs, Committee insiders remain deeply invested in efforts to improve the world by advancing the legalization of human rights. In informal discussion, however, some question the utility of the treaty body model established decades ago for today's changed world.

The Committee members are mindful of the perils of the shift from "real reality" to "legal reality," a transformation elaborated in Chapter 5: as they often comment in Constructive Dialogues, what they ultimately hope to see are changes to—and the ICCPR's impact on—"real reality," rather than merely the introduction of new laws.[38] Additionally, members may express reservations over excessive legality. In one instance, during drafting of General Comment No. 35 discussed below, Sir Nigel noted, "Certain legal formalism has crept in that might make legal enforcement rather difficult," indicating that excessive legalism may be detrimental to the advancement of human rights.[39]

Furthermore, caution regarding excessive legalism is present in the OHCHR's instructions for submitting Individual Communications, which explicitly state that there are no formal criteria for the communications. These guidelines differ from court-filing requirements and stress that one does not need to be a lawyer or even familiar with legal or technical terms to file a complaint. The guidelines' open-ended nature can be seen as an attempt to eliminate another peril of human rights legalization: that such bodies as the Human Rights Committee become accessible only to lawyers, thereby excluding others, thus undermining the foundational premise that UN treaty bodies should be open and accessible to laypersons. In practice, legal competence is paramount, as the issues raised in complaints must be translated into "UN reality" and embedded strongly in the law in order to be visible to and admissible before the Committee.[40]

A Historical Vision

The vision for a world order anchored in human rights and the rule of law is connected to the events of the 1940s, when World War II was ravaging the globe and the future of the planet and humanity appeared uncertain. At the time, various activists began to lobby for human rights. The culmination of these efforts is today commonly recognized as the adoption of the UDHR in 1948, celebrated as one of the most significant milestones of the dawning post–World War II order.[41] What is less well known is that many activists lobbied for a legally binding treaty, an international Bill of Rights modeled after the US Bill of Rights.[42] The Bill, so the activists envisioned, would be backed by robust implementation mechanisms, ideally an international human rights court.[43] It was a vision for a utopian form of deterritorialized governance aiming for "universality, with an authority that derives from everywhere and is thus beyond any sovereign 'somewhere.'"[44]

Due to a lack of political support, or rather, the firm opposition of the world's leading superpowers—the US, the UK, and the Soviet Union—the plan never came close to realization.[45] Instead, in 1946, soon after the UN Human Rights Division began its work, the plan for a binding legal document was sidelined. The Division focused on the drafting of the legally non-binding UDHR, while a treaty was to be completed later. In the European context, plans for a solid legal framework to support human rights gained favorable momentum soon thereafter with the adoption of the European Convention of Human Rights (ECHR) and establishment of the European Court of Human Rights in 1950.[46] At the UN, however, human rights initiatives struggled.

In 1952, the plan to draft one unified human rights treaty was split into two covenants: the International Covenant on Civil and Political Rights (ICCPR) and the International Covenant on Economic, Social, and Cultural Rights (ICESCR).[47] By that time, the momentum surrounding human rights at the UN had waned, with Secretary-General Dag Hammarskjöld opposed to their inclusion at the core of the organization's mandate.[48] In the 1950s, the major global challenges were the Cold War and national struggles for self-determination and decolonization, accompanied by struggles against totalitarianism and fascism.[49] These developments halted the drafting of the two covenants, prompting John Humphrey, director of the UN Human Rights Division, to state in 1955 that there had been "no progress."[50]

Finally, in 1966, almost two decades after the UDHR's adoption, the ICCPR and the ICESCR were completed and opened up for state ratification, and a decade later, they entered into force.[51] By then, the momentum around human rights had shifted once more. The 1970s became the decade of the "human rights breakthrough" accompanied by the expansion of human rights ideology and discourse, as well as the growth of the global apparatus and community surrounding them.[52]

There was nevertheless one significant caveat: the covenants would not be backed by a court, but rather by "lawlike" treaty bodies. The creation of these bodies differed significantly from the visions of activists who advocated for the covenants' creation. For example, Roger Baldwin—founder and long-term chair of the American Civil Liberties Union (ACLU) and chair of one of the world's first human rights NGOs, the International League for the Rights of Man—wrote to the UN Human Rights Division in 1959 to express his concern: "We do not think the covenants worth more than the Declaration unless provisions for implementation are included."[53] Such a lack, he feared, would water down the influence of the covenants, just like the lack of binding force had watered down the UDHR.

Baldwin, along with many activists, believed robust enforcement mechanisms were needed to eliminate the greatest Achilles' heel of international human rights law, namely, "the culture of impunity" that the absence of enforcement mechanisms with binding legal force had caused.[54] The aim of completing the international legal order by constitutionalizing it as a "domestic analogy"—as well as, more generally, humanizing international law by placing the individual at the center—continues to the present day.[55] Together, these efforts by human rights advocates can be seen as seeking to advance the supposed march of humanity away from irrationality and "primitive customs" toward rationality, human rights, and the rule of law,[56] thus "ending history"[57] and "realizing utopia."[58]

From Guidance to Progression

These historical events provide the broader context in which the Human Rights Committee operates and negotiates its relationship to the law, a dynamic that was visible in the debate over the General Comment No. 35 that opened this chapter. In the first reading of a General Comment, the Committee members discuss the draft document, agreeing on exact wording. Afterward, the document is shared for feedback from various stakeholders, including states and NGOs, on the OHCHR website. The second reading then follows in which the Committee members agree on the final wording, and finally the General Comment is adopted, accompanied by its publication.

In the discussion following General Comment No. 35's first reading, Committee members reflected on the purposes for which General Comments are adopted, as well as the Comments' role once published, both of which touch upon the relationship between the Committee's operations and the law.[59] The discussion illustrated divergence among the members, as well as what was seen as strategically prudent in negotiating the Committee's mandate. One member suggested that in their interpretation of the article, "we are lagging behind" current world events, referring to the increasing emphasis that states place on national security instead of human rights. The member noted that the proposed wording of the General Comment "codifies many of the Concluding Observations we have done over the years, going beyond them by establishing a guiding framework."

This raised the broader question of whether establishing such a framework was an appropriate task for the Committee. One member said that General Comments are "not law but rather guidance," directed toward both future conduct of states and the Committee's work.[60] Sir Nigel joined the debate by noting that the question "is about what [the Comment] does" rather than its specific wording. He continued that General Comments "provide our interpretation of the scope and nature of the provision. From the beginning, this is what General Comments have offered to NGOs and the academic audience." He continued, "One only has to look at the now numerous rulings of the ICJ [the International Court of Justice] to confirm that this is *indeed* what the content of General Comments is supposed to be about. The purpose is to guide states, and of course, guide others, as there is no reason this should be restricted to states."[61]

"What are the consequences of General Comments?" he asked, and responded, "States and others benefit from the Committee's understanding of the scope of obligations through the process of codification." This codification, he continued, forms "a progressive development" that summarizes "how things evolve." According to Sir Nigel, General Comments function as progressive devices that advance the prevailing legal human rights framework and the interpretations of specific ICCPR provisions.

Another member echoed his characterization by commenting on the wording proposed to address the right to security of person, noting, "This is the first time ever that such a clear definition on the right to security of person has been offered, and I think that it is an important new element in a General Comment." The formulation likewise emphasized the progressive quality of General Comments in advancing legal thinking rather than merely summarizing a pre-existing understanding.

Members discussed what kind of legal grounding distinct paragraphs should have, illustrated by a debate on Paragraph 3, for which Sir Nigel proposed the following formulation: "I'll read it slowly. Article 3 of the UDHR begins with the proclamation that everyone has the right to life and liberty and that this is the first substantive right proclaimed in the UDHR, and so indicates the profound importance of Article 9 both for individuals and society as a whole." He elaborated, "I had already signaled to the rapporteur that I wanted to refer to Article 3 of the UDHR, as the Covenant is based on it. This is the first substantive article in the Declaration."

The reference to the UDHR prompted caution from another member, who commented, "The ICCPR gives us solid grounding, as it is a legally binding document. If we refer to the UDHR, this may give the impression that we need more grounding. I am hesitant, therefore." The statement illustrates how distinct members may have different views on how the Committee's operations should be grounded in law: whereas by mentioning the UDHR, Sir Nigel leans toward the view that human rights provide reasons for legislation, to paraphrase Kennedy's analysis of how rights claims straddle the border of the law,[62] the other member emphasized that human rights are law, full stop, and thus need no additional grounding.

The discussion of the General Comment's language was incredibly detailed, focusing on specific words and their connotations. As the debate continued, disagreements remained, with the rapporteur, Mr. Neuman, the member from the US, ultimately summarizing, "You have made clear you want the whole paragraph back, and the whole paragraph will come back to the first reading. Thus, no portion of it has yet been adopted." Sir Nigel responded, "But collective thinking on it has moved forward a lot"—a testament to the Committee's accomplishments during the previous ninety minutes spent discussing a few short lines. The slow pace elicited occasional dry humor from the other members, prompting Mr. Neuman to comment, "I want to congratulate us for moving into a new paragraph within Article 9."

Following the work the members invest in adopting a General Comment is a stretch even for the most engaged observer: it is characterized by an enormous level of detail and a protracted pace, with consideration of individual sentences—and even individual word choices—extending into hours, and the entire first reading of a General Comment possibly stretching into weeks, even months. In these qualities, the drafting of General Comments can be described as a distinctly legalistic enterprise.

That the level of detail was indeed intricate was mirrored in the scarce audience attention that these sessions gather: although the session in question was public and thus open to general observers, the Palais Wilson conference room was almost empty, in contrast to many of the Committee's other sessions.[63] Whereas to insiders of the Committee, drafting a General Comment may be an exercise of paramount importance to the realization of human rights, that sentiment is not reflected in broad outside attendance. The drafting work is too detailed and specific, and thus fails to capture wide attention outside the Committee's immediate vicinity.

The exchange among Committee members on the roles and purposes of General Comments captures the Committee's complex role vis-à-vis the law: in addition to serving as a review body assessing state compliance with existing human rights obligations, many members aspire for the Committee to be an authoritative, progressive interpreter of human rights law, in a manner that resonates with the role of a legislature—even if members would unlikely use such language. Beyond summarizing what states and the Committee currently recognize within the scope of specific articles, General Comments articulate what their scope *should* be, drawing on the Committee's earlier jurisprudence. In its expansive interpretations, the Committee—via the contributions of its members—advances the vision of a world order governed by human rights and law.

In committing to such detailed, painstaking work, Committee members go clearly beyond the bare minimum of the Committee's mandated functions of examining state reports and individual communications. Instead, they assume the role of the Guardians of Vision, engaged in ensuring that the Committee's operations remain relevant and legitimate as the world continues to evolve after the ICCPR's adoption. These individual contributions are largely invisible in most scholarly accounts as the Committee officially operates as an entity basing its views on the consensus of its expert members. Thus the session offers also an insight into how the Committee's operations shift agency from individuals to the collective.

Between a Rock and a Hard Place

The aspirations for robust influence were visible in the exchange between the members over the meaning of "everyone" that opened this chapter. What the exchange fundamentally addressed—and what was eventually reflected in the elaborate list of subcategories—were ongoing tensions over state sovereignty and the extent of states parties' Covenant-based obligations. It offers another avenue for reflecting on the Committee's multifaceted relationship with the law as well as how the members navigate this relationship. If the Committee were to appear too influential and "lawlike" in its operations, it might provoke criticism and resistance from states that are averse to international human rights oversight.[64] Together, these elements create vulnerability and frustration for the Committee's operations, casting them, to use Koskenniemi's term, as ongoing navigation between the "utopia" of a robust, binding legal framework and an "apology" for actual state conduct.[65]

Given that the Committee, like other UN human rights monitoring mechanisms, has no means to compel states to participate in its proceedings, its authority is vulnerable to states failing to report, either on time or at all, and subsequently not appearing for the Constructive Dialogue, as well as cancelling their sessions. One such instance occurred in October 2013 when the US abruptly cancelled its appearance due to a government shutdown, which had frozen most government operations.

The cancellation came at very short notice, giving rise to speculation among those convened at the Palais Wilson as to whether there was an intentional element linked to it due to the US's fraught relationship with the international human rights monitoring framework and multilateral collaboration more generally. The cancellation further resulted in what can only be described as a shared anti-climax, as the Committee, instead of examining the US's report in one of the large conference rooms of the Palais des Nations with robust NGO participation, as initially planned, continued its first reading of General Comment No. 35 at the Palais Wilson.[66]

More recently, Burundi withdrew from its Constructive Dialogue scheduled for July 4, 2023, informing the Committee only moments before the dialogue was due to begin that it would not participate. The state explained as the reason that certain audience members were "convicted criminals posing as civil society members."[67] The individuals in question, however, had been accredited to attend the sessions by the UN Human Rights Office and thus, as the Committee informed Burundi's state delegation, could not be excluded from a public UN meeting. The Committee therefore decided to continue its examination of Burundi's state reports, emphasizing that the state had the usual forty-eight hours to respond to the Committee's queries.[68]

Soothing Tensions with Constructive Dialogue

"This has been an excellent dialogue with an excellent, trilingual delegation, wonderfully balanced in gender [*laughter from delegation*]. It has been very useful for us to have such a knowledgeable report with much statistical data available," Sir Nigel noted in a spring session of 2013 when Macao submitted its first report to the Committee.[69] The language that he used was almost conscientious in its positive, even exaggerated tenor, even if customary in the Committee's sessions.

Although the Committee uniformly utilizes the term "Constructive Dialogue" to refer to its sessions with states parties, no clear-cut definition exists for what "constructive" means in international law, a finding that applies equally to the concept of "dialogue" prevalent in international collaborations and UN operations.[70] Riles suggests that "dialogue" stems from the ability to link seemingly separate actions and documents into long, contiguous chains, giving increased visibility and legitimacy to these individual, constituent elements.[71]

In the subsequent section, I focus on the significance and manifestations of "constructiveness" as a tool the Committee members use to maneuver and continually renegotiate the Committee's mandate within its contentious operational space, as well as to soothe potential clashes with states parties. Here the human interface between Committee members and states parties plays a crucial role, specifically in terms of language: in the Committee's sessions, an observer is struck by the elaborate compliments that the members pay states parties. When a new Constructive Dialogue commences, members praise state delegates for their diligence in reporting and commend them for their commitment to the ICCPR, signaled by their participation in the Committee's hearing.

Members extend particular praise to states with high-level delegations that include broad civil servant representation from different government offices and ministries. The participation of such high-profile delegates as members of Parliament, supreme court justices, or ambassadors is likewise highlighted. Members often mention how well prepared state delegates are in responding to the questions they pose. Further, they thank state delegates for making the long journey from their respective home states to Geneva for the hearings.

At times, praise is combined with recognition of direct personal connections, such as collegial ties between Committee members and state delegates, illustrating that the two groups professionally belong to the same community of practice. When Peru's state delegation appeared at the Palais Wilson during the spring 2013 session, the country rapporteur, Fabián Salvioli, the Committee's member from Argentina, stated: "Let me join my voice [to the conversation] and extend a welcome to the delegation. The state report is a wealth of information which is excellent for us; it is important to proper dialogue." He then acknowledged, seeking to lighten the mood as well as to pre-empt state criticism that the subsequent questions might provoke, "Vice Minister of Justice is a dear colleague of mine . . . I am going to be a little more demanding with you, as one often is with one's friends. So be patient with me as I will be as demanding as I can."[72]

In another instance, regarding Ukraine's seventh state report, Sir Nigel remarked, "We use the term 'Constructive Dialogue' a lot, but this time I think that it *has* been a Constructive Dialogue. We have learned a lot. It was some seventy years of Soviet rule, and there will be a transition period. That does not mean that there is nothing to learn. There is a lot to learn. That is the meaning of transition."[73] Emphasis on learning underlies the reciprocal nature of Constructive Dialogue, casting it as an instance in which—in addition to expertise flowing from the Committee to the state delegation—the Committee received new knowledge. The language of mutual learning further contributed to an atmosphere that eased potential underlying tensions over the Committee's operations vis-à-vis the state party.

Soothing language emphasizes the Constructive Dialogue's importance, highlighting the special nature of particular states' participation, as was illustrated in the Constructive Dialogue on Indonesia's first state report in July 2013. Concluding the session, Sir Nigel noted, "Of course every country is important. Every report is important. But I do take special pleasure in having Indonesia here for the first time. Indonesia is a big country with big influence and a lot of population, and it is good to have you on board. The coming on board happened in 2006, and we received the report in 2011, so it was a bit later than we hoped. But we are very, *very* happy to have you here to get to know you." He highlighted Indonesia's involvement in the then-ongoing treaty body reform by saying, "I have a particular pleasure as I was able to meet [one of the state delegates] in the meeting of the chairs in the treaty reform process that you are leading, together with Iceland.[74] I am sure that you are continuing to make a magnificent contribution. . . . As a member in the meeting of treaty bodies, I feel that the whole system has to be grateful to the magnificent work that the two facilitators were doing."[75]

Constructive language is characteristic of much UN human rights monitoring today, particularly in the UPR, which sought to replace the confrontational "naming-and-shaming" practices of the former Human Rights Commission.[76] Instead of being empty of significance, I argue that such sustained emphasis carries decisive weight in cultivating an atmosphere of mutual trust and learning in the human interface of the Committee members and state delegates, thereby alleviating tensions related to questions of state sovereignty and the extent of the Committee's discretion in assessing state conduct. The exaggeratedly "constructive," performative language of the Committee's sessions can be seen, as Bens phrases it, as "actually designed to create affect and emotion and to regulate them in specific ways."[77]

Thus, just as in more "strictly" legal proceedings, success in the Committee's operations depends "to a large degree on lawyers' ability to create courtroom atmospheres and manage affective arrangements."[78] Further, success hinges on the Committee members' capacity to ease underlying tensions by cultivating an atmosphere of constructiveness and pleasantness.

Partial Transparency as a Safeguard

"Thus, with apologies to those supporting this motion and to the representatives of civil society who would have liked to see us moving ahead with the notion of transparency, we will have to revisit the issue. I do hope that when we revisit it, we will not always be reminded that we have discussed it as that really does not help us in moving forward. For the moment, we do need to continue with the existing policy. Unless there are any requests for the floor I have to conclude the issue. [He looks around the room inquisitively.] The discussion is concluded, as is also the discussion on working methods."

With a bang of his gavel, Sir Nigel declared the meeting over, concluding the Committee's 107th session.[79] The room sprang to life as people rose from their seats in good spirits, exchanging handshakes and thanking each other for their diligent work over the previous three weeks of the session. Some exchanged kisses, with a few hesitating over the appropriate number—three in Geneva.

Despite the celebratory mood, an undertone of disappointment lingered in the background. The preceding hour had been consumed by an intense debate over a crucial issue for the Committee's operations: transparency. Specifically, the discussion focused on whether the names of task force members and country rapporteurs, who take the lead role in the examination of specific states' reports, should be made public or remain confidential, as had been the Committee's practice. A debate that, at first, seemed a minor technicality ultimately occupied most of the final session, with almost all members weighing in on the matter.

Sir Nigel opened the debate by noting that the Committee's "bureau"[80] had discussed in a closed session whether the Committee should align its approach with the other UN treaty bodies, all of which favor full transparency. He summarized that the bureau had not reached a consensus on the issue and had instead decided to open it to public debate in the plenary of all eighteen members.

In the subsequent debate, a few members expressed their unequivocal support for transparency, with one member stating, "Our bloodline depends on openness and transparency." The member then noted, "Many civil society organizations and individuals might feel more confident in sharing information with specific Committee members due to a number or reasons, including linguistic ones," implying that such direct contacts could only be realized if civil society representatives knew whom to contact within the Committee. Another member echoed the view, emphasizing that the Committee "needs to guarantee total transparency" and disclose the names of country rapporteurs. A third member said, "Our image as a Committee that values transparency would be somewhat weakened if the Committee did not step in line with the other treaty bodies."

These views find broader context from the Human Rights Committee's elevation of transparency as one of the core values of human rights protection. In Article 3 of General Comment No. 34, focusing on Article 19 of the ICCPR on "Freedoms of Opinion and Expression," the Committee avers, "Freedom of expression is a necessary condition for the realization of the principles of *transparency* and accountability that are, in turn, *essential for the promotion and protection of human rights*."[81] The Committee likewise expects transparency from the state delegations that appear before it, and periodic state reports are, at their core, an aspiration for transparent and reliable depictions of "real reality" within states.[82]

In the discussion, by contrast, other members emphasized the need for varying degrees of confidentiality. Several highlighted past experiences in which states had mounted attacks against Committee chairs, with one member recounting how a treaty body member was "strongly criticized by states" for expressing views in their capacity as a treaty body member of which the state did not approve. Another member referred to their personal experience as a Committee chair, noting that they could share personal anecdotes of pressures, including an instance in which a state party criticized a treaty body severely for its choice of country rapporteur. Sir Nigel likewise acknowledged that "if a country rapporteur's name is made known, they can face serious pressure from various sources, including obviously states parties but arguably also other stakeholders." Numerous members echoed these sentiments, with one asking, "Why we would want to depart from a practice that I think has served us well?"

A Shred of Mystery

The debate on transparency illustrated members' differing approaches to its role in the Committee's operations. In contrast to the earlier views, a few members highlighted the future perils that full transparency about country rapporteurs might create. One member noted that they were "not concerned for themselves or even others here," but rather for "Committee members in the future," as "we do not know from which countries they will come, or what is the situation in those countries." Another stated that transparency might jeopardize certain members' re-election if their past actions as country rapporteurs were criticized by states parties. Both comments made clear that members saw full transparency as potentially jeopardizing the Committee's future operations. Also in this instance, the members were playing the role of Guardians of Vision, seeking to increase the scope of human rights in the world with the Committee's unimpeded operations.

A third member argued for maintaining the current practice by emphasizing the Committee's collective agency, raising "some concern over the dichotomy of secrecy-confidentiality," which, the member noted, did not capture the Committee's operations. Instead "putting too much emphasis on the task force by naming names," the member continued, "conveys the wrong message: it creates the impression that only members of the task force stand behind [the Committee's] conclusions." The member further emphasized how important it is for the "Committee to give states the impression that its documents are something that we have been working on together—where everyone was invited to contribute."

A fourth member challenged these arguments, highlighting that the problem was, in fact, "the need to know if it is possible to keep and preserve confidentiality." The member emphasized that it was "not a theoretical question" but instead a factual one related to the mechanisms needed for maintaining confidentiality, which the Committee, in the member's opinion, realistically lacked. The member reminded those present that "there are eighteen of us," and "people know who the special rapporteurs are. . . . When two or three people know, the information becomes public. . . . We do not have the kind of confidentiality mechanisms" that "only exist in armies, et cetera." Thus, the real question was, the member emphasized, "Is it possible to maintain total confidentiality or not?"

Other members continued by suggesting that what I call "opaque transparency" was, in fact, both realistic and desirable. The member who had mentioned occurrences of state delegates pressuring country rapporteurs said that even if the rapporteur's identity was an "open secret, it would nevertheless assist people from becoming victims of attack." The member elaborated that such "official secrets" mean that rapporteurs "at least have official protection," thus eliminating opportunities for states "to attack them directly," a statement that played cleverly on formality and informality.

Another member commented that they hoped the Committee could "strike a balance, find a halfway house between full disclosure and full confidentiality" as "keeping everything private is never good and we need a degree of transparency." The member proposed a practical solution: "publicize the names of the five members of the task force and *not* the rapporteur" during the Constructive Dialogue rather than beforehand when the List of Issues is adopted. Thus, the Committee member continued, "No one will know exactly who is the rapporteur," allowing the Committee to maintain "a shred of mystery." A few others highlighted the special nature of the Human Rights Committee's operations, emphasizing that it works with the "hard core of human rights issues" and should not necessarily change its approach simply because other treaty bodies had adopted a different practice.

As the discussion wound down, it was evident that there was no consensus. Sir Nigel noted that it was "not a majority-minority issue," continuing, "Unless those who have been resisting change have been persuaded by those favoring it, I feel that we cannot change the rule." He was candid about his feelings toward this outcome, stating: "I regret it." He then elaborated upon arguments made by the various members to outline the perils of full transparency, but he stated that he did not find them persuasive.

Nevertheless, he repeated, the Committee "tends to operate by consensus,"[83] and thus he saw it as "not appropriate to change the rule by a simple majority." Consequently, the Committee maintained its earlier practice: the first member who took the floor in the Constructive Dialogue after the state delegation would be the country rapporteur. If states parties inquired about the matter, the Committee would share information with them. Thus, the identity of the country rapporteur remained an open secret—an additional example of fuzzy logic in the Committee's and the UN human rights apparatus's operations.[84]

The arguments for partial opacity find support in scholarship. Reflecting on the potential downsides of absolute transparency in international law—including the tendency of states to conceal their positions before decisions are finalized—Peters concludes that "in light of the positive and negative effects of transparency on deliberations and negotiations, institutional designers should envisage both opaque/confidential and transparent elements or phases for international law-making processes." She continues, "Total transparency of international law is neither appropriate nor realistic." Instead, she notes, "International law- and policy-makers should treat transparency as a variable of institutional and legal design" and "balance the potential negative effects against the positive ones."[85]

The Committee's inclination toward confidentiality reflects a long diplomatic tradition that privileges confidentiality over transparency as is illustrated by Cowan's analysis of the Minority Petitions of the League of Nations.[86] In her discussion of the continuities and discontinuities of rights oversight from the League to the UPR, she identifies a change in approach to transparency as one of the most significant discontinuities between the two.

Whereas transparency is a core guiding principle of the UPR, in the League's processes "non-transparency was an explicit value among most League bureaucrats and statesmen," as it was argued that "behind-closed-doors negotiations around minority problems allowed the Minority State to cooperate and to make concessions without losing face, as they would in a formal and public investigation."[87] This echoes the stance of those members who opposed full transparency: that the Committee would be better positioned to protect human rights by keeping certain operations behind closed doors and thereby shielding itself from potential attacks.

In the debate among members, the central concern was trust—the assumption that the states parties were not fully trustworthy, whereas a high level of trust prevailed among the Committee members as representatives of the Guardians of Vision's community of practice. Trust, the members' statements suggest, was reciprocated by members of the civil society, who are commonly likewise seen as Guardians of Vision motivated in their engagement by the greater realization of distinct rights. The sense of shared commitment accounts for why many Committee members believed that trust between the Committee and civil society would not be compromised by the Committee's continued practice of "open secrets."

Further, the members' comments indicated that trust did not depend on or demand full transparency. On the contrary, full transparency might jeopardize the Committee's ability to most effectively serve the realization of the ICCPR around the world. Thus, despite the opposition of some members, the Committee ultimately endorsed the UN human rights apparatus's opaque transparency as an ideal tool for human rights protection.

The discussion about transparency illustrates an instance where Committee members both sought to and refrained from incorporating central elements associated with the practice of law in the Committee's operations. Linking this finding back to the Committee's complex relationship with law, it results in an unexpected conclusion: law—including transparency as a core element—appears in such instances more as a means than as an end for the Committee members. Rather, the exchange frames the greater realization of human rights as the ultimate end, and where the excessive technicalities of the law—such as demands for absolute transparency—threaten to compromise that aim, the members prefer to set these technicalities aside and keep the realization of human rights at the center.

Conclusion

This chapter has addressed the complex relationship between the Human Rights Committee and law: on the one hand, an analysis of the Committee's operations reveals aspirations to operate as a distinctly legal body with robust authority, including the adoption of General Comments, which are akin to lawmaking. On the other hand, in practice, the Committee must continually negotiate its mandate with states parties, treading carefully around states that are inimical to international human rights oversight. In the accompanying navigation, Committee members play a key role in maintaining a human interface that remains unfailingly "constructive" toward states parties, thus helping prevent state initiatives aimed at curtailing its operations.

I have suggested that the relationship between the Human Rights Committee and law is far more complex than the mere question of the binding force of the Committee's operations and documents. Undoubtedly, the Committee incorporates such elements as legal aesthetics and a high level of precision akin to that used in drafting legal documents, illustrated by the first reading of General Comment No. 35, supported by the members' high degree of expertise and commitment.

In other, sometimes surprising respects, the Committee clearly departs from what one might expect of a legal body. Its emphasis on exaggeratedly "constructive" language belongs more to the tradition of diplomacy than to legal proceedings. The discussion of transparency illustrates that Committee members both seek and resist elements associated with the rule of law. Transparency is a value the Committee promotes when reviewing state reports, intended to curb corruption and increase good governance. At the same time, Committee members do not regard full transparency as intrinsic to the Committee's own practices due to the high degree of trust and integrity members invest in the Committee's operations, and in the human rights community more generally.

In recent decades, the Committee has undoubtedly contributed to the overall legalization of human rights. Committee members emphasize the rule of law connected to modern states as a desirable societal goal, thus—via the Committee's operations and documents—creating a hierarchy over other types of social norms and effectively continuing the civilizing mission of international law. In all of these outcomes, the Committee's eighteen expert members hold central roles as the Guardians of Vision who creatively maneuver to expand the Committee's realm of operations under the UN's fuzzy logic and opaque transparency. They embody a vital human interface, fortifying trust within the Guardians of Vision's community of practice and safeguarding NGO participation.

CHAPTER 5

From "Real Reality" to "UN Reality"

It is a little after 11:00 a.m. on a Friday morning, and the Constructive Dialogue between the Human Rights Committee and the state delegation of Finland has been ongoing for a good hour.[1] Thus far, the bulk of the time has been taken by the presentation of the state delegation, beginning with the customary compliments expressing appreciation for the Committee and its expert members. The delegation head then elaborated issues covered in Finland's sixth state report, responding to the List of Issues the Committee had sent in advance.

Moments before the session started at 10:00 a.m., the atmosphere in the Palais Wilson felt calm, especially when compared with the preceding days, when Constructive Dialogues on the state reports of Ukraine, Tajikistan, and Indonesia drew significantly larger NGO representation than Finland's. However, as the head of Finland's delegation concluded his statement and the Committee members began asking questions about the realization of the ICCPR in Finland, the atmosphere electrified. Members of Finland's state delegation, seated at the center of the Palais Wilson conference room, listened attentively and took diligent notes. A few of them began shuffling thick piles of documents—background briefs on questions they anticipated from Committee members. In the middle of the room, an NGO representative recorded every exchange with a webcam.

This chapter traces the translation of "real reality" to "UN reality" in the life cycle of Finland's sixth state report to the Human Rights Committee. It examines the patchwork-like quality of the report's drafting, which restricts individual drafters' personal influence and ties state reports intrinsically to ongoing human rights dialogue. I then consider how the draft document's circulation shapes its content and how circulation constitutes a standardization exercise that creates the legal fiction "legibility" and robust statehood. In echo with the findings of Chapter 4, I conclude that, in a telling paradox between human rights ideology and practice, documentation such as periodic state reports consolidates rather than erodes state power over its citizens.

The second part of the chapter places Finland's sixth state report in longitudinal perspective by contextualizing it, on the one hand, in the bulk of reports examined by the Committee, and, on the other, by examining all the seven documentary cycles on Finland. This section engages with the question of impact: do these reporting cycles yield in actual societal changes? The outcome of analysis suggests mixed outcomes, thus paving the way for the subsequent chapters' discussion on the multifaceted consequences of the Committee's work.

From "Real Reality" to "UN Reality"

Despite the air-conditioning generating a cooling breeze, the room started to heat up. There were no signs of clouds in the sky, and Mont Blanc was visible in her full beauty. A few cars passed by. Across the street, schoolchildren rushed outside for recess. The severity of issues being discussed inside the Palais Wilson seemed a million miles away from their laughter. Through the back windows of the conference room, their merriment felt within an arm's reach. Still, it was a part of a different reality: a "real reality" existing in the present moment, free of the layers of bureaucratic translations that characterize the sessions of the UN Human Rights Committee—scripted speech acts, careful translation of documents into depersonalized UN language, and the formatting of societal ills into the human rights vernacular.

As there are no regular audio microphones in the Palais Wilson conference room, speakers can be heard only through the headphones. During Human Rights Committee sessions, when members intervene in English, audience members listen to the speaker either directly through the headphones or via simultaneous translation offered into the UN's working languages—French, Spanish, Russian, Arabic—as well as, usually, an official language of the state presenting its report.

When listening to the speaker's voice directly, it adds an element of personal presence to the proceedings. In other aspects, the interventions are translated into the particularities of "UN reality": anyone attempting to follow the proceedings without headphones encounters a soundscape of near-total silence, punctuated only by the occasional keyboard clacking and other inconsequential sounds from the conference room's various corners.

The sensory detachment that characterizes the Human Rights Committee's sessions intensifies when speakers intervene in a language unfamiliar to most participants. Simultaneous translation filters their words, stripping away personal elements from communications such as tone and pace. Thus, the intervention of a passionately articulating elderly gentleman from the South Pacific may be transformed into the unemotional human rights lingua of a native female Oxbridge speaker.

Further, as each treaty body session includes a fixed roster of interpreters covering a predetermined set of languages, the layers of simultaneous translations can multiply. An oral intervention delivered, for example, in Tzotzil—an Indigenous language of southern Mexico—may first be rendered into Spanish, then from Spanish to English by another simultaneous interpreter, and, in the most extreme cases, from English to Russian or Arabic by a third.

Most often, attendees cannot see the speaker's face. Committee members sit in a semi-circle along the walls at the front of the conference room, and state delegates occupy a smaller semi-circle in front of them with their backs to the Committee, whereas only heads of delegation sit at the front podium facing the Committee. When I conducted the bulk of my ethnography, seeing speakers' faces was even more difficult for general observers seated at the back of the room, as they were both separated by distance and blocked by the sea of heads located in front of them.[2] Consequentially, the oral interventions that dominate the Human Rights Committee's sessions are devoid of personal cues such as facial expressions and gestures. More often than not, general observers do not know the speakers' names, as they are mentioned only in passing at the beginning of lengthy interventions.

Formal UN transcripts—typed by press officers in the back row—document what transpires and fortify the sense of personal detachment. The transcripts disseminated after the sessions through official UN channels condense each session to exactly six pages, omitting much of what occurs: when the Committee chair tells a state delegate to slow down as they start speed-reading responses from documents not provided to the interpreters, making interpretation impossible; or moments when Committee members express frustration at the Secretariat's personnel shortage that delays preparing documents that the Committee needs for its operations.

The official transcript does not capture the jokes Committee members share among themselves, with UN staff, or the occasional state delegate—instances that function almost like glue for the community of practice of the Guardians of Vision, and attest that the work of UN treaty bodies is indeed the work of real people, with real senses of humor, experiences of frustration, nervousness, and occasional boredom.

Instead, the formal transcript, issued as a press release, highlights the List of Issues addressed in the exchange, likely mentioning women, children, Indigenous peoples, LGBTIQ+ groups, persons with disabilities, and other groups customarily considered vulnerable in Human Rights Committee sessions. It typically denotes the treatment of prisoners, freedom of speech and information, and police brutality—all classic civil and political rights issues. It will refer to states, Committee members, and NGOs, emphasizing their roles as constitutive elements of the monitoring mechanism. It summarizes both the progress made and further steps the state must take to continue advancing implementation of the ICCPR, and its human rights situation more generally, thus moving the world in the rights direction.

Bureaucratic Layers of Translation

A key goal of UN treaty body proceedings—as Committee members frequently note in their Constructive Dialogues with state delegates—is to offer Committee members the sense of "real reality," by which they mean an accurate account of how states are realizing human rights in general and the ICCPR in particular. The notion of "real reality" recurs in varied guises during Committee sessions. Primarily, it is an attempt to grasp people's lived experiences—outside action plans or social programs—which states, by contrast, tend to offer as examples of societal progress in their interventions.[3]

As the opening sections nevertheless illustrate, what UN treaty bodies capture instead is "UN reality," which is the outcome of multiple layers of translation.[4] Some layers are literal: for instance, interventions are translated from one language to another, while simultaneously being rendered in the official UN human rights lingua. These translations, nonetheless, are constrained by the fact that English is the de facto language of discussion and the one in which members most often pose their questions.[5]

Other layers are figurative and aesthetic: documents are formatted—first by state delegates and later by UN staff—to comply with the logic and structure of UN style, including what Hull has described as the "rubrics of classification and graphic elements such as paragraphs, tables, subtitles, fonts, margins, and bullets."[6] Together these surface graphics "serve a range of semiotic functions,"[7] such as conferring legitimacy on the data states parties provide as reliable information.[8] Some layers are temporal: discussions at the UN Human Rights Committee and other UN treaty bodies rely on documents submitted to the UN perhaps two years earlier, themselves the product of compilation processes that may take more than a year. Even though NGOs offer corrections and updates, which I elaborate upon in Chapter 7, most of what is discussed in the present moment rests on outdated data.[9]

Layers of translation likewise eliminate personal influence: individual names mentioned during Human Rights Committee sessions vanish from official transcripts, replaced by the names of governments and the Committee as a whole. The outcome erases the community of practice of the Guardians of Vision from view in a quintessential technique of contemporary bureaucracies, whose discourse is often, as Hull notes, "impersonal and anonymous on the basis of lexical and semantic features: the prevalence of passive verbs, abstract nouns, and the like."[10]

These linguistic choices are not accidental, but instead blur agency by obscuring responsibility for particular formulations and documentary processes. They furthermore depoliticize contested issues, while, as Müller observes, "naturalizing economic inequalities."[11] During the Committee's sessions, such choices transfer action from individuals to the legal fictions propagated by the state and the Committee, resulting, in Hull's words, in the "construction of collective agency from the agency of individuals."[12]

Also the state reports are the product of multiple translations: literal ones that render source material, such as constitutions and other laws, from national languages into English, and figurative ones that cast societal ills into the human rights vernacular articulated in UN human rights treaties.

Within the Human Rights Committee's cycle, the latter translation inserts state action plans, programs, acts, and legislative initiatives into the reports to show how the state has advanced fulfillment of its obligations under the ICCPR. In state reporting, these elements feed into what Babül calls the "standardization of administrative procedures, and fostering a pro-human rights organizational culture within administration," which together present themselves as "important steps towards establishing human rights in countries."[13]

Finland's Sixth State Report as Ongoing Dialogue

Local and global bureaucracies commonly deem documents "rationality badges" that increase transparency and predictability.[14] Both scholars and bureaucrats alike see the ability to create and maintain files as the emblem of modern bureaucracy and part of what Osborne calls the establishment of "the ethical competence to rule."[15] Concurrently, over the past decade, anthropologists of documents and bureaucracy have shown how, rather than the Weberian fantasy of stability and rationality, documentation processes are dynamic and in constant flux, accompanied by affect and prone to contradictory outcomes.[16]

As Hull argues, "documents are not simply instruments of bureaucratic organizations, but rather are constitutive of bureaucratic rules, ideologies, knowledge, practices, subjectivities, objects, outcomes, even the organizations themselves."[17] By extension—and contrary to Scott's notion of making populations "legible"[18]—research shows that bureaucracies can render populations illegible while concealing bureaucracies' constructive nature behind a seeming veil of objectivity.[19]

Finland submitted its sixth periodic report on the ICCPR to the Human Rights Committee in August 2011.[20] A tightly packed, thirty-eight-page document organized in treaty-like paragraphs emphasizes the documentary genre's legalistic nature—and by extension, the legalistic nature of the Human Rights Committee's reporting cycles. The state report exemplifies the thousands of documents states produce annually to UN human rights treaty bodies and other human rights monitoring mechanisms at the local and regional levels.[21] Finland's state report was compiled in the Legal Division of the Ministry for Foreign Affairs, specifically the Unit for Human Rights Courts and Conventions. About ten civil servants staff the unit; in 2023 all were women with a legal background. Beyond the ICCPR, the unit prepares reports with regard to six other UN human rights treaties, as well as four Council of Europe instruments.[22]

The front page of Finland's state report includes a UN document's customary "surface graphics"—the document number and the UN emblem—and notes that English is the document's original language, Finnish and Swedish being the state's official national languages. The detailed table of contents on page 2 lists both page numbers and paragraphs, a presentation that resonates with legal aesthetics. Page 3 opens with a brief description of the report's content and cites the Human Rights Committee's "harmonized guidelines on reporting," which shaped the document. The page further notes that the report covers "developments after the submission of the previous report in 2003, mainly until the end of 2009."[23] Here we see the temporal translation of UN human rights monitoring: by the time the Committee discussed the report in summer 2013, much of its content was already more than four years old.

Section II of page 3 likewise captures the translation of "real reality" into "UN reality." It discusses "responses to the recommendation contained in Paragraph 7 of the Concluding Observations (CCPR/CO/82/FIN)," referring to the document the Committee adopted after processing Finland's fifth state report in 2004. References to paragraphs from the fifth report continue for the subsequent seven pages without ever specifying what these paragraphs contain.[24]

Finland's sixth state report is, in other words, impossible to read as a stand-alone document. Instead, to make sense of it, a reader must either be already familiar with the Concluding Observations from 2004 or have the text readily available. Analytically, such documents must be construed as intrinsic parts of ongoing human rights dialogue, not as stand-alone documents. As Riles notes, individual documents acquire significance less from their concrete wording than their link to documents that both precede and succeed them, forming ongoing progressive chains.[25] The interview with Finnish state delegate "Sam" in Chapter 6 likewise highlights the chainlike quality of individual events within UN treaty body monitoring cycles as a core element of these documentary cycles' significance.

Moreover, Finland's sixth report references Finland's fifth periodic report (CCPR/C/FIN/2003/5), on which the Committee's Concluding Observations were based. For example, paragraph 82 on page 14 addresses Articles 4 and 5 of the ICCPR concerning "restrictions upon and derogation from Convention provisions," noting that "the question was covered in the fifth periodic report of Finland." Thus, a reader seeking to make sense of Finland's sixth state report would need access to Finland's fifth state report in order to know Finland's position on restrictions and derogations.

The reference to Finland's fifth state report illustrates a key component of documents produced for UN treaty bodies: rather than being written from scratch, they are compiled on top of each other. As interlocutors at both the Unit for Human Rights Courts and Conventions and the UN Secretariat shared in interviews, they commence drafting a new document by reviewing previous reports, and copying and pasting relevant sections to form the foundation of the new report. For Finland's sixth state report, these source documents included Finland's fifth state report and the most recent reports Finland submitted to other UN treaty bodies, including the CESCR, CEDAW, and CAT committees. Staff at the Unit for Human Rights Courts and Conventions then revises the copy-pasted data in line with developments since the last reports.

A practical explanation clarifies drafting logic: the same individuals often compile reports for multiple monitoring bodies. The same finding applies moreover to UN staff who prepare documents for treaty body proceedings as also they typically work on specific states' files for two or three different UN treaty bodies. Thus, the staff member who prepares the List of Issues on Finland for the Human Rights Committee will likely prepare the same document as well as other background papers on Finland also for other UN treaty bodies such as the CEDAW or the CRC committees. Staff therefore hold intimate knowledge of documents related to Finland produced for other monitoring bodies, and consequently, when drafting new documents, staff commonly begin by consulting lists of issues by the other treaty bodies.[26]

These examples show that seemingly separate documents not only connect but actually embed one another. Sometimes, interdependency yields undesired outcomes: in numerous interviews, Finnish civil servants voiced frustration that certain recommendations were "simply copied and pasted" from earlier ones. Their comments suggest disappointment with treaty body proceedings constituting "merely going through the motions" without solid anchoring to substantive issues regarding how to realize treaty obligations.

"The State Is One"

While preparing documents for the Human Rights Committee's reporting cycles, individual civil servants and UN staff members play a key role in translating "real reality" to "UN reality," as intermediaries.[27] In practice, a compiler's judgment shapes the document's content—including which action plans or programs they include—as well as the document's structure and the emphasis given to different areas of concern.

The final state reports mask the drafter's personal influence, since the reports speak in the voice of the state. Further, the idea of state unity is the civil servants' single most important guideline when they draft state reports. One Finnish civil servant characterized the drafting as "acting like the state" while withholding personal views. Another governing value, the same civil servant noted, is that "from the viewpoint of information the state is one." In practice, when drafting state reports, civil servants treat all information the government generates and shares on official government websites as equally valid. Thus, in state reports, the perceived veracity of information depends on who produced and disseminated it. Consequently, government-issued data trumps, for example, the most recent discoveries in science, unless a formal government source has transmitted those findings as official knowledge in some formal channel such as a government website.[28]

Compared with many other document genres, individual influence in state reports remains limited due to the clear format, embedded in a distinct legalistic aesthetic, that governs state reports' organization. The format's importance has further increased under the "simplified reporting procedure" the Committee has adopted,[29] in which the Committee provides states with a list of questions to answer, effectively dictating what the reports include.

At the same time, the movement that accompanies a report's drafting and life cycle shape its content. After the Unit for Human Rights Courts and Conventions staff prepared the initial draft of Finland's report, they circulated the document among relevant officials in different Finnish ministries, who updated it in turn.[30] Consultative meetings often accompany the document's circulation, during which civil servants from various ministries discuss the report's contents.

In the final version of Finland's sixth state report, the Ministry of Justice commented on non-discrimination legislation, explaining that it has "set up a non-discrimination Committee to prepare the [legislative] reform" (p. 12, par. 68). The Ministry further noted it "is drafting a legislative amendment to extend the scope of application of the compensation to legal proceedings before administrative courts, special courts and administrative appellate boards" (p. 26, par. 176). The Ministry of Social Affairs and Health summarized that it "published the first national action programme for the promotion of sexual and reproductive health" for 2007–2011 (p. 15, par. 91). The Ministry of the Interior shared that it "commissioned a survey on children's and young persons' experience of discrimination" (p. 33, par. 226), and the Ministry of Education and Culture detailed that it had "increased the number of student places for sign language interpreters and instructors" (p. 37, par. 250).

Circulating draft state reports among ministries and relevant government offices helps ensure that the information contained in the report's segments reflects the most recent legislative and policy initiatives. Simultaneously, documentary movement has additional creative consequences. The cited inputs from different ministries show how circulation and consultation "construct in concrete forms the very corporate order that it appears to reproduce"[31]—projecting the image of "the state as one."

As draft reports move between ministries and across the desks of civil servants, they forge alliances and, to return to Hull, "draw . . . particular bureaucrats into a matter or exclude . . . them as the file moves across their desk or is routed around them." Circulation "creates associations among people that often differ from formal organizational structures and draw people outside the bureaucracy into bureaucratic practices."[32] In the case of state reports, it connects dispersed civil servants in shared documentation practices, which translate their everyday work into the human rights vernacular. These shared bureaucratic endeavors integrate dispersed civil servants into the human rights community, even when, in their regular duties, they do not engage with human rights. Thus, document circulation solidifies and expands the community of practice of human rights professionals, pushing the scope of human rights further.

Invisible Municipalities

The documentary cycles characteristic of UN treaty bodies entail further implications vis-à-vis the state by fostering the impression of state legibility and "it-ness."[33] This is evident when one examines who is included in—and excluded from—Finland's sixth state report and, by extension, its consultative cycles. The bulk of actors the report identifies are state representatives, not unexpected considering that state reports communicate specifically how the state has, or has not, fulfilled its obligations under the ICCPR. The report refers to Finland, the President of the Republic, the Government, Parliament, the Prime Minister, the police, and different courts, including the Supreme Administrative Court.[34] It mentions numerous ministries, in addition to those listed above, including the Ministry of Defense and the Ministry of Employment and the Economy. It lists several ombudsmen, including the Parliamentary Ombudsman and the Ombudsman for Equality.

The report mentions actors operating at the boundary between the state and civil society, such as the Center for Non-Military Service, the Investigation Committee of Conviction of Persons Liable for Military Service, and the National Institute for Health and Welfare—all likely recipients of some state funding. The document further refers to the Advisory Board of Romani Affairs and the Sámi Parliament as bodies overseeing the realization of human rights among Roma and Sámi people, respectively.

The report names several NGOs. One is the Coalition of Finnish Women's Associations (Nytkis), which was consulted about discrimination against women for the report, including discrimination Roma and Sámi women face (p. 13, par. 75). Another is Monica, Multicultural Women's Association, which contributed the statement that "every fourth woman who dies as a victim of family violence has an immigrant background" (p. 16, par. 97). The report mentions HeSETA (Helsingin seudun seksuaalinen tasavertaisuus ry), a non-governmental LGBTIQ+ organization that organizes the annual Helsinki Pride Parade.

In addition, the report cites the Association of Finnish Local and Regional Authorities, which has adopted a child policy program. Further, it mentions the Mannerheim League for Child Welfare and the Central Union for Child Welfare, which are "concerned about the insufficiency of the support provided to divorce families" (p. 33, par. 225). Finally, the report refers to the Finnish Association of the Deaf, which, together with the Research Institute for the Languages of Finland, has "prepared a sign language policy program for Finland" (2010–2015) that aims to increase awareness among authorities and members of the sign language community of the latter's linguistic rights (p. 37, par. 251).

Mentioning these actors in the report contributes to the impression of a unified state, in which a broad range of functionaries engage with human rights and the ICCPR's provision as part of their professional duties. The focus on NGOs likewise underscores the importance of the civil society and signals Finland's investment in human rights protections, a theme elaborated in Chapter 6. Equally relevant, nevertheless, are the actors absent from the report: municipal authorities. In light of Finland's legal and political system, the absence is unexpected, as municipalities hold significant powers and responsibilities in Finnish social life.

The pivotal role of municipalities is communicated by another genre of documents, namely, the Core Document that states may submit to UN bodies alongside their individual state reports. Core Documents offer a comprehensive introduction to the state, its political and legal system, population, and economic model.[35] Finland's Core Document explains that, "based on the Constitution of Finland, *municipalities have strong autonomy* arising from the self-government of municipal residents." Further, according to the Core Document, the scope of Finnish municipalities' autonomy—the total number of which was 310 in 2020—is "among the broadest in the world."[36]

The Core Document continues that "as a rule, a municipality is responsible for organizing the social and health care services for its residents," as well as "obligated to organize basic education for all of their residents who are of compulsory education age." In addition, municipalities are responsible for "extensive educational and cultural services, sports and exercise services, green area and road infrastructure, and fire and rescue services." The Document adds that the role of municipalities has "grown significantly with regard to promoting the health and wellbeing of the population and maintaining and enhancing demographic, economic and operational vitality."[37] To fund these tasks, the Constitution safeguards the right of municipalities to levy taxes, and municipalities receive central government transfers to local government. In other words, municipalities are central actors in the effective realization of rights, including those under the ICCPR. Under Finland's Constitution, they are both enabled and required to safeguard rights independently of the state.

The significance of municipalities, nevertheless, is impossible to deduce from Finland's sixth state report, which names no municipal authorities. By extension, few, if any, municipal authorities took part in the circulation of draft state reports. Finland's sixth state report mentions municipalities only a handful of times, including in connection with "activities to improve skills of multiculturalism" (p. 9, par. 48). Additionally, it notes that the Health Care Act of 2010 "obligates all municipalities to provide residents in their territories with contraception counselling and other services promoting sexual and reproductive health" (p. 15, par. 93). In addition, the report refers to reforms to the Municipality of Residence Act (201/1994), which increases "individuals' freedom of choice in respect of institutional care, housing services and family care" (p. 23, par. 158).

The section on policy programs for children likewise mentions municipalities: the Association of Finnish Local and Regional Authorities "recommended that municipalities prepare municipal or regional child policy programs" (p. 33, par. 220). The Mannerheim League for Child Welfare and the Central Union for Child Welfare note that "municipalities should allocate more resources for support services to divorce families" (p. 33, par. 225). Elsewhere, the report refers to municipalities with regard to child and family counseling (p. 32, par. 224), people with disabilities, the Sámi homeland, the status of immigrants, and multiculturalism.

A Robust Sovereign

All in all, Finland's sixth state report assigns municipalities a marginal role. The report neither names distinct municipal authorities and actors nor introduces distinct municipal initiatives. Thus, without prior knowledge of Finnish municipalities' significant autonomy and extensive responsibilities, a reader cannot discern their significance in realizing the ICCPR in "real reality." Instead, Finland's sixth state report leaves readers with the impression governing "UN reality": that from a governance viewpoint, the state of Finland is both unified and robust in realizing the obligations enlisted in the ICCPR, with occasional assistance from NGOs.

Importantly, downplaying municipalities does not merely stem from the state report's drafting or wording. Rather, it is a direct consequence of the very legal foundation and purpose of these reports. As has been noted, the Human Rights Committee, like the other treaty bodies, has a covenant-based mandate to examine how the state meets its obligations under the ICCPR. The expectation, in turn, derives directly from the fact that only states—not municipalities, cities, provinces, cantons, autonomous regions, clans, or chieftainships—are, or can be, parties to the ICCPR as an instrument of public international law. Consequently, only state actions fall within these reporting cycles.

Additionally, when we consider the consequences of state emphasis for "real reality," state reports appear as standardization exercises that create the legal fictions of legible states with the "invention of units that are visible."[38] Finland's sixth state report presents the state of Finland as the sole governing unit for the issues that the report addresses, omitting other levels of governance. "Unity of a state" masks multiple domestic governing levels, forming an "everyday site . . . of standardization"[39] that both produces and conceals state centrality in Finnish societal life.

Downplaying all other governance levels and institutions has significant consequences for delimiting the authority of local leaders or for regional autonomy as Indonesia's first state report in 2013 illustrates. During the ensuing Constructive Dialogue, Committee members emphasized that regional autonomy was not an excuse for deviating from ICCPR obligations, citing reports of corporal punishment in schools in the Special Autonomous Region of Aceh.[40] Because only the state of Indonesia is—and can be—a party to the ICCPR, the state bears the legal responsibility for such conduct. Nevertheless, if the state acts on the matter, it will curtail local autonomy and strengthen the state authority in the Aceh region, despite the region's autonomous status.

In research on human rights policymaking in Costa Rica, Clark notes the same tension in the Committee on the Elimination of Racial Discrimination's document cycles. He observes that "the holes in the actual Costa Rican delegation's knowledge reminded me once more how untenable is the premise of this forum: that 'the state' is to speak, to give an account, to take stock reflexively, and to respond coherently of 'itself'—in fact an unsettled and non-unitary subject."[41] These observations underscore that documents such as state reports "carry both a descriptive and a prescriptive mandate" as Moon has noted,[42] while, as Hull reminds us, "much of what is important about the use of files is not documented within them."[43]

State reports thus have, as Brohman describes of documents more generally, "the capacity 'to make things come into being.'"[44] As Hull observes, like "other forms of material culture, such as uniforms, cars, and official buildings," documents are central to "how the state comes to be imagined, encountered, and reimagined by the population."[45] Further, Kelly reminds us, the reports "hide as much as [they] reveal."[46] The outcome engenders several paradoxes. The UN treaty body framework exists to curb state power by ensuring the greater realization of individual rights. In treaty body proceedings, states are the objects of scrutiny and potential rights violators, and the very task of UN treaty bodies is to ensure that states live up to their lofty treaty commitments.

Simultaneously, state reports themselves, as well as the Constructive Dialogues, strengthen—rather than curb—the state's centrality as the key reference point in the eyes of the international community by sustaining, and actively producing, the fantasy of legible statehood while erasing from view the multiple levels of governance that operate in "real reality." Under the Human Rights Committee's mandate, it treats any apparent divergence from treaty obligations as the state's fault. Accordingly, the Committee expects the state to take corrective action. For example, if the Committee finds that schooling is not offered in required languages—national or minority—it will expect the state to intervene, thereby expanding the state's realm of operations while delimiting that of minority groups. From this perspective, treaty body operations amplify the importance of the state, running counter to scholarly expectations that transnational collaboration and human rights work would diminish it.[47] These dynamics illustrate how, as Mathur observes, "certain laws do not work as they ought to and how they are capable of producing absurdity."[48]

The analysis of Finland's state report shows that the state's growing salience as the dominant legal and political institution in treaty bodies' monitoring cycles is not explained solely by the fact that only states are—and can be—parties to the ICCPR. Rather, state reports actively produce it, state centrality forming one of the "immutable mobiles" of the Committee's operations. As Latour notes, the more such ideas spread, "the more powerful they become."[49] Thus, the analysis of Finland's sixth state report, and the municipalities' marginal role in it, shows how treaty body monitoring also functions as a state-building exercise, connected to the civilizing mission embedded in treaty body monitoring discussed in Chapter 4.

Movement of Issues in Finland's Concluding Observations

To say that UN organs generate massive quantities of documents is an understatement. As Niezen and Sapignoli summarize, they "generat[e] documents that heighten obscurity, while producing ideas and policies behind closed doors"[50]—to the point where document production appears as *all* that they do while hindering what IOs should *actually* be doing. What follows from these massive quantities of documents? What kind of tangible effects do they generate in "real reality"? The remainder of the present chapter answers these questions with an analysis of Finland's seven documentary cycles under the ICCPR.

Finland's sixth reporting cycle commenced with Finland's thirty-eight-page state report sent to the UN Secretariat in August 2011,[51] accompanied by an eleven-page Core Document.[52] The next step was the three-page List of Issues that the Committee sent to Finland in November 2012.[53] Finland reciprocated in May 2013 with a thirty-two-page response, two months before the Constructive Dialogue in July of the same year.[54] After the Dialogue, Finland submitted two short documents, one and three pages long, with further information the Committee had requested.[55] The Committee then adopted its seven-page Concluding Observations, requesting additional information on three issues: the detention of asylum seekers and irregular migrants (par. 10); the maximum number of detention hours for individuals arrested on criminal charges (par. 11); and Sámi rights (par. 16).[56]

The following summer, Finland provided the Committee with additional information on these three issues in a seven-page document.[57] In April 2015, the Committee requested further clarification in a two-page document,[58] and Finland reciprocated by sending a six-page document with additional information in May 2015.[59] In December 2015, the Committee sent its three-page follow-up to Finland.[60] On April 2016, in the third round of follow-up,

Finland submitted a seven-page document with further information.[61] The following year, in August 2017, the Committee concluded the reporting cycle with its final seven-page follow-up to the Concluding Observations, while noting that the dialogue will continue in Finland's next reporting cycle, with Finland's seventh Constructive Dialogue taking place in spring 2021.[62]

In total, Finland's sixth reporting cycle generated sixteen documents of 165 pages exchanged between Finland and the Committee over six years. Of these pages, 110 were produced by Finland and 55 by the Committee. In addition, eight NGO reports totaling 70 pages accompanied the cycle, raising the total to 235 pages. To place these figures in broader context, during the 108th session, when Finland's report was processed, the Committee additionally examined the reports of six other states, accompanied by seventy-five NGO submissions. The Committee further adopted Lists of Issues for six states and issued views on sixteen individual communications.[63] Across its three sessions in 2013, the Committee reviewed 16 state reports and received 186 NGO reports, adopted Lists of Issues for another 20 states, and issued views on 55 individual communications.[64]

These figures highlight the volume of documents the Human Rights Committee processes. If each state had submitted the same number of pages as Finland, the Committee's 2013 sessions would have involved approximately 3,680 pages of documentation. Extending the figure to the full eight-year period encompassing Finland's sixth and seventh reporting cycles—processed in 2013 and 2021, respectively—the figure grows to a staggering 29,440 pages.[65] Document flows have since been reduced by the introduction of the simplified reporting procedure.[66] At the same time, the Committee has introduced additional follow-up cycles, intensifying concern about the high volume of documentation that persists among Committee insiders and scholars.[67]

What substantive consequences ensue from these massive documentary flows? An analysis of Finland's seven reporting cycles suggests that unequivocal answers remain elusive. The first Concluding Observations on Finland were adopted in August 1977. Brief reflections of only two pages, the observations focused primarily on issues at the core to the ICCPR's implementation: the compatibility of the ICCPR with the Finnish Constitution and ordinary legislation, and questions of jurisdiction. The Committee likewise asked whether the Covenant applied to all persons residing in Finland, not just citizens.[68] Another substantive issue concerned Finland's reservation to Article 20(1) of the ICCPR, prohibiting war propaganda.[69]

Both of these issues have since disappeared from the Committee's Concluding Observations, suggesting that internal changes in Finland have made further engagement with them unnecessary. Another example where an issue first appeared then disappeared from subsequent reporting cycles comes from the third Observations from 1991.[70] In them, the Committee expressed concern that the new Passport Act might restrict citizens' fundamental right to travel abroad.[71] Finland revised the act, and the issue has not reappeared in subsequent Observations. These examples illustrate substantial shifts in the issues the Committee has addressed over the past decades, reflecting broader changes in the rights landscape both in Finland and the world.

Similar conclusions emerge from the significant expansion of issues the Committee now considers, when compared to when its reporting cycles commenced. Whereas Finland's first Observations make no mention of women's or Sámi rights, for example, by the second reporting cycle both these topics were discussed, if only in passing. In subsequent reporting cycles, these issues became integral to the Concluding Observations, mirroring the general post–World War II expansion of the human rights concept. These findings suggest that the Committee's work aligns with the world's general movement in the rights direction.

It is difficult, however, to determine the Committee's precise role in these changes. Have shifts in the Committee's focus resulted from incorporating issues that NGOs have introduced into the proceedings, reflecting evolving NGO priorities and strategies? Or do these shifts emerge from proactive stances adopted by the Committee itself? Also, have the Concluding Observations prompted changes in local conditions that have resulted in the issues' disappearance from the Observations, or is this the result of other factors, such as domestic advocacy?

Toward Greater Covenant Realization?

Close examination of Committee proceedings suggests a complex picture of causes and consequences: even the Committee's sustained attention to specific issues does not guarantee tangible changes in "real reality."[72] One of the most persistent concerns in Finland's Observations—the pay gap between men and women—offers an illustration. Since the second reporting cycle, with the exception of the fourth one, the issue appears in all Observations. In the second one, the Committee raised the matter directly. Finland responded: "With regard to salary disparities, parity existed in the public sector but had unfortunately not quite been achieved in the private sector."[73] The Committee continued to highlight the issue in subsequent cycles, noting in the fifth one that although "steps . . . have increased the number of women in senior posts within the administration, including the directors of several ministries, . . . the Committee observes that there are still sex-related differences in rates of pay."[74]

In its seventh Concluding Observations in 2021, the Committee shifted its approach by noting recent positive legislative changes, which it lauded.[75] Still, the underlying issue persists in Finland: in 2022, various sources estimated that women's salaries averaged roughly 84 percent of men's salaries for comparable positions.[76] The discrepancy cuts across sectors and has prompted local initiatives such as "Women's Payday."[77] The persistence of wage inequality, despite orchestrated national efforts, raises the question of whether it is reasonable to expect external input from a UN monitoring body to overcome it, considering that a gender-based pay gap stems from a complex, deep-seated mélange of cultural and social factors—even in a state such as Finland with a strong reputation for being progressive and egalitarian. Of course, the assumption that external pressure can influence domestic dynamics lies at the core of the Committee's operations and its legitimacy. Still, one might argue that wage inequality may exemplify an issue the Committee cannot meaningfully affect due to its complexity.

Simultaneously, a review of the Concluding Observations reveals how repeated efforts have not produced the desired changes even in straightforward civil and political rights issues. This is evident in the Committee's comments on Finland's reservations to Article 14(7) of the ICCPR dealing with a right to a fair trial and equality before the courts.[78] The Committee questioned the need for the reservation already in its first Concluding Observation.[79] Over the years, the issue has remained one of the Committee's most persistent concerns: it is explicitly mentioned in every one of the seven Observations on Finland, with the exception of the second, which only notes general concern over Finland's Covenant reservations.[80] Finland has continually not amended the reservation, instead stating that it has no plans to do so in a direct challenge to the Committee's position.[81]

Another area in which Finland's actions have run counter to the Committee's recommendations concerns the rights of conscientious objectors. The issue likewise appears in all Observations except the first. The core concern regarding the matter can be summarized in three points: first, the length of civil service for conscientious objectors exceeds that of regular military service, which the Committee interprets as punitive and contrary to the Covenant; second, total objectors have faced imprisonment; and third, Finland has exempted Jehovah's Witnesses from such penalties due to their religious convictions.[82] By contrast, across the reporting cycles, the Committee has repeatedly emphasized that this exemption should apply to all conscientious objectors.[83]

In the seventh Concluding Observations, the Committee noted that Finland had repealed the exemption for Jehovah's Witnesses. However, this move runs counter to the Committee's consistent recommendations. Rather than ensuring that no one faces criminal prosecution for refusing all forms of military and non-military service on grounds of conscience, Finland now permits the prosecution of *anyone* who refuses military service, *including* Jehovah's Witnesses.[84] This reflects movement as a result of domestic developments in the Committee's reporting cycles—but, in the Committee's views, in the opposite direction from the "rights direction" it seeks.

Sámi Rights and Persistent Fluctuation

Sámi issues offer an another example of uncertain outcomes.[85] Sámi rights first appeared in the second Concluding Observations in 1986, when one member requested additional information regarding the implementation of the provisions of Article 27 of the Covenant in respect to the "Lapp people" and asked for clarification of the functions of the "Lapp parliament."[86] Using "Lapp people"—anchored in the geography of Lapland where most Sámi reside—rather than "Sámi" indicates that Sámi rights had at the time not become a staple issue for the Committee with consistent terminology.[87]

This soon changed as Sámi rights became one of the Committee's most consistently addressed topics. In the third Concluding Observations in 1991, the Committee commented on developments regarding language rights,[88] an area in which the Committee viewed Finland's actions favorably.[89] Concurrently the Committee's tone on core Sámi rights—land rights, reindeer herding, and the definition of who is recognized as Sámi and who decides—remained critical, flagging shortcomings of Finnish legislation. Further, the Committee asked why Finnish law, unlike Sweden's, kept reindeer herding open to all instead of restricting it to the Sámi, and whether Finland had a law governing the recognition of ethnic minorities.[90]

The third and fourth Concluding Observations from 1998 and 2004 reiterated that Sámi land rights remained unresolved, affecting the Sámi's traditional subsistence and endangering their culture, way of life, and identity.[91] The Committee urged Finland to resolve the issue swiftly in conjunction with the Sámi people, as well as to follow up on an individual communication regarding Sámi rights, on which the Committee had recently issued its Views.[92] Yet little had changed by the sixth Observations in 2013.[93]

Again, the Committee noted that the Sámi "lack participation and decision-making powers over matters of fundamental importance to their culture and way of life, including rights to land and resources."[94] In sum, despite repeated urgings, movement on foundational issues regarding the Sámi was limited across Finland's first six reporting cycles. By contrast, core legislative issues regarding land rights and the Sámi traditional way of life remained unresolved, as Finland had consistently not ratified ILO 169. Likewise, revisions to domestic legislation were halted.

In hopes of speeding up changes, the Committee selected Sámi issues as one of the three follow-up topics in Finland's sixth Concluding Observations.[95] In August 2014, in its additional information requested by the Committee, Finland detailed its intent to "strengthen the dynamics of the Sámi Parliament's operation and its active obligation to promote the rights of the Sámi as an indigenous people,"[96] thus signaling that Sámi issues would advance under Finnish legislation as the Committee desired. In summer 2015, the Committee found that movement had again halted, as plans to both revise the act pertaining to the Sámi Parliament and ratify ILO 169 had stalled.[97]

Finland's third follow-up reply in 2016 again showed improvement on Sámi issues, embodied in a new act that focused on state forestry and included a reference to the Sámi Parliament Act.[98] The Committee welcomed this as a positive development, while recognizing that this act represented only a fraction of the changes that the Committee sought.[99] This suggests that the accelerated exchange of documents between the Committee and Finland in the follow-up procedure had some, though limited, impact on outcomes. Yet progress remained still slower than the Committee hoped, prompting it to urge Finland in the seventh Concluding Observations, in plain language, to "speed up the process" of revising the Sámi Parliament Act and implement the Committee's Views from November 2018. It further urged Finland to "step up its efforts to provide government and local officials, police officers, prosecutors and judges with appropriate training on the need to respect the rights of the Sámi as an indigenous people."[100] The Committee's seventh

Observations on Finland's state again comment on Sámi issues, reiterating familiar concerns about Finland's failure to revise the Sámi Parliament Act and ratify ILO 169.[101]

In sum, developments in Finland suggest movement in ambivalent directions regarding Sámi rights. As a positive outcome, finally in 2025 the Act on the Sámi Parliament was revised.[102] As a negative one, two recent Views by the CRC and the CESCR Committees found that Finland had violated the Sámi people's rights to culture and land in its recent conduct. Both communications concerned the granting of mineral exploration permits in Sámi territory without an impact assessment or an adequate participatory process.[103] These Views suggest a continuation of long-term patterns in which Sámi rights are recognized at the level of discourse while often infringed in practice by Finland.

Reflecting on "Impact"

This analysis of Finland's reporting cycles suggests that the translation of "real reality" concerns into "UN reality" in the Committee's Concluding Observations does not yield guaranteed consequences in "real reality," even when the same issues recur, a finding aligning with earlier analyses of these documents' impact.[104] Given Finland's reputation as a model human rights student, one might infer that if *even Finland* fails to follow the Committee's recommendations, the record of other states is unlikely to be better, and may be worse.[105]

Even so, the Concluding Observations trigger manifold activities with wide-ranging effects, in which state civil servants play a significant role as Guardians of Vision.[106] When Finland receives them from the Human Rights Committee and the other UN treaty bodies, the Unit for Human Rights Courts and Conventions issues a press release and translates the Observations into the national languages, Finnish and Swedish, and often into minority languages such as Northern Sámi. The Ministry for Foreign Affairs then distributes the document to the Parliament, the judiciary, advisory boards, churches, state-level public authorities, the national human rights institution, municipalities, and NGOs.[107]

The significance of the government's press release was evident with the Concluding Observations on Finland's sixth state report.[108] Major Finnish outlets—including the public broadcaster Yleisradio and the country's largest newspaper, *Helsingin Sanomat*—picked the press release up, giving the document broad national visibility.[109] Nonetheless, that visibility was brief and focused on a single issue, namely, gender and wage inequality, even though the Ministry's press release highlighted all seven issues raised by the Committee.

Another disseminating channel is the Government Network of Fundamental and Human Rights, which includes representatives of Finnish ministries, independent observers, and members from the Office of the Parliamentary Ombudsman and the Ministry of Justice. The network reviews Finland's Observations from various UN treaty bodies and develops action plans for their implementation.[110]

Additionally, whereas the direct impact of individual Concluding Observations remains elusive, the ICCPR itself has been invoked in Finnish courts in numerous cases. In 2021, the head of Finland's state delegation for the seventh Constructive Dialogue—held online due to the COVID-19 pandemic—summarized that "the Supreme Court has referred to the covenants at least fourteen times and the Supreme Administrative Court has referred to it in hundreds of decisions since 2013."[111] The delegate furthermore emphasized that the Covenant is used in lower courts and legislative processes. The court practice alone confirms that, despite mixed outcomes and uncertain impact of Finland's Constructive Dialogues, over the past decades the ICCPR has become deeply embedded in Finnish society and judicial practice.

Conclusion

This chapter has explored the translations incumbent in the drafting, circulation, and processing of state reports, simultaneously tracing the aesthetic, temporal, and depersonalizing acts that transform "real reality" into "UN reality." Following the circulation of Finland's draft state report, this chapter demonstrates how the document's continual movement forges a human rights community among Finnish civil servants, creating new alliances. At the same time, circulation excludes key domestic actors responsible for implementing core ICCPR provisions at the municipal level, an exclusion replicated in the state report's text.

The examination of Finland's seven documentary cycles illustrates how tangible impact in "real reality" in regards to specific issues under the ICCPR remains elusive and difficult to reach. Simultaneously, the Committee's operations influence public debate, inform political agendas, and impact court proceedings and legislation. Together these outcomes help move practice in a rights-affirming direction by making the ICCPR a central domestic reference point. The impact following the press release issued on the Concluding Observations on public debate raises awareness of issues in Finnish society that a highly respected UN expert body identifies as problematic.

This analysis has further shown how one consequence of translating "real reality" into "UN reality" in treaty body cycles is the strengthening of the state as an institution of internal governance. Thus, contrary to prevailing expectations, the post–World War II human rights regime has not only curtailed states' sovereign powers; it has concurrently, through UN treaty body proceedings, consolidated and amplified the state's role. In this sense, the story of human rights monitoring is one of state-making—and movement in the rights direction entails an increasing, rather than decreasing, centrality of states.

CHAPTER 6

The Feeling of Reporting

"We welcome back the state delegation and look forward to their responses to the questions Committee members posed before lunch," Sir Nigel concluded from the podium. The lunch hour had been a welcome break after three intense hours of questioning by the Committee members, followed by answers from the state delegates. Once the morning session had adjourned, members of Finland's state delegation rushed off to combine lunch with preparing answers for the afternoon session starting in two hours.

Most people in the conference room had headed across the hallway to the cafeteria, where some settled on the terrace to enjoy their lunch together amid the beautiful rays of the July sun with a view of Lac Léman. The mood was lively as people discussed how the session has gone, the performance of both the state delegation and the Committee members. Once the session reconvened, the head of Finland's state delegation took the floor again, thanking the Committee members for their insightful questions, proceeding to read a statement from a document prepared in advance. The mood of the state delegation appeared attentive. Would they be able to respond appropriately, balancing concision with sufficient detail?

This chapter explores the affective elements that UN treaty body cycles awaken[1]—as Cowan phrases it, the "feeling of pursuing an ideal."[2] Following the processes that led up to and followed the Constructive Dialogue on Finland's sixth state report, this chapter traces what Mathur has described as "the labours of a heterogeneous group of actors and, especially, the marshalling of things in the process of making a law real."[3] I ask why civil servants choose to engage, often voluntarily, in treaty body documentary cycles, which commonly entail additional work without extra compensation. This question is intensified by the analysis of Chapter 5, which showcased the uncertain impact that these documentary cycles may have. The chapter contextualizes its query in a historical perspective by connecting diligent adherence to human rights obligations to Finland's role as an integral part of Western Europe, particularly in the post–Cold War period after decades of imposed proximity to the Soviet Union.

I consider the role successful professional performance plays in motivating state delegates, and the affective elements that state reporting awakens in many civil servants. I further probe beneath the layers of bureaucratic translations to underlying, loaded emotions: nervousness and excitement paired with commitment to the notion of what Bear and Mathur call "the public good."[4] The chapter contrasts these emotions with a narrative of a "burned-out bureaucrat," a civil servant with decades of experience in treaty body reporting cycles who questions the meaning of this work.

The bureaucrat's sentiments resonate with broader experiences that I encountered during research for this book, including frustration and occasional boredom. The significance of these sentiments in the Committee's reporting cycles captures the ice-like fragility of human rights monitoring: UN treaty body cycles remain vital and robust only as long as they generate commitment and belief. Were these sentiments replaced by disappointment, cynicism, and exhaustion, the future of robust monitoring would be jeopardized, as would sustained movement in the rights direction.

Why Participate? Civil Servants and Reporting Duties

For state civil servants, participating in treaty body cycles is hard work and, in the case of Finland, commonly results in no overtime or other compensation from the employer. The itinerary of Finland's state delegation when presenting Finland's sixth state report to the Human Rights Committee on Friday, July 12, 2013, illustrates the work involved. On Thursday, the day before Finland's report was processed, the state delegation arrived in Geneva—in the middle of Finland's traditional holiday season—on a morning flight that departed from Helsinki at 8:00 a.m., meaning that delegates had arrived at the airport by 7:00 a.m., having left their homes circa 6:00 a.m. They arrived in Geneva at 10:30 a.m. local time and were at their accommodation by noon. After quickly settling in, they went to lunch, and from there to Finland's permanent mission by 1:00 p.m. to prepare for the Constructive Dialogue the following day. They remained at the mission until 7:00 p.m., after which it was time for dinner.

The day of the Dialogue, the delegation left the hotel by 9:00 a.m. to arrive at the Palais Wilson in time to take their seats and organize themselves. The proceedings commenced at 10:00 a.m. and continued until 1:00 p.m. The session resumed at 3:00 p.m. and lasted until 6:00 p.m., during which they provided the answers prepared during lunchtime, followed by another round of questions from the Committee and more answers from the state delegation. After the session ended, the delegates returned to their hotel and then departed for a dinner hosted by the Finnish ambassador. They returned to Helsinki the next day, possibly preparing further follow-up information the Committee requested for transmission within forty-eight hours after the Dialogue had ended.

These days, while intense, constitute only a fraction of the work required to participate in a Constructive Dialogue: in interviews, many civil servants described preparing for the sessions for days, even weeks. Due to the open-ended nature of the exchange, civil servants do not know in advance what questions the Committee will pose and thus try to prepare answers to as many potential questions as possible. The list of issues the Committee shares in advance is a helpful tool, yet nothing guarantees that Committee members will stick to the list, and often they do not. Thus, civil servants usually arrive at the sessions with thick binders of detailed information on a wide array of topics under the purview of the government office they represent. Whether this material is sufficient or not they will only learn during the hearing.

Existing scholarship on UN treaty body proceedings usually approaches the motivations for participation from the perspective of the state as a holistic, legal unit. Hathaway proposes that governments ratify human rights treaties because this embodies a costless expression of support for the principles the treaties contain, and allows governments to receive approval and validation from the international community for respecting these "new standards of civilization."[5] Riles notes that participation by Pacific countries in drafting international human rights documents rendered the region "visible" at the next level of negotiation in future UN meetings, and this newfound visibility was something the Pacific delegates spoke of with pride.[6]

A third possible motive for joining bureaucratic cycles builds on Strathern's work on university mission statements that "create no knowledge."[7] In analyzing why universities might produce what "from an academic viewpoint is nonsense," Strathern equates mission statements to "bullet-proofing" by the army of Naparama of Mozambique, which the Comaroffs discuss.[8] Bullet-proofing refers to a practice whereby warriors rely on marks drawn on their chests to protect them from their adversaries' bullets. Strathern argues that universities draft mission statements in a similar effort to shield themselves. Applying this to the human rights framework, this suggests states participate in human rights monitoring in the aspiration of protecting themselves from critiques of not taking human rights values and obligations seriously.

Reflecting on these potential motivations for state participation in the UN treaty body framework is important. Concurrently, for a more nuanced understanding it is imperative to examine the actions and motivations of the individuals who participate in the proceedings. After all, as Hull reminds us, constructing the collective agency of the state "requires the cooperation of even the most humble members of the bureaucratic collective, including runners and pieces of paper."[9]

Weber argues that "bureaucracy develops more perfectly, the more it is 'dehumanized,' the more completely it succeeds in eliminating from official business love, hatred, and all purely personal, irrational, and emotion elements."[10] Later scholarship significantly challenges this view, illustrating that to secure the participation of those "most humble members," bureaucracy needs to elicit affective responses. Otherwise, they may view bureaucratic tasks as tedious obligations that collectively constitute "bullshit jobs," to quote Graeber's memorable phrase.[11]

Guardians of Vision Within the State

As was noted in Chapter 5, the bulk of human rights scholarship builds on the opposition between states and the international human rights community. In regards to UN treaty bodies, this characterization assigns an adversarial tenor to the relationship between state delegates and Committee members. The Committee's operations embody this adversarial relationship, although it is softened by unfailingly courteous language, as was discussed in Chapter 4.

In recent years, research has explored the role of state civil servants in international human rights work.[12] Concurrently state delegates—together with UN staff—arguably remain the most understudied group of actors in international human rights bureaucracies. This oversight hinders our understanding of the operations and impact of treaty bodies, including the subtle maneuvering used to defend the broad discretion of the bodies in the face of challenges from adversarial states, such as that by Belarus described at the beginning of Chapter 3.

Below, I contribute to this scholarship by drawing on an in-depth interview with a seasoned Finnish civil servant, whom I call by the pseudonym Sam.[13] Sam's candid reflections clarify central aspects of being both a committed civil servant and a Guardian of Vision, including long-term and multifaceted participation in international human rights bureaucracies. Sam's interview finds broader context from the insight that, on closer examination, the dynamics among state delegates, Committee members, and UN staff are not solely or simplistically adversarial.

Instead, many state delegates belong to the Guardians of Visions' community of practice, which becomes clear when we examine the profile of civil servants who produce state reports. Due to the legal nature of treaty body proceedings, many of these civil servants have legal backgrounds, and thus belong in the "invisible college" of lawyers. In addition, many are likely specialists in, and perhaps devotees to, human rights. Thus, when they participate in UN human rights cycles, civil servants represent their states, on the one hand, and on the other hand, they are committed to protecting human rights.

This situation creates a double consciousness: in their involvement with UN treaty bodies, individual state representatives need to balance their positions as civil servants supporting a state's policies, and their roles as Guardians of Vision aspiring toward greater realization of human rights as well as the optimal functioning of UN human rights monitoring bodies. As other members of this community of practice, many civil servants have been socialized into the human rights field as interns of NGOs or the UN OHCHR. Some long-term civil servants may have been involved in UN treaty body work for significant periods of time, even their entire careers, making them carriers of institutional memory as well as vast personal connections and indirect relations within the UN human rights apparatus defined by incessant staff rotation.

An Interview with Sam

I meet Sam at the beautiful, turn-of-the-century headquarters of the Finnish Ministry for Foreign Affairs in downtown Helsinki. My arrival is accompanied by a brisk ocean wind that surrounds me on all sides, reminding me that we are on a peninsula and that the ice around us has barely begun to thaw after the long winter. A security guard clears me at the front desk, and we go into Sam's office, which, compared to the polished floors, large mirrors, and uplifting artwork of the front lobby, appears slightly mundane, ordinary—the site of business as usual rather than a venue for the unusual and the unexpected.

We begin our discussion with a brief exchange about the ongoing UN treaty body reform, one additional international human rights process in which Sam has participated. I have already learned that this is hardly the only activity outside the Ministry in which Sam is currently engaged or has been engaged over the years. Indeed, Sam seems to be everywhere to a startling extent, considering that Sam is "just" a civil servant working for the Finnish government.

We talk briefly about the "usual suspects" in the international human rights regime and how their "resistance" is incarnated this time—Russia emerges as a key antagonist, as does Belarus, which, over the past few years, has assumed a leading role in challenging the authority of UN human rights bodies. Sam explains that one key source of ongoing controversy is the reluctance of a few states to accept treaty body recommendations, comparing this to the UPR. Sam notes: "We learned fast during the first cycle of the UPR that one needs to be careful when mentioning recommendations by UN treaty bodies. It is safest to remain vague—talk only of 'Concluding Observations by the CEDAW Committee,' for example, and not include verbatim quotes on anything."

We turn to Finland's report, and I ask what the Finnish delegation expects from the upcoming Constructive Dialogue in Geneva. Sam grows tentative, noting how things have not always proceeded as smoothly as hoped:

> We have had serious problems with different members of UN treaty bodies, who have simply failed to grasp what is expected of them. A few years back, Finland appeared before the CRC Committee, and the members had simply failed to do their homework! They hadn't studied any of the background papers and posed questions that were extremely embarrassing. They were asking Finland whether we could tell them anything about [our] paramilitary groups![14] These questions vanished from the Concluding Observations, but there were other recommendations related to sexual harassment that simply were off target.

This statement clearly identifies Sam as a civil servant of the state of Finland: someone whose professional duty is to ensure that the state they represent appears in a good light and is accurately portrayed in such international contexts as human rights monitoring mechanisms. Simultaneously, Sam comes across as expressing concerns that clearly surpass the views of a detached bureaucrat. Sam appears as someone who is *committed* to the proper functioning of the monitoring mechanism. This attitude becomes clearer as Sam describes their views of UN staff:

> I don't trust some of the new top people in UN human rights offices. Some of them have never liked the treaty body system. Instead they really like the [Human Rights] Council. I find that people are much more cautious in sharing and discussing things within the UN human rights framework today. Earlier, people in the Secretariat shared information easily. The atmosphere was genuinely one oriented toward human rights. People worked insanely long hours in a field that was extremely difficult. Now, many feel too intimidated to speak, it seems. There are a lot—the majority, I would say—who are devoted to their work as a part of the UN treaty body system. But then there are the high-profile political nominations, such as those of former ambassadors. That's the problem right now. I do not entirely trust everyone in the relevant positions on the UN human rights side.

As Sam continues describing the UN human rights system, it becomes evident they know it intimately. Furthermore, their concerns take on a different form: they are no longer about whether Finland is accurately represented or depicted in a favorable light—they are *not at all* about Finland. Rather, Sam's comments regard the integrity of UN human rights monitoring generally.

Expressing a lack of trust in people working at the UN, and implying that they suffer from a lack of commitment and integrity, constitutes stark criticism of the UN staff's commitment to the underlying values of the UN human rights framework. Indeed, Sam does not speak solely as a civil servant of any individual state but as someone whose dedication extends much further: as someone defending the very integrity of the bureaucratic mechanism.[15] This fluctuating self-positioning emerges as Sam describes the members of UN treaty bodies: "In each Committee, there are always a few great legal minds who take the entire human rights framework further. They carry the responsibility for the hard substance. Then, there are a large number of good members who do their job very well, even if they are not the cream of the crop—and then there is always that tiny little group which . . ." A tiny little group, I finish the sentence in my mind, which has ended there because of political agendas that have little or nothing to do with human rights concerns. I am not surprised when I learn later in our discussion that Sam worked for the UN Secretariat for a few years, a period during which they were formally on a leave of absence from the Foreign Affairs Ministry of Finland. Having professional experience in both their national government and the UN, Sam bridges the two prime categories around which most UN operations, human rights work, and the bulk of scholarship remains structured: the UN as representing "the international" and the Foreign Ministry of Finland as representing the state, the "local," and a potential violator of human rights obligations.

Sam's fluctuating representative status is strengthened by their involvement with NGOs in treaty body proceedings. I ask Sam whether any Finnish NGOs have submitted shadow reports or will be present in Geneva. Sam exclaims:

> I don't know what the NGOs are up to! I don't know if there will be any parallel reports or not, but I hope so. These reports are hugely important! The Human Rights Committee is the "biggest" of all the UN Committees and doing good work. The [Committee] usually does its background work—but the report of a state is just that, a report from and by a state. I don't usually read them myself. I read the reports from NGOs. They offer Finns themselves the opportunity to contribute to the information supplied by the state. We need these reports! Parallel reports have a hugely important role—they can help move things forward, something that otherwise can be difficult. I wish NGOs would see treaty body proceedings as a medium for change!

Here, Sam appears both as someone concerned about societal reform in their state and as a universal defender of the UN treaty body system. Concurrently Sam respects the conventional division of labor: their intense tone indicates that it is of paramount importance that, as a representative of the state, they *should* be unaware of what NGOs are doing. This stance has a dual motivation: on the one hand, being unaware aligns with the formal, pragmatic division of labor that characterizes Sam's work on UN human rights reporting as a state civil servant. Thus, while participating in UN human rights monitoring, Sam upholds the state's contractual obligations while being disconnected from NGO contributions.

On the other, Sam's statements reflect a broad devotion to human rights values and the integral role of NGOs in upholding these values. From this viewpoint, it is not mere pragmatism or technicality that separates NGOs from the state. Rather, it is precisely their outside status that allows NGOs to serve the integral role Sam assigns them. Sam continues: "In fact, we are seeing far fewer Finnish NGO reports in UN treaty body proceedings than what was the case in the early new millennium. I have sometimes talked with the previous director of the Finnish League for Human Rights about why this is so, and they said that the League was disappointed by the proceedings: they felt that submitting these reports made no impact at all. They made similar comments on the UPR, that there is no impact. It's terribly worrying if people start giving up!" In this statement, Sam reassumes the position of a Guardian of Vision who seeks to protect UN human rights treaty bodies' capacity to protect universal values and truths. This likewise emerges in how Sam describes one of the central perils to the treaty body system, a reform that would build on total transparency and make all the information and documents that treaty bodies process public.[16] Sam comments:

> It would be extremely dangerous if nothing were kept from states anymore. All states would be informed which NGOs are talking with the treaty bodies. This would lead to inevitable reprisals both against UN Committees and possibly the NGOs in question. Now, Committees can decide themselves to whom they listen, from which sources they receive information. Otherwise, they would often lack relevant information for their work. There are demands circulating in the UN system to unify everything. Here, Finland is on a slightly different track: we consider that the discretion to decide what should be confidential and what publicly available belongs to the Committees themselves. We wouldn't dare release all information to everyone!

Once again, Sam balances between serving as a representative of an individual state and a Guardian of Vision who is engaged in the general mission of developing and protecting the UN treaty body system. Sam speaks not only for Finland, where the position of human rights NGOs is stable and secure, but additionally assumes the role of an intermediary,[17] safeguarding the confidentiality of NGO activists who may face harassment for disseminating information critical of their states. In the process, like members of the Human Rights Committee in Chapter 4, Sam advocates for opaque transparency: the need to keep certain information confidential to secure the UN treaty body framework's ability to safeguard continually greater rights protection.

As I followed the processing of Finland's sixth report, I came to learn the full extent to which Sam's conviction about the importance of NGOs in UN treaty body proceedings translated into action. First, during spring 2013, before the Dialogue on Finland's report, Sam actively informed Finnish NGOs of the relevant deadlines for submitting their parallel reports. Sam attended an NGO meeting organized to brief Finnish NGOs on the upcoming hearing and, in person, explained what UN treaty body proceedings are and how—and why—NGOs could and should participate. As the spring progressed, Sam circulated further information to encourage participation in the ongoing documentary cycle. Sam even sent out last-minute reminders as the deadline for parallel reports approached.

However, Sam did not stop there. As elaborated in Chapter 7, despite these efforts, only a few NGOs from Finland contributed to and participated in the Constructive Dialogue in July 2013: the lunchtime hearing between NGOs and Committee members featured only three people representing Finnish NGOs, only one of whom was actually Finnish—a representative of the Sámi Council. Further, that representative was present at the Palais Wilson because of Sam: not only had Sam encouraged the representative to come to Geneva, but, with Sam's help, the Ministry for Foreign Affairs of Finland covered the representative's attendance.

More accurately, the Sámi Council had received funds from the Ministry for Foreign Affairs to attend another expert meeting at the Palais des Nations held during the same week. Since the representative was already in Geneva, Sam encouraged them to participate in the hearing of the Human Rights Committee at the nearby Palais Wilson. Thus, without Sam's urging, there would have been *no* Finns representing NGOs at the Human Rights Committee's hearing. This outcome would have disappointed both Finland's state delegation and the Committee, given that many Committee members already criticized the scarcity of Finnish NGOs after the Constructive Dialogue.

Together, Sam's actions manifest the blurring of lines between the state and NGOs, revealing Sam's ambiguous position. In conversation, Sam expressed both interest in and concern for the position of Sámi people in Finland, an expected stance for someone working in human rights in the country.[18] It would, nevertheless, be misguided to describe Sam as a Sámi activist. Thus, Sam's urging of the Sámi Council representative to participate in the Human Rights Committee's proceedings appears not to stem solely, or even predominantly, from specific concerns for the Sámi. Rather, their actions come forth as a devotion to something else: to being a Guardian of Vision committed to the effective operation of the Human Rights Committee and the UN human rights framework. This becomes clarified as I ask Sam what participation in treaty body sessions means. What values does Sam invest both in their own participation and the delegation of Finland as a whole? Sam's answer is fascinating:

> I see everything as forming a chain. There are many layers involved: a personal level, that of the group, a holistic level, the level of consequences. How do I feel myself? What kind of feedback do we get? What do we concretely achieve? What kind of discussions unfold? The government often does things in a bubble. Thus, to have NGOs participate has an enormous importance; it pushes us [government representatives] toward better performance too, just due to the fact we are being observed. We need the surge of adrenalin [to perform well]! I always feel that whenever Finland goes into the session room of a UN treaty body, there are huge expectations. This is also a burden. The high reputation [of Finland in human rights issues] creates expectations that we need to meet. Finland needs to aspire toward good performance, and to respond correctly, meaning that the state delegation's performance is well orchestrated and constructive.

Sam reflects on what this means for the Constructive Dialogue with the Human Rights Committee at the Palais Wilson, reflecting on both the performance of individual civil servants and their expectations of these sessions:

> What if one member of the Finnish state delegation gets nervous and doesn't stop reading from their notes, despite urging from the delegation leader? These are simply awful situations! Also, even though the UN Human Rights Committee as a whole is really good, I am nervous if members of the delegation of Finland lose their faith and trust in the Committee [due to lack of advance preparation or knowledge]. What if they become disappointed and feel it is all nonsense?
>
> I see that here there are terrible risks! In Finland, human rights have for such a long time been central on the agenda of the Ministry for Foreign Affairs. We participate in so many human rights

> networks and treaty bodies. Human rights are on the agenda of every meeting. That is why it is particularly important that the Committee is sharp and has an edge, and that the recommendations are specifically crafted for Finland, not merely copied and pasted from previous documents and bizarre!

This answer clarifies how, in addition to being a state civil servant of Finland, Sam aspires to safeguard continued trust and faith in the operations of UN human rights treaty bodies. Here, Sam emphasizes the importance of individual Committee members: subpar performances, lacking sharpness or expertise, may jeopardize state delegates' faith in the Human Rights Committee and the UN treaty body framework generally. By contrast, excellent, sharp dialogue may do the opposite and strengthen belief—which, by extension, may motivate state delegates to defend both the importance of, and funding for, UN bodies in domestic decision-making processes.

Being Like a State

How do other civil servants feel about attending treaty body sessions, and the Human Rights Committee's sessions specifically? "Going to UN hearings feels a lot like preparing for a large oral exam. You try to think in advance which questions might be asked and prepare answers for them. And many others too." This was how one civil servant characterized participation in treaty body sessions in an interview. Thinking of the Constructive Dialogue as an oral exam opens new approaches for exploring civil servants' motivations to participate in the Committee's proceedings and helps us understand the affective qualities that state reports and UN documentary cycles assume.[19]

A simple answer to what motivates civil servants to participate in Constructive Dialogues is professional duty, since they work in ministries that oversee how Finland meets its obligations under the ICCPR. In interviews, civil servants working on the documentary cycles likewise emphasized upholding Finland's Covenant-bound obligations. This view was particularly pronounced among civil servants with a legal background.

An answer emphasizing mere duty nevertheless fails to account for the diverse motivations civil servants shared. In numerous interviews, civil servants mentioned how, rather than being assigned—let alone forced—to take on treaty body duties, they had volunteered for it.[20] They furthermore highlighted that treaty body tasks were often allocated to colleagues in their ministries who had expressed interest. This has resulted in the emergence of a like-minded community of civil servants, with a few civil servants noting with concern how small this community was.

In discussion it became clear that treaty body work goes beyond the mere call of duty: my interlocutors repeatedly stated that participation requires days, even weeks, of preparation. One has to command vast substantive areas related to the work of different ministries, including the Ministries of Interior, Justice, and Education. From this perspective "being like a state"—the instruction civil servants follow as they construct state reports, as was discussed in Chapter 5—boils down, at a mundane level, to careful advance preparation and the successful performance of professional duties. In practice, this means arming oneself with masses of documents as a shield against criticism, akin to the "bullet-proofing" in Strathern's analysis.[21]

During the hearings, advance preparation translates into feelings of excitement and nervousness: Did I guess correctly which questions the Committee members will pose? Will I be able to answer them adequately? Will my colleagues in the delegation think I performed well? Many wonder if their English will be professional and understandable enough. While all civil servants participating in the sessions have a good working command of English—foreign affairs usually constitutes some portion of their professional tasks—English is rarely anyone's native language, as the bulk of civil service work occurs in Finland's official national languages, Finnish and Swedish.

Sentiments of nervousness are particularly intense for newcomers in the sessions, and they travel with participants from their home offices to the Palais Wilson—and back again—and remain evident in interviews conducted long after the substantive details of the hearing have faded from memory. At the same time, many civil servants are undoubtedly excited to join the Human Rights Committee's sessions. During the proceedings, this excitement is communicated by the interested gazes with which both state and NGO delegates inspect the Palais Wilson conference room. Many take photographs inside the Palais Wilson and snapshots in front of the Palais des Nations. Later, such images are often shared on social media with captions confirming the importance and excitement of appearing before UN human rights bodies. Civil servants may describe representing their countries before an important UN body, and the UN Human Rights Committee specifically, as a career highlight. Undoubtedly the UN and its human rights monitoring mechanisms, combined with the glamour of "Genève internationale," continually attract many civil servants.

National Branding

Treaty body reporting additionally appears to have broader significance for civil servants in "bureaucratizing utopia." Many highlighted that Finland's active participation offers tangible evidence to the international community of the seriousness with which Finland treats its Covenant-bound obligations, and from this perspective strengthens Finland's positive image in the international human rights regime. Fulfilling Finland's treaty-bound obligations coincides with how "actors maintain a sense of agency in spite of the tedious and burdensome nature of the administrative procedures in which they take part."[22]

The importance civil servants placed on Finland's positive role in the international human rights community is compounded by Finland's history since World War II.[23] After being part of Sweden for centuries, Finland became an autonomous grand duchy within the Russian Empire in 1809. Finland gained independence from Russia in 1917, but nearly lost it again during World War II when the USSR attacked. Although Finland remained a sovereign state, the postwar decades were an era of *Finlandization*, marked by a close relationship with the Soviet Union, embodied in the Agreement of Friendship, Cooperation, and Mutual Assistance.[24] Finland's imposed alignment with the USSR manifested itself most clearly in its foreign affairs: Finland joined the UN only in 1955, after the Soviet Union withdrew its opposition to Finland's membership.

Formally, the principle of *neutrality* intended to keep Finland outside the Cold War's bipolar conflicts, governing Finland's foreign policy at the time. In the 1960s and subsequent decades, Finland followed the momentum of the other Nordic countries—commonly seen as progressive leaders in human rights issues—by ratifying the principal human rights treaties at the same pace as them. In 1956, Finland joined Sweden, Norway, Denmark, and Iceland in the Nordic Council. Beginning in the 1960s, Finland participated in the Organization for Economic Cooperation and Development (OECD), and became a full member of the European Free Trade Association (EFTA) in 1986. By contrast, Finland remained outside the Council of Europe until the Soviet regime started crumbling and the Cold War ended.[25] In 1990, Finland finally joined the Council of Europe—the last Western democracy to do so—only months before the first formerly socialist state, Hungary, ratified the European Convention of Human Rights (ECHR).[26] The following year, the Agreement of Friendship, Cooperation, and Mutual Assistance ended, and in 1995, Finland joined the European Union following a favorable referendum.[27]

As part of this history, Finland was both a peripheral actor in the post-war international human rights community and a country in which human rights were peripheral to its foreign and domestic policy.[28] For example, the Finnish chapter of Amnesty International was established in 1967, yet it remained marginal during the 1970s, while Taistolaiset, sympathetic to the Soviet Union, was a much more prominent youth group up until the end of the decade.[29]

After subtle societal changes during the 1980s around the role of human rights in Finland's internal and foreign policy, in the 1990s things altered rapidly, aided by Finland's first female minister for foreign affairs, and later its first female president, Tarja Halonen, who shifted the focal point of Finland's foreign policy from disarmament to human rights. This was followed by broader changes, including the constitutional law reform of 1995, which effectively ended the separation between constitutional rights and human rights—previously constitutional rights had been seen as rights bestowed on Finnish citizens by constitutional provisions, whereas human rights were regarded as Finland's Covenant-bound obligations and thus a matter of foreign affairs.[30]

In the new millennium, Finland's human rights activeness has continued to intensify, and human rights have moved from the periphery to the center of Finnish policymaking.[31] As one example, in 2007, Finland issued a new educational policy that made human rights education mandatory for all schoolchildren.[32] Finland's relationship to human rights—whether measured in terms of participation in the UN and the European human rights regimes, active commentary on the internal human rights records of other countries, alignment of public policy with human rights, or the robustness of its civil society—no longer differs from that of the other Nordic countries.

Instead, the Nordic countries are jointly regarded as the global leaders in human rights and have ratified the main UN human rights treaties. All Nordic countries are active in the UN diplomatic and political community, with numerous citizens in high positions in various UN human rights bodies. They provide substantial funding for the UN OHCHR, with Finland among the largest contributors together with the European Commission, Sweden, and the Netherlands.[33]

The importance of presenting Finland in a positive light in front of a high-profile UN body was mentioned with virtual uniformity by the civil servants who participated in Finland's state delegation at the Palais Wilson in July 2013. In discussion, civil servants from different ministries consistently mentioned Finland's leadership role in human rights as a source of pride. Thus, an earnest commitment to UN treaty body reporting strengthens the national sentiment that human rights activity forms an important part of Finland's national self-identity as a state at the core of Western European collaboration, after decades of being pushed toward the Eastern bloc.[34]

This aligns with Babul's observation regarding Turkish human rights training in which "human rights are formulated as a requirement for expertise and professionalism to which all government workers should subscribe in order to better perform their jobs."[35] Compared to Turkey, however, there are important differences in how Finnish civil servants view human rights: whereas Turkish officials may be critical of the values they embody, associating human rights with colonialism, such views are notably absent from discussions with Finnish civil servants.[36]

The national history on Finland's relationship to human rights described above seldom came up in my interviews. Civil servants commonly do not consider Finland's role within the international human rights regime to have differed from that of the other Western nations or the Nordic states.[37] There is no discourse among civil servants that suggests that human rights might involve elements of cultural imposition, let alone colonization. By contrast, adherence to the values embodied by human rights is strong and unquestioned, with shared emphasis on their universal nature and origins.

Finnish civil servants are thus socialized to conceive human rights as embodying a new "standard of civilization,"[38] which they see as indigenous to Finnish society. Likely this conception forms an element of rewriting history and national identity that downplays Finland's close ties to the former Soviet Union in the Post–World War II decades, while emphasizing Finland's place in the liberal Western world—a self-understanding sealed in spring 2023 when Finland entered NATO.

The Feeling of Reporting

As the hearing on Finland's sixth report continued at the Palais Wilson in the July heat, individual delegate members took the floor to answer the

Committee members' questions from the viewpoint of the government offices they represented. At the podium, the head of delegation kept a watchful eye on their troops, hoping everything would go smoothly this time. Just a few moments earlier, sentiments of tension accompanying the state delegation's performance were revealed in one delegate's vigorous smoking outside the Palais Wilson's main entrance. During the session, nervousness revealed itself in occasional garbled words, and after the session, in clammy handshakes and flushed cheeks.

I realized that I was surprisingly nervous myself. This was not something that I had expected: even though anthropologists aspire to achieve an empathetic understanding of their interlocutors, nervousness had not been a part of my participant-observation—on the contrary, I felt enthusiasm, exhaustion, and the inevitable, occasional boredom. I tried to figure out what—and for whom—I was nervous: Was it for my state, Finland, or rather for the state delegation, the individuals on it, and their performance? How would they do? Would all their hard, preparatory work carry them through? Was I nervous for my research assistant seated with the state delegation, worried we might not end up with the kind of material we hoped to collect?

Maybe I was nervous for the Committee members, wondering whether their advance preparations were sufficient to make the delegation of Finland think that they had "done their homework." Or was I nervous for "the other side": the NGOs? Would their concerns be addressed in the proceedings and, if so, how? Would the issues of the Sámi people and LGBTIQ+ groups be addressed seriously enough? Perhaps I was nervous about my own modest contributions—whether the background material I supplied to a Committee member regarding pretrial detainees, and the last-minute data I delivered the day before about LGBTIQ+ issues, were useful and reflected the needed expertise.

Building on Cowan's analysis of the UPR, the Constructive Dialogue can be described as a "review ritual." The Dialogue is "highly ordered in terms of time, space, and language, its repetitiveness contributing to its ritual power." It "transforms the subjects of ritual [here, officials from the state under review], confirming them into the community of rights-respecting states." Subsequently, the dialogue "elicits state performances" as "each State under Review adopts a posture and tone and decides how to present the balance between achievements and challenges, often calibrating its performance for the domestic audience as much as for the community of states."[39] In the case of the UPR, the direct audience of the ritual is formed by other states, and for the Human Rights Committee, the Committee's expert members.

Affective elements hold a pivotal, and thus far underexplored, role in solidifying and contributing to the momentum of UN treaty body cycles.[40] Positive sentiments build on state delegates' own experiences of having succeeded at their professional tasks: being well prepared and responding appropriately to the Committee members' questions. Particularly significant for assessing a session's success is how the Committee performs—whether Committee members are up to par with their questions and whether state delegates consider the Observations as being on point. A glimpse into the Constructive Dialogue between the state delegation of Finland and the Human Rights Committee illustrates this.[41]

The questions Committee members posed to the state delegation had been divided in advance among the members of the task force that had prepared for the Dialogue. The broad range of themes that Committee members addressed in response to Finland's report showcased the expansiveness with which the Committee interprets its mandate, whereas the questions illustrate the level of detail a Constructive Dialogue ideally embodies. Members addressed issues related to the Sámi people, the Roma, and LGBTIQ+ groups, including expectations that Finland would pass legislation to eliminate the requirement of sterilization as part of gender-affirming treatment, and questions about maternity and paternity leave rights among LGBTIQ+ adoptive parents. They asked about the situation of migrants—including discrimination within migrant groups—and inquired into Finland's previous hearings before the UPR and the CEDAW Committee, specifically what actions Finland had taken, since the hearing, on issues those bodies had raised.

Some questions were particularly detailed. One Committee member asked why "Russian-speakers must file more job applications before being interviewed for a job than non-immigrant job seekers with corresponding education and work experience." This question was somewhat surprising, since it referred to the hiring practices of private companies far removed from state-bound Covenant obligations. Two Committee members raised a familiar issue from past reporting cycles—Finland's reservations to the ICCPR upon ratification—arguing that, in light of existing national legislation, those reservations could be withdrawn.[42]

One Committee member noted that, even though Finland ratified the Covenant in 1975, there have been scarce references to it in national legislation and the judiciary, prompting the member to ask how much awareness of the Covenant exists in the legal profession and whether training is provided. Another Committee member raised non-refoulement in the context of counterterrorism. He noted that although Finland does not allow its airports to be used for illegal activity, reports circulated about a specific Boeing 737 flight landing in Lithuania in March 2006, according to information released by Finnish authorities. The member asked whether this was a cover-up for a rendition flight.

Examining gender inequality in the workforce and anti-discrimination legislation, Committee members requested information on how relevant Finnish laws are applied to private and public sectors alike, raising a familiar theme from previous reporting cycles, as Chapter 5 discussed. One Committee member noted that Finland should take measures to ensure that employers comply with the requirement of equal work for equal pay, asking how Finland aims to reduce the current gap between men's and women's salaries—another familiar theme from Chapter 5—as well as what penalties it plans to implement. He emphasized the seriousness of anti-discrimination: "Lack of proper pay does not just have an impact on society. It is also a human rights issue." This Committee member provided a detailed example of workplace discrimination against women who are pregnant or recently gave birth, and are subsequently held back at the workplace. He noted that while Finland has extensive legislation to address this, he sought evidence from the "real reality," namely, "concrete measures to prevent illegal dismissals of women who gave birth."

The detailed quality of the questions illustrates the extensive level of legal and human rights knowledge that Committee members must demonstrate during the Constructive Dialogue—as well as the level of knowledge that state delegates expect of them, as interlocutors emphasized to me. Questions attuned to recent societal developments and legislative changes confirm that Committee members had prepared appropriately, and reward diligent preparation by state delegates, translating the ritualized dialogue between a UN Committee and a state into a substantive exchange between real individuals.

State delegates' sense that the Committee members' engagement is substantive helps inculcate a belief in the importance of UN treaty body documentary cycles. Committee members' diligent engagement is cast as what Cowan calls a "mode of acting virtuously,"[43] which convinces delegates that such practices can bring about change. When I spoke with the state delegation after the Dialogue, they praised the level of engagement, and occasionally the contributions of individual Committee members, with Sir Nigel Rodley being the Committee member who was positively singled out by numerous commentators.

Concurrently, some questions and comments were seen as falling short of expectations and out of touch with local conditions. This reaction followed a lengthy intervention on violence against women, a prevalent societal problem in Finland, as in many other countries. The Committee member addressing the issue took an expansive approach, stating that change required "not just legislative work" but a "change of culture to stop violence against women." The comment highlighted crimes of sexual violence, emphasizing that there was a large number of unreported crimes with few cases reaching courts and even fewer resulting in prison sentences. The Committee member added that "if [victims of domestic violence] were assisted, this might help break the cycle of violence, whereas now "women are sometimes encouraged to take a settlement and not take the cases to court."

The Committee member then asked: "How do you work with the concept of masculinity?," noting that, in order to introduce change, one has to "work with the perpetrators." He listed issues related to reform of the criminal code, noted a lack of investigations of sex crimes, and asked whether minor sexual assaults were treated as crimes or resolved by alternative settlements. Additionally, he requested official statistics on how many prosecutions result in prison terms and how many do not, along with statistics of repeat offenders.

He continued by inquiring what compensation victims receive, what role male perpetrators play, and how to deconstruct the structure of violence against women. Finally, he asked about trends of domestic violence and whether there had been any progress, the impact of the police and the judiciary, the inclusion of gender and LGBTIQ+ perspectives in trainings, and immigrant centers for women. His last question concerned female genital mutilation, seeking details on measures to prevent the practice in Finland.

In discussions after the session, multiple civil servants singled out this intervention as off target, for being both too general and too specific. They saw his remarks as emanating from a standardized list of issues related to violence against women, rather than focusing specifically on the Finnish context. The question as to how Finland "works on the concept of masculinity" appeared out of place, not the least because, with the exception of the male delegate head, Finland's entire state delegation consisted of female civil servants, in notable contrast to most other state delegations.

Apart from this individual criticism, satisfaction within Finland's state delegation regarding the Committee's engagement appeared high after the session.

Before Finland's Constructive Dialogue began, some NGO participants had wondered whether the hearing on Finland's report would be as intense as those of many other states, as did some Committee insiders. "How could the Committee spend an equivalent amount of time discussing the human rights situation in Finland as those in Indonesia and Ukraine?," both of which had been discussed the same week, a seasoned Committee member remarked.

In the end, the prediction that Finland's report would not take equivalent time proved grossly misguided, as the exchange between Finland and the Committee in no way waned in intensity. In fact, the hearing was almost exceptionally precise. It was as if the legal predictability, the high degree of available quantified data, and the overall bureaucratization of the Finnish state machinery formed an ideal match for the monitoring instrument the Committee embodies. Ultimately, the Constructive Dialogue exceeded its allotted time—even if, admittedly due only to the delegation head's verbose final statement.

When the intense one-day hearing concluded with another bang of the chair's gavel, all parties exited the conference room wearing smiles of satisfaction. Members of Finland's state delegation—both immediately and in interviews over a year later—praised the Committee for being, on the whole, very well informed. Apart from a few questions that, the delegates noted with dismay, "circulate from one UN report on Finland to the next,"[44] they considered the issues the Committee raised as valid and justified.

Finland's state delegation also approved of most of the recommendations in the Concluding Observations, even if one or two experienced civil servants again called a few of them the "same old." The Committee members, in turn, praised Finland's delegates for their careful advance preparation and diligence, while noting the high number of internal Committees the Finnish civil servants cite as solutions to problems of various kinds. Together these experiences strengthened the shared feeling that the ritual in which state delegates and Committee members had participated mattered; the session, in Bens's words, "affect[ed] audiences, grab[bed] their attention, and connect[ed] to their sense of justice."[45]

The Tale of the "Burned-out Bureaucrat"

In my interviews, the vast majority of sentiments toward the UN treaty body framework appeared notably positive. Simultaneously, I encountered differing opinions worthy of closer examination. These surfaced in the following interview with an interlocutor I dubbed the "burned-out bureaucrat." During the interview she was sitting behind her desk, covered in thick piles of documents and binders. She looked visibly exhausted. I asked what she remembered from the Constructive Dialogue that took place in Geneva some eighteen months earlier.

She exclaimed: "I remember nothing of it! There are always multiple reports being processed simultaneously; it's all just sort of mush. I do remember that I had done massive preparatory work as I am also doing now. These preparations take up so much time and are so demanding. In the hearing, you have to be able to respond to questions quickly. There is no time to start going over papers. That's why I always prepare my own background dossiers for my own sector. I trust that I'll have the dossiers memorized so that I will be able to respond directly."

She contextualized this preparatory work in light of the hearing itself, noting: "It's really difficult not knowing what the Committee will ask. Many of the questions are always the same from one report to the next. Sometimes there are incomprehensible ones. It frequently feels like the Concluding Observations have been determined before the hearing, that it makes no difference whatsoever what we say. Often the Committee members have no idea what they are talking about, especially when compared to the civil servants who work on these issues every day. It feels like their views are based solely on personal opinions!" She spoke candidly, with an intensity surprising for a civil servant. But she knew what she was talking about: she had worked at a Finnish ministry for over twenty years and participated in the preparations of most human rights reports Finland produced for international bodies both at the UN and the EU. She reflected on the notion of a unified state in treaty body proceedings discussed in Chapter 5, commenting:

> There's this theoretical discourse of engaging NGOs. But far too often it is the Committee members' view of the world and distinct problems that rule. They give too many recommendations, far too detailed. They do not know the countries in question or the details of its systems! How, for example, in Finland many of the issues that the Committee raises do not fall under the jurisdiction of the state, but rather the municipalities!
>
> The municipality is never considered in these hearings. It is always only the state. This is why this reporting discourse is severed from actual reality. But I can't say that as a representative of the state.

> I can't say that in one municipality things are going well, [but] in another they are not. To the outside, I have to represent the state that is unified.

She then shared her frustrations about the monitoring mechanism as a whole: "Finland is very hard on itself and takes its human rights obligations very seriously. It feels unfair that we get so many recommendations compared to many states where human rights are not being realized at all! Sometimes enormous attention is given to some small detail, whereas foundational questions are ignored." She had a distinct view of how the UN treaty body framework had changed over the years, noting: "During the past several decades reporting fluff has definitely increased. Now, the Committees often pose additional questions. There are interim reports. Also the factual number of human rights instruments has increased. Additionally, there are more recommendations inside the Finnish government, plus internal follow-up."

She considered this intensification of pace to have adverse consequences, summarizing: "The problem is that all of our work time goes toward monitoring and follow-up, instead of actually doing the work! These reports [she flicks through Finland's human rights report], they are all the same, with the same guidelines. It is always the same groups of people: the disabled, Roma, ethnic groups, immigrants, LGBTIQ+. Nobody ever asks about the elderly, for example!" Why are these hearings arranged, and what purpose do they serve? I asked her. She exclaimed, irritated: "I don't understand! If they say that it's a dialogue, it should mean that there is an actual conversation. But it does not feel like a dialogue. It feels like an inquisition! One where it is weighed how well the Finnish delegation is able to respond. There is no feeling that we are being listened to!"

Could the UN system be changed, and how? She responded again with notable intensity: "I don't know! I have the impression that UN processes are almost impossible to change. They are so cemented. I don't even know how change could occur. In CEDAW, there are Committee members whose life is essentially the Committee. Their entire life mission revolves around being on a Committee. There are those members in each Committee, and they are not likely to give this position up." What makes her feel that a particular hearing was successful? She connected her answer to the performance of her professional tasks: "If I am able to respond to the questions in my sector in an appropriate manner." This seemed a modest reward considering the shortcomings of the monitoring system she outlined.

In summary, she said, "As a whole, this is not an assignment that people at the ministry want to undertake; these reports are a pain! It's really difficult work, having to memorize all these data and answer quickly—in English—on the spot! Nobody wants to go on these delegations. They take weeks of preparations. And there is no extra compensation, no overtime calculated! Nobody knows at the ministry that I'm going to another hearing soon. Nobody cares! I get no credit for it, for how I perform—nobody cares. It's just something that is forced on me!"

This interview stood out from most discussions and interviews for its intensity and candid tenor, both exceptional for a Finnish civil servant—and simultaneously, it was by no means the sole instance of a civil servant expressing frustration, disillusionment, alienation, and exhaustion. Rather such expressions became an unmistakable undercurrent as my research progressed. They emerged during unexpected encounters in half-empty UN offices in Geneva, whose occupants were preparing to leave after failing to secure new contracts due to staff rotation. They were shared in cramped rooms, covered from floor to ceiling with documents, occupied by long-term civil servants at Finnish ministries in Helsinki. Often communicated in semi-hushed tones, such sentiments clearly did not belong to the mainstream narratives human rights functionaries use to describe their work. At the same time, it was undeniable that they were more prevalent than initially evident.

A frequent source of complaint was the repetitiveness of the work, both the reporting itself and the issues captured in the documents.[46] On more than one occasion, people referred to these reporting cycles as "always talking of the same people or issues," a characterization of sameness rather than reports producing something new in the world. Another complaint was a sense of being overwhelmed and exhausted: the feeling that reporting "fluff" continually increased, referring to the proliferation of documentary tasks devoid of substantive significance. The consequence entailed "going through the motions" that Brown, Reed, and Yarrow describe as "boringly, even achingly familiar routines"[47] to comply with requirements.[48]

Another common frustration was that the work was not appreciated sufficiently—or to put it bluntly, that "nobody cares." Among UN staff, such sentiments were cloaked in complaints about internal UN professional hierarchies, specifically that certain secretarial positions should have a higher "grade," yielding in higher pay as well as greater prestige and recognition of the importance of the work, as was discussed in Chapter 3. These sentiments—just like those of commitment, excitement, hope, and belief—are crucial for the continued movement in the rights direction embodied by UN treaty bodies, in general, and the Human Rights Committee specifically. Just as positive feelings generate momentum, negative ones may lead to delays in state reporting due to the unavailability of staff volunteering for the task, and to this work being seen solely as a Covenant-bound obligation rather than a devotion.

Conclusion

This chapter shows that, in order to gain a comprehensive understanding of UN treaty body cycles, we need to translate "UN reality" back into "real reality" by paying attention to the people behind the drafting and processing of the state reports that accompany these cycles. To do so, I have reflected on the affective elements that reporting awakens in Finnish civil servants, linking human rights reporting to Finland's post–World War II history and to the civil servants' sentiments of professional success and failure. I have connected this analysis to the sentiments that Constructive Dialogue sessions elicit in state delegates, as well as highlighted how experiences of fatigue and loss of meaning generate feelings of alienation. The chapter further illustrates the key role that individual Committee members' personal contributions play in reaffirming belief in the importance of the Committee's monitoring cycles in state delegates participating in its sessions.

Due to incessant UN staff rotation and the Committee's recomposition after elections every two years, some of the longest-serving participants in the Guardian of Vision community of practice may, in fact, be state delegates who may spend their entire careers in their ministries, making regular appearances in front of UN treaty bodies to present state reports. In the process, these state delegates build impressive social connections, both with key staff at the UN and civil servants in like-minded states.

In their engagement with UN treaty bodies, civil servants balance professionalism with the commitment of the Guardians of Vision to contribute to UN treaty bodies' effective operation. This results in high motivation to perform tasks related to Finland's human rights Covenant obligations diligently—and when possible, in a timely manner. It also helps maintain civil servants' sense of agency in the face of bureaucratic tasks that may occasionally appear repetitive and devoid of meaning.

Such affective elements constitute the human factor that brings the impersonal monitoring cycles of UN treaty bodies to life, while imbuing them with solidity and momentum. When the experiences of state delegates are positive, this strengthens participants' commitment to—and belief in—the UN human rights monitoring system. Under such circumstances, "what is discussed in Geneva does not stay in Geneva" but rather "add[s] fuel to mobilization and prompt[s] demands for implementation"[49] back home in local government offices.

Positive sentiments will likely be shared with colleagues, contributing to the understanding that the Committee and UN human rights monitoring hold importance. As this chapter has shown, enthusiasm, hope, and belief play vastly underappreciated roles in spreading and reproducing the global regulatory human rights framework, as well as contributing toward these monitoring mechanisms' ability to sustain movement in the rights direction. At the same time, negative sentiments are equally consequential; feelings of exhaustion, ineffectiveness, and repetitiveness erode belief and commitment, slowing the momentum surrounding the treaty bodies and increasing their fragility in the face of state critique.

CHAPTER 7

Moving in the Shadows: NGOs in the Human Rights Committee

"Is there anyone here who knows of the situation of the Roma people in Finland? What about claims that the Finnish government was aware of Guantanamo Bay prisoner transfer flights by the US military through Finnish air space? The treatment of underaged asylum seekers? LGBT issues,[1] gender-corrective surgery, and forced sterilization?"

Committee members look inquisitively at the NGO delegates from diverse Finnish organizations seated on the opposite side of the oval table. The NGO representatives squirm slightly; these issues do not fall under their competence, and thus they have no information to share. The week has been intense as the Committee has examined reports from numerous high-profile states with conflicting human rights records. All week, the seats of the Palais Wilson conference room have been packed, as have the lunchtime NGO hearings taking place in this smaller meeting room. The contrast with today's calmer hearing is striking, as shown by the lower number of attendees. Even so, the NGO delegates appear every bit as committed to advancing their causes as their counterparts from other states. With slight reluctance, it seems, Committee members abandon their questions, and the meeting is declared over well in time for the next session commencing after lunch.

This chapter explores the role that NGOs play in the Human Rights Committee's operations. It traces NGO delegates as they lobby their causes in the Palais Wilson conference rooms, as well as in the cafeteria and the corridors. It continues the discussions of Chapter 5 of the translation processes required to transform "real reality" into recognizable human rights issues within "UN reality,"[2] and the importance of both direct personal connections and indirect social relations[3] within the UN human rights apparatus. It further discusses how over the past decades Guardians within the Committee, the UN Secretariat, and states have maneuvered within the UN human rights apparatus's opaque transparency to expand NGOs' role in the Committee's operations.

Tracing NGOs from Finland and elsewhere reveals the multifaceted roles of the Guardians of Vision as intermediaries in the Committee's operations: they instruct NGOs about minute details of the sessions as well as direct lobbying within the Committee. Finally, this chapter connects its analysis to the theme of movement by reflecting on the consequences of incessant flows—of people, discourses, and expertise—that NGO participation instigates. It connects this movement to historical patterns of North-South collaboration within the NGO sector and reflects on these patterns' relevance to present-day action.

Curious Grapevine with Historic Anchoring

NGOs have long enjoyed prominence in both human rights practice and scholarship. Korey calls NGOs the "curious grapevine" that would bring the UDHR to life.[4] Today many see them as forming, to quote Reiners, "transnational lawmaking coalitions"[5] that impact the content of international law and its interpretation.[6] In UN treaty body operations, scholars and practitioners praise NGOs for providing critical information that fills gaps in an overburdened system, creating a form of global "participatory democracy."[7]

Despite NGOs' prominence in international collaboration, no clear-cut or widely agreed-upon definitions exist as to what constitutes one. Rather, the term serves as "an umbrella under which highly diverse projects, policies and organizational structures can co-exist,"[8] including differing views of what "doing good"[9] entails. Some scholars argue that this definitional unclarity is precisely where the NGOs' power lies.[10] Simultaneously, due to this conceptual open-endedness, no one knows for sure how many NGOs exist today, with estimates ranging from tens of thousands to millions.[11]

The term "non-governmental organization" is most commonly linked to Article 71 of the UN Charter, which mandates the UN Economic and Social Council to make "suitable arrangements for consultation with non-governmental organizations which are concerned with matters within its competence."[12] When discussing non-governmental actors, formal UN sources commonly use the term "civil society."[13] This includes the Human Rights Committee, the website of which labels NGO reports as "Info from Civil

Society Organizations."[14] In informal Committee parlance, the acronym NGO is common, and thus this chapter likewise utilizes the term.

O'Sullivan traces the roots of modern NGOs to the late eighteenth century.[15] The nineteenth century saw the emergence, particularly in Europe, of organizations involved in the peace movement and socialist rights experiments, among other issues.[16] During the League of Nations era, many of these organizations—referred to as private organizations or learned societies rather than NGOs—remained active, one of the most visible rights organizations being the French Ligue des Droits de l'Homme.[17] The Ligue united European leagues—especially in French- and German-speaking countries—in 1922 into the Fédération Internationale des Ligues des Droits de l'Homme (FIDH), becoming the era's most prominent "rights of man" coalition. In the US, the American Civil Liberties Union was founded in 1920,[18] and in Britain, the National Council for Civil Liberties in 1934.[19] Unlike later human rights NGOs, these organizations focused primarily on domestic civil liberties.

In the first decades after World War II, human rights NGOs remained marginal, as both their visibility and following were low, echoing the slow pace at which the international human rights movement developed. The 1940s and the 1950s saw the emergence of only a few human rights NGOs, with the International League for the Rights of Man becoming the most prominent of these. The League was originally the French Fédération Internationale, which was regrouped in New York in 1943 after the organization's key members immigrated to the US.[20]

Things changed rapidly in the late 1960s and 1970s—timing that both coincided with and contributed to the "human rights revolution" of the same period.[21] Aided by swift developments in media technologies, newly established NGOs found growing following via a combination of targeted human rights and mass media campaigns. Amnesty International's membership numbers reflect these developments: in 1974 the organization, founded in 1961, had 20,000 members. By 1976, its membership was almost 100,000—only to double again in the next few years.[22]

Within the international human rights movement, NGOs are often celebrated for decolonizing the field by introducing global grassroots mobilization to advocacy, thus embodying "global democracy."[23] Close examination challenges this narrative, as the NGO field has been strongly dominated by actors and funders from the Global North, with program recipients located particularly in the Global South. A few examples of prominent human rights NGOs illustrate this pattern. In spring 1945, at the UN's founding conference in San Francisco, all forty-two participating civil society organizations were American, with no organizations from other countries.[24] Amnesty International was founded in London, where its headquarters remain,[25] and Human Rights Watch was founded in the US in 1978, with its headquarters in New York.[26] Among other prominent INGOs, Save the Children was founded in the UK in 1919,[27] Plan International in the UK in 1937,[28] and Oxfam in the UK in 1942.[29]

The 1980s saw a dramatic increase in NGOs based in the Global North focusing on Africa in particular.[30] This geographic division connects NGOs to earlier missionary projects and the broader "civilizing mission" dating back to the fifteenth century.[31] By extension, the civilizing mission echoes in the economic structural adjustment programs that the World Bank began to promote in the 1970s targeting the Global South and aiming to downsize state institutions. These programs promoted neoliberal policies that favored channeling development funds through NGOs instead of states.[32] The outcome was an "NGO moment"[33] that dramatically increased both the number of NGOs and the funding they received from Global North actors.[34] The figures involved are massive: according to some estimates, by the mid-1990s, more than $1 billion in aid globally was being channeled through NGOs.[35] In the new millennium, NGO funding has increased at an accelerating pace.

In formal terms, NGOs are distinguished from states and from National Human Rights Institutes, whose mandates derive from the 1993 Paris Principles.[36] In practice, NGOs often operate in close entanglement with states, as many organizations receive the majority of funding from them.[37] This applies particularly to NGOs located in the Global North, where up to 90 percent of funding may emanate from the state.[38] Funding dependency has tangible consequences, as states often monitor NGOs to "ensure they do not abuse their nonprofit status."[39]

NGOs' proximity with states is linked also to the civilizing mission. For example, donor states in the Global North may require states in the Global South receiving financial aid to involve local NGO sectors in development work or demand that NGOs provide certain social services.[40] Thus, whereas partnerships between states and NGOs may appear voluntary, in reality external factors may impose them.[41] NGOs' centrality to international collaboration has awakened considerable criticism. Scholars highlight how the "patchwork of donor-funded parallel structures"[42] duplicates governance structures, complicating efforts aimed at coherent development policy. Critics describe neoliberal policies as creating a "humanitarian marketplace" that relies increasingly on business models favoring short-term projects over long-term oversight, as well as publicity and fundraising to pay for professional global advocacy.[43]

These developments have made the international NGO space increasingly competitive. As a result, NGOs' PR campaigns may lean on essentialized conceptualizations of culture and progress, producing neocolonial continuities while reproducing racial stereotypes. Accompanying imagery "usually exploits the image of passive, poor, ignorant people, usually people of color, waiting for a white Western hand to rescue them."[44] Together, these features contribute, in Biraben's words, to a "reconfiguration of Global North-South power relations and to a new type of political order, where 'human rights' (gender equity, the rule of law, transparency, etc.) serve the North as a means to exercise surveillance and intervention across national borders."[45]

From "Prestige-Seeking Charities" to "Providers of Objective Knowledge"

The formal mandates of UN treaty bodies recognize no official space for NGO involvement.[46] Over the past decades, nevertheless, NGOs have become increasingly conspicuous in treaty body operations, aided by careful maneuvering by the Guardians of Vision. Today, many attend treaty body sessions regularly, and their delegates skillfully use the UN human rights system in their lobbying.[47] NGOs' significance to the UN human rights monitoring framework is widely recognized, with the OHCHR noting that the work of UN human rights bodies is "inconceivable without civil society input, which adds to the relevance and credibility of the conclusions and recommendations resulting from the experts' deliberations."[48]

NGOs' growing influence at the UN echoes the general pace of their development internationally. Pivotal moments were the Stockholm Environment Conference of 1972,[49] the World Population Conference in Bucharest in 1974,[50] and, in the 1980s, the drafting of the UN Convention on the Rights of the Child (CRC).[51] Another core moment was the drafting of the Convention Against Torture, and Other Cruel, Degrading or Treatment or Punishment (CAT), in which NGOs played a key role.[52] These developments coincided with a shift of public perception. In the 1980s, as Martens describes, NGOs were widely viewed as "prestige-seeking" charities and often "regarded as ineffective."[53] By the 1990s NGOs appeared increasingly as "neutral experts"[54] providing "objective expertise."[55] Growing professionalization supported this shift, marked by exponentially expanding staff numbers and budgets.

Professionalization spurred job exchanges between NGOs and the UN. Staff rotation was aided by the UN's internal developments as the organization, for the first time, needed large numbers of personnel prepared for human rights posts in peacekeeping and field operations. Due to the scarcity of qualified professionals, Martens notes how NGOs became the "main source of experts, both at the rank-and-file and the managerial levels."[56]

Today, NGO delegates are often welcomed by the OHCHR to feed information to different human rights programs, and they are even invited to consultations with UN Security Council members. That many state civil servants working on human rights have some previous association with NGOs, as do many UN staff and Committee members, as discussed in Chapter 3, confirms the high status of NGOs.[57] One might even suggest that NGO affiliation is synonymous with activist commitment in the human rights field, and that this commitment forms the bedrock of the community of practice of the Guardians of Vision.

Robust Informal Information System

NGOs made a surprisingly late entry into the Human Rights Committee's operations as publicly recognized participants in its reporting cycles. The first mention of NGOs in the Committee's minutes occurred during the third informal meeting with states parties in 2004. In the minutes, a familiar name, Sir Nigel Rodley—then in his second term on the Committee—addresses the matter. Rodley notes that "under the Covenant there was no provision for dealing with information supplied by NGOs." He continues, "When the Committee had first begun its work, individual NGOs had approached members of the Committee to brief them on concerns regarding States parties whose periodic reports were due for consideration." The Committee has since continued the practice, the only amendment to this practice being, Rodley adds, "that such information was now often transmitted to the Committee via the secretariat."[58]

Given Rodley's long-term association with NGOs, and Amnesty International specifically,[59] it is no surprise that he would be the Committee member to address this issue. The records, however, show how he was not unequivocally in favor of NGOs' increasing role, instead noting that "the Committee did not assume that the information from NGOs was well founded." Rodley emphasizes that "the aim of the Committee's dialogue with the delegation was to allow the State party to provide its own information and express its point of view." In light of this, "the most important information at the stage of formulating Concluding Observations was the State party's input."[60]

Rodley notes how the Committee "agreed that it would be good practice to encourage NGOs to make the information they provided to the Committee available to delegations as well." According to him, sharing NGO reports publicly is unproblematic because "for the most part . . . that information was in the public domain and [state] delegations were already aware of it." Still, he cautioned that "it would not be appropriate, under the terms of the Covenant, to convert the information system to a formal advocacy procedure."[61]

These minutes yield two prominent insights. First, by sharing how individual NGOs had been in direct contact with individual Committee members prior to 2004, Rodley acknowledges that NGOs had informally participated in the Committee's operations since their inception. Committee insiders that I interviewed confirmed that NGO reports had been submitted for virtually all states well before 2004. What had changed most was the reports' media: Today NGO reports are disseminated electronically on the Committee's website. By contrast, up until the new millennium, they were shared in paper form, and deposited together with such documents as the special rapporteurs' country mission reports, submissions by UN agencies, and Concluding Observations from other Committees, in a filing cabinet still present in the Palais Wilson's conference room.[62]

Second, in describing the NGOs' informal engagement, Rodley articulates the fuzzy logic of the UN human rights apparatus: even though formal procedures and mandates exist, informal procedures, in place since the Committee's establishment, help secure continuously increased realization of the ICCPR and human rights—in this instance meaning the gradually growing role of NGOs. Under the UN human rights apparatus's opaque transparency, Guardians of Visions have, over the past decades, delicately maneuvered to increase and consolidate NGOs' influence in the Human Rights Committee's work. As a consequence, NGOs are today viewed as integral and routine participants in the Committee's operations.

Stating that "it would not be appropriate, under the terms of the Covenant, to convert the information system to a formal advocacy procedure,"

Rodley confirms that arrangements with NGOs *must* remain informal and off the record today as well as in the future.[63] Although the ICCPR provisions that laid the foundation for the Human Rights Committee's mandate leave discretion regarding their working methods to the Committee, this discretion only extends to practices realized informally. Thus, the Guardians of Vision can only support NGOs' growing role when they continue to operate under the guise of opaque transparency but remain formally in the shadows.[64]

This conclusion aligns with the Committee's 2012 statement on its relationship with non-governmental organizations. The Committee notes candidly that "since the early 1980s NGOs have been playing an important role in the implementation of the Covenant and have been making contributions at all stages of the Committee's activities." It explains that contributions include "submitting alternative/Shadow Reports for the Committee's consideration in connection with State party reports and the follow-up procedure to Concluding Observations, assisting authors in the submission of individual communications, providing briefings to the Committee during its sessions and overall improving the visibility of the Committee and its activities." In sum, the statement characterizes NGOs as "provid[ing] important information relevant to the conduct of the Committee's activities and hav[ing] a catalytic role in enhancing the implementation of the Covenant at the domestic level."[65]

Furthermore, the statement recognizes the creative maneuvering behind NGOs' greater role, noting how "the Committee has over the years created a space for NGOs to play a constructive role in relation to the reporting process and the review by the Committee of States parties' compliance with their obligations under the Covenant." As justification for this maneuvering, the Committee notes how it "*considers . . . necessary* that this dialogue is based on information received not only from States parties, United Nations entities and national human rights institutions, but from NGOs, to ensure a well-informed and Constructive Dialogue."[66]

The Committee further "emphasizes that it is highly desirable to receive input from NGOs at an early stage of the reporting process." The statement concludes with the Committee noting it "welcomes and encourages the efforts of NGOs to enhance outreach and awareness of the Covenant and its Optional Protocols, and of its Concluding Observations, Views and general comments."[67] In other words, the Committee views NGOs' increased influence in its reporting cycles as essential for the greater realization of the ICCPR and, by extension, sustaining the world's movement in the rights direction.

The Shadow Report

NGOs' most tangible contribution to the Human Rights Committee's documentary cycles is the submission of ancillary reports called shadow reports. These reports, maximum ten thousand words in length, are submitted to the Committee in English, French, or Spanish to highlight distinct human rights violations in the target state, with the aim of complementing—and challenging—the periodic reports states submit. Shadow reports must be delivered to the Committee by the deadlines set for each Committee session and, according to the UN's guidelines, should be "as specific, reliable, and objective as possible." They should further utilize "non-abusive language" while "highlight[ing] priority concerns and suggest[ing] possible country-specific recommendations."[68]

The first shadow reports available online complemented official state reports on the Central African Republic and the United Nations Interim Administration in Kosovo in 2006.[69] Reports posted online proliferated soon thereafter, and already the next year, in 2007, for the committee's ninetieth session, shadow reports were posted on the Committee's website for virtually all the states under review.[70] The weight given to NGO reports in the Committee's review cycles today is significant: they can contest the veracity of state-provided information and challenge the states' legitimacy to represent their populations.[71] Committee members often rely on shadow reports while preparing for Constructive Dialogues, with some members stating that they focus particularly on these reports rather than the state reports. The significance many Committee members assign to NGO reports is evident in the Dialogues, as members may expressly challenge state submissions using content from them.

Shadow reports find broader context in the document production of human rights NGOs, which Ron characterizes as "the single most important activity that human rights organizations . . . undertake to promote human rights."[72] The logic behind reporting is simple: bring human rights violations to light and "promot[e] change by reporting." Here the guiding notion is that, as Moon phrases it, "if only people knew, they would act"—a credo that "underpins a key cultural form of the human rights movement, the human rights report." Significantly, NGO reports are advocacy tools intended to yield particular results. Concurrently their power lies, both during Human Rights Committee sessions and more generally, in public perceptions of their seeming objectivity as a "correspondence model of truth," marked by distinct "elevator words" such as "facts," "reality," and "knowledge."[73]

To translate "real reality" to "UN reality," since the 1980s, statistics have acquired increasing salience in human rights advocacy. Moon notes how this has resulted "in a complex reciprocity between the authority of [human rights organizations] and the metrics they deployed,"[74] resonating with the "seduction of quantification"[75] characterizing modern bureaucracies. Another predominant feature in NGO reports are narratives that focus on individuals. This approach aspires to and often succeeds in revealing concrete Covenant violations. Simultaneously, scholars and victims of abuse have criticized the approach, noting the challenges in narrating traumatic experiences due to shame, stigma, or other social consequences. Focusing on individual stories may lead victims of human rights abuses to feel that their stories have been "appropriated, commodified and circulated"[76] without their consent by human rights entrepreneurs.[77]

The Role of Intermediaries

The first NGO reports posted on the Committee's website were uneven in content and quality,[78] whereas the vast majority were soon submitted by large international NGOs, such as Amnesty International and Human Rights Watch, embodying more professionally formulated content. This emphasis on INGOs awakened concern across the treaty body framework that these organizations, with their headquarters in the Global North, did not truly represent NGOs from around the world, thus challenging the idea of NGOs as embodying global democracy and universality.

One response was the emergence of international facilitative NGOs that assist grassroots organizations seeking to participate in UN treaty body sessions. These organizations offer training, arrange interpretation, and set up meetings between grassroots NGO staff and treaty body members.[79] For the Human Rights Committee, the most significant facilitative NGO is the Center for Civil and Political Rights (CCPR Center), a Geneva-based organization founded in 2010.[80] The Center supports report drafting and editing in diverse localities around the world, and works with a range of funding agencies to secure resources that allow NGOs, particularly those from the Global South, to participate in Committee hearings. CCPR Center further assists with travel and visa arrangements, and organizes many of the NGO lunchtime hearings and other closed NGO briefings described in this chapter.

In Merry's terminology, the CCPR Center acts as an intermediary[81] that helps grassroots NGOs translate their "real reality" concerns into "UN reality." In her study among OHCHR staff and treaty body members, McGaughey found "a preference for domestic NGO input being channeled through an international NGO as they felt this brought added legitimacy and credibility." This preference, her research showed, stems from the operational logic of UN treaty bodies: although the Economic and Social Council has a system for NGO accreditations, this is not generally required for NGO engagement with human rights treaty bodies.[82] Subsequently, any organization, without limitations, may submit shadow reports, whereas Committee members have restricted opportunities to verify the reliability of the information they receive.

Grassroots organizations, furthermore, may lack the knowledge needed to make effective interventions in treaty body proceedings. As a consequence, they may end up drafting reports that appear to Committee insiders, as McGaughey observed, "quite long and not very good, sometimes confusing."[83] Facilitative NGOs thus serve a twofold role: they act as a seal of approval that helps treaty body members rely on the information included in NGO reports, and they help NGOs translate their interventions into the appropriate vernacular, increasing the intervention's impact.

The CCPR Center's favored role among the Committee and the UN Secretariat was clearly noticeable during my field research: the Center was frequently thanked at the end of Committee sessions for the webcast it provided at the time. Its special position was embodied by an assigned table in the center of the Palais Wilson conference room, close to the Committee, setting the Center staff apart from the rest of the audience seats, including representatives from other NGOs. During breaks one could often spot the Center's staff in informal interactions with both Committee members and key UN Secretariat staff. Many Committee members expressed their appreciation for the Center's work in citations in the Center's annual reports, with some previous Committee members joining the CCPR Center's board and even serving as the organization's president.[84]

Importantly, echoing the role of NGOs in the Committee's operations, the CCPR Center's special role hinges on informal arrangements that rely on direct personal connections and indirect social relations, rather than a formal written mandate. These connections and relations allow the CCPR Center to fill a gap the Guardians of Vision among Committee members and relevant UN staff perceive to exist. This gap concerns grassroots NGOs from around the world who lack knowledge on the appropriate formats in which to submit information to the Committee as well as organizations that may have questionable reliability. Thus, the CCPR Center's facilitative role enables greater global representation by NGOs in the Committee's operations. Simultaneously, the Center's connections and relations transform its core personnel into integral members of the community of practice of the Guardians of Vision.

The role of such facilitating NGOs nevertheless has raised reservations among scholars. For example, Lewis, Kanji, and Themudo note how "within their work, NGOs may consciously or unconsciously control information and create informal networks which create potentially exclusionary knowledge."[85] This exclusionary potential is embodied in the integral role that the CCPR Center held, for example, in disseminating speech slots in collective NGO hearings discussed at the end of this chapter. Exclusions additionally arise from the Center's decisions on which NGOs, from which states, it selects as collaborators for specific documentary cycles.

Another source of critique, resonating with what was discussed earlier in this chapter, relates to the facilitative NGOs' funding that emanates from the Global North while their operations target NGOs in the Global South. This geographic pattern applies to the CCPR Center's operations: its funding comes mostly from Swiss sources together with select countries in Northern Europe, whereas the bulk of its target countries are in the Global South.[86] These funding patterns reproduce the dynamic whereby expertise and training flow from the Global North to the South, whereas money, in the form of travel possibilities flows to the Global South, and in the form of personnel resources to the CCPR Center staff remains in the Global North. Simultaneously, the Center's operations transform only its core staff into true insiders and members of the Guardian of Vision's community of practice, who remain in Geneva, while grassroots NGO staff continue their nonstop movement between Geneva and diverse localities around the world.

Making an Impact

In addition to submitting shadow reports, NGOs have various lobbying opportunities during the Committee's sessions. One is the adoption of the List of Issues that occurs two sessions before the Constructive Dialogue takes place, the List forming the Dialogue's basis. The sessions where the Lists are adopted include direct consultations with NGOs, and concerns NGOs raise during these consultations often appear among the issues the Committee addresses in the eventual Dialogue. Participating in these sessions may be tricky for NGOs, however, mainly because funding to attend them is difficult to secure.

Numerous lobbying opportunities exist also in session where the state report is processed. These include joint sessions at which NGOs from all states presenting reports make interventions. The most important opportunities are the lunchtime sessions with NGOs from one specific state described at this chapter's opening. In these sessions, NGO staff can engage directly with Committee members and flesh out particular concerns with the hope of making last-minute impacts on the Constructive Dialogue.

Taking advantage of these lobbying opportunities requires significant insider knowledge, of both the formats that information needs to assume and the sessions' "rituals and ritualism."[87] NGO delegates from small grassroots organizations who travel to Geneva only for a few days often lack this knowledge. This is where the CCPR Center's facilitative role becomes instrumental, as the below exchange between three NGO delegates and a CCPR Center representative illustrates, all addressed through pseudonyms.

I spot Susan and Jonas at the Palais Wilson cafeteria with Rosa from the CCPR Center. We are soon joined by Charles from a Geneva-based NGO that had agreed to represent another Finnish NGO unable to send its own representative to Geneva for the session. The group discusses the details of the forthcoming closed briefing, where NGOs from all the states presenting reports will make appearances. Rosa explains the session's choreography, with Finland scheduled last. Given how many NGOs from the Global South are present, the CCPR Center had to defend the right of Finland to make its case, Rosa says.

"Do the Committee members come back with questions?" Charles asks. Rosa answers that they do not have time. However, she adds, the Committee members will have the opportunity to ask questions in the closed lunchtime briefing, limited only to Finnish NGOs, scheduled a few days later. Rosa notes that Jonas and Charles will each have two-minute slots. "Theoretically, you could have three minutes but it is better to say two minutes so that there is time for the handover. Mind you," she continues, "this is assuming that the session actually starts at the scheduled time, which is wildly optimistic," she notes, referring to earlier delays when previous sessions ran overtime.

"Do we know who is the rapporteur for Finland's state report? Could we speak with them?" Jonas asks. Rosa says that, unfortunately, the Committee has decided that this information needs to remain confidential. "That's new," Jonas says, prompting Rosa to reply, "That has always been the policy of the Human Rights Committee and never of the others. We keep on suggesting harmonization." She continues, "You could identify the country rapporteur on the basis of which committee member speaks first, but up until that point we are not allowed to learn this," Rosa concludes, highlighting the opaque transparency surrounding the rapporteur's identity discussed in Chapter 4.

"Which committee member might be good on Indigenous peoples?" Jonas inquires. Rosa considers a few members. "The problem is that we have a group of new members who only joined the Committee on the last session. It is difficult to know their views," she notes, alluding to the nonstop rotation of Committee members that contributes to opaque transparency. Rosa names one member who was not re-elected. "He would otherwise have been the one to talk to," she adds, before noting that one of the new members appears strong on these issues.

"It also depends on who is on the task force," she notes, prompting Susan to ask, "What is the task force?" Rosa explains that the task force is a group of five Committee members responsible for responding to the state report. In her response, Rosa illustrates relevant insider knowledge for making effective interventions for the Committee's sessions that Susan, working in a grassroots NGO, lacks. "Of course, all Committee members can engage," Rosa continues. "Do you know who the task force members are by now?" Susan asks. Rosa responds, "No, for each state they are confidential, in theory," again referring to the opaque transparency and the "public secrets" that accompany the Committee's operations.

Charles asks how long the session on Finland's report will last. He adds that he will not be in Geneva for the hearing but that he has copies of their NGO's report that he would like to distribute to the Committee members. Rosa instructs him, "You want to give four copies to the conference services that go to the interpreters. For the rest," she continues, "you can give them directly to the Committee members." These instructions, including the need to share reports with the conference services so that they reach the interpreters, again embody crucial insider knowledge that Rosa, as a representative of a facilitative NGO, holds but Charles lacks.

Soon the meeting concludes and everyone leaves the table. As we depart, I ask Susan whether the Sámi are ever represented in such international contexts by facilitative NGOs based, for example, in Geneva. She says no. "Why would we want or need to be represented by others when we can really do it by ourselves?" she notes. I later learn that Susan is trained as a lawyer, like so many NGO delegates appearing before the Committee. This gives them undoubted insider knowledge of how to frame their concerns in the appropriate vernacular and, in particular, to translate "real reality" concerns into violations under the ICCPR.

Concurrently this exchange between Susan, Jonas, Charles, and Rosa illustrates how even such specialized knowledge is insufficient for impactful in-person lobbying, which, instead, requires detailed insider knowledge of the Committee's operations. One needs to know which Committee members to approach directly and understand the existence and significance of such roles as "rapporteur" and "task force." Additionally, one needs to know the expected parameters for direct interventions in NGO sessions with Committee members, including the strict two-minute slots and the need for precise statistics and personal narratives.

This information is impossible to gain from the UN's written guidelines, which focus primarily on technical instructions for drafting shadow reports.[88] Instead, it resides in the bodies of experienced intermediaries who know the intricacies of the sessions—down to what is public knowledge about the Committee's operations and what is a secret, at least "in theory." This knowledge makes the intermediary powerful. The power rests both on tangible elements—assigning time slots for NGO interventions and instructing NGO delegates to keep their lunchtime interventions—and on informal knowledge, such as which Committee member may be particularly sympathetic to which kind of issues. The intermediary's power renders some voices and concerns audible while pushing others to the margins, erasing them from view.

Lunchtime Briefing

It's 2:00 p.m. and the meeting room doors close. The NGO lunchtime briefing—open only to the Committee's expert members, their interns, representatives of NGOs, relevant UN Secretariat staff, and the occasional scholar—is about to start. It is *hot* in the room. Someone opens a window. In the background, distant sounds of a protest unfold in a language impossible to identify. This is unusual, as protesters usually stay farther up the hill in front of the Palais des Nations. No demonstrators are visible, and it is impossible to make out their complaints. Soon, traffic of the lakeside road muffles the protest noises. Someone closes the window, and silence sets in.

The mid-sized meeting room located on the Palais Wilson's first floor corridor has ornate ceilings and is divided by a large, oval table. One can easily imagine high-caliber international diplomacy taking place here for decades. To one side of the doorway sit eight members of the Human Rights Committee. The scorching afternoon sun pouring through the large windows must feel uncomfortable in their eyes. The remainder of the room is filled to the brim with NGO delegates and a few representatives of international NGOs from London or Geneva headquarters, as is often the case when developing states of the Global South are under review.

By contrast, hearings on established democracies from the Global North, such as Finland, commonly draw significantly smaller audiences. These lunchtime briefings are the most intimate encounters between NGO representatives and Committee members. They are usually the only moments when NGO delegates and Committee members see each other face to face, apart from occasions when they have lunch at adjoining tables in the Palais Wilson cafeteria, oblivious to each other's presence.

The Committee members listen attentively; a few look visibly exhausted. These weeks of sessions from 10:00 a.m. to 6:00 p.m.—often extended by breakfast meetings and dinners, as well as reading and drafting documents outside session time—take their toll. All signs of fatigue nevertheless vanish as the members begin to question the NGO delegates. In principle, the members and NGOs are on the same side, so to speak: both aim to advance realization of the ICCPR by criticizing state conduct and thus safeguard the well-being of humanity. The briefing dynamic is therefore set for a positive exchange.

Even so, in these lunchtime meetings the members often come across as rather strict. Their questions are pointed, targeting minute details of national legislation and recent local events. Members may request exact figures, such as the number of inmates in a given prison or the percentages of minority children in higher education. This exchange is not for dilettantes as providing satisfactory answers challenges even the most seasoned NGO delegates. After the hearings, many delegates confess to feeling surprised or overwhelmed by the level of precision sought by members. "It feels like one should have learned the entire constitution by heart," one delegate shared.

There is, nevertheless, distinct logic to the members' strict tenor. NGO lunchtime briefings, while providing additional information, serve as personal checkups offering the members one last opportunity to test whether their understanding from the massive background information for each state report is accurate. It forms their final opportunity to obtain specific knowledge with which to challenge data in the state party's report.

"New" Mechanism of Low Impact

NGO participation at the Committee's sessions generates recurring discussion among Committee insiders, including comments on the size of NGO delegations as well as the number of NGO shadow reports. Finland's sixth state report was accompanied by eight shadow reports.[89] Of these, two were by international NGOs: one by Amnesty International and the other by a small Geneva-based NGO, the International Fellowship of Reconciliation, which focuses on conscientious objection. Finnish NGOs submitted four reports, including one by the Union of Conscientious Objectors, likewise addressing the issue of conscientious objectors to military service; the Coalition of Women Association NYTKIS; the Union of Freethinkers; and SETA, an NGO focusing on LGBTIQ+ issues. Two reports were collaboratively authored by Finnish and international organizations: one on disability and another by the Sámi Council.[90]

Amnesty's submission was well versed in the Constructive Dialogue's organizing logic: it was arranged in the paragraph style characteristic of documents produced by both the Committee and states. The report highlighted concrete issues and presented information in a clear and concise manner, showing great familiarity with the forms that effective treaty body submissions require.[91] In thematic terms, the report was broad: it addressed rendition flights, which had garnered broad media and civil society attention at the time; LGBTIQ+ rights; and established civil and political rights issues such as human trafficking, the detention of asylum seekers, and freedom of thought, conscience, and religion.

The other seven shadow reports were likewise professionally written, though varied in format. Many cited both ICCPR provisions and Finnish legislation, including the Constitution, giving these documents a distinct legal bent. Six of eight reports included no footnotes or references to supporting data. Many of the eight reports offered direct recommendations for actions the Committee should demand of the Finnish government, with the Sámi Council's report including direct proposed wording for the Committee's Concluding Observations.[92]

Viewed from the shadow reports alone, NGO participation in Finland's Constructive Dialogue appears satisfactory, even if eight reports are on the low end of what the Committee typically receives as states with controversial human rights records tend to generate dozens of reports. The closed lunchtime briefing between Committee members and NGO delegates on Finland, however, was less successful. In the end, only three people represented Finnish NGOs, and only one was from Finland herself: the representative of the Sámi people. The other two delegates were representing the Sámi from Sweden—the Sámi inhabit a unified geographic territory extending across Finland, Norway, and Sweden, which sometimes generates occasional joint representation for UN human rights bodies—and a representative of a Geneva-based NGO focusing on conscientious objection.

The tepid participation of Finnish NGOs was discussed after Finland's Constructive Dialogue by Committee insiders, and the absence of Finnish NGOs was singled out as the sole disappointment of the proceedings on Finland. To these Committee insiders, this lack of Finnish NGOs came across as the session's failure to "embody universality,"[93] undermining the Committee's legitimacy. Why were no other Finnish NGOs present, and why was the contrast so stark when compared with the proceedings regarding numerous other states, some of which drew NGO delegations with dozens of participants? As Finland lies on the same continent as Switzerland, one might assume that Finnish NGOs could find the resources for the trip, which, on a global scale, formed a modest expense. Discussions with Finnish NGO delegates suggested otherwise: they consistently highlighted the difficulty of securing funding to attend UN sessions in Geneva.

Lack of resources, however, did not emerge as the most significant reason for low participation. Instead, discussions pointed to organizations' operational logics and priorities—combined with restricted familiarity over UN treaty body operations—as the pivotal causes for NGOs' absence. For Amnesty Finland, organizational priorities were primary: by that time the UPR had been placed higher on Amnesty's lobbying agenda than treaty bodies.[94] This emphasis aligned with what some other NGOs shared, highlighting UN bodies as the Permanent Forum for the Rights of Indigenous Peoples, which were seen as offering broader networking opportunities than the treaty bodies.

Importantly, some of the most significant human rights NGOs in Finland had no awareness of the forthcoming Dialogue and thus logically had no plans to submit reports or send staff to Geneva. This applied to the Finnish League for Human Rights, one of the country's oldest human rights NGOs, often seen as an "umbrella association."[95] During the spring leading up to Finland's Constructive Dialogue, I interviewed the League's newly appointed director, who said she was unaware of the hearing. Thus, understandably, the League had no plans to submit a shadow report or send staff to Geneva for the hearing.

SETA, the NGO working on LGBTIQ+ issues, had heard about the hearing, but a shortage of personnel meant its report had remained on the back burner. Eventually, SETA submitted a report, which was discussed during the Committee's hearing. The organization did not send a delegate to Geneva, however, and arranged for a Geneva-based umbrella organization to represent it instead. SETA's decision not to send a representative resembled Amnesty International's in that presence at UN treaty body hearings was a low organizational priority.

In interviews, many Finnish NGO staff described the UN system as distant, unfamiliar, and of uncertain usefulness because of its low impact and visibility. Despite nearly five decades of existence, many NGO workers characterized UN treaty bodies as "new" and, because of the bodies' "recent nature," still unfamiliar. This latter characterization was particularly unexpected from staff at the Finnish League for Human Rights. I later learned in my interview with Sam, discussed in Chapter 6, that, in the 1990s, the organization had in fact been active in submitting shadow reports and even attending sessions in Geneva. The sentiment of "newness" was, in this instance, the new director's subjective view. This shows that movement in the rights direction is not linear, indicating continually greater awareness of the ICCPR and the Committee sessions accompanying its realization. Rather, factors such as personnel changes can redirect attention away from treaty body sessions, capturing how the movement around the Committee remains volatile and fragile, easily disrupted and undone.

Lobbying with Tacit Insider Knowledge

"I will have to cut you short. You have distributed a note [to the Committee] so there is no concern that [the issue you represent] will not be included. There is also the NGO briefing this afternoon in which you can engage with the Committee members," Sir Nigel concludes at the podium in his customarily courteous yet frank tone.

Heather finished her intervention and sat down. We were in the middle of a closed NGO session at which NGO representatives from states whose reports would be examined later in the Committee's session made their oral interventions. The audience was packed with dozens of NGO delegates hoping to direct the Committee members' attention to the issues they represented. The schedule for the ninety-minute session was crowded as each NGO representative had only two to four minutes—a few interventions were even timed for two and a half minutes. Timekeeping is challenging in the Committee's regular sessions, but here the chair was seriously pressured to stay on top of it.

NGO delegates did their best to stick to the schedule. Many tried to compensate for the brevity of available time by speed-reading to fit maximum information in these precious minutes. On numerous occasions Sir Nigel asked the speakers to slow down, noting that their speed rendered it impossible for the interpreters to follow. Often, the encouragement backfired as some speakers, visibly flustered by the nervousness caused by the momentous occasion, sped up even more as nerves started to take over.

One speaker joked about keeping his intervention short in order to be "a good boy," generating audible laughter from the audience in a collective release of nervous energy. Many delegates struggled to formulate their message in specific human rights terminology, and heavy English accents occasionally clouded comprehension. These factors prevented their interventions from being translated from "real reality" into "UN reality," and, as a result, their message remained inaccessible to Committee members, even after all the effort involved in traveling to Geneva, and the rare opportunity to present their concerns to the Committee.

For Heather, the reasons her intervention remained beyond the members' reach were different: not a lack of skills, but the opposite. Confident and eloquent, she came across as one of the most experienced NGO delegates in the room. Her intervention demonstrated notable talent for framing her intervention in the appropriate human rights language, and furthermore, the boldness to push the boundaries of her allocated slot. Unlike every other NGO delegate, she did not stop when Sir Nigel first tried to cut her off, but insisted on continuing for as long as she could. Her determination signaled that this was hardly the first time she had lobbied before a high-profile human rights body.

Going over one's time slot was not very collegial and scarcely elicited sympathy from other participants. Each delegate must work within severe time constraints, and if one person took up more time, the others had less. Taking up additional time further suggested that the issues Heather represented were more compelling than those for which others lobbied—a conclusion the other delegates could scarcely be expected to accept.

Given how competitive human rights advocacy is, this is, of course, precisely what one must do: find ways to persuade the world—in this instance the Committee's eighteen expert members—that one's issue is more urgent than others, worthy of the time and attention it requires, even if this means exceeding a pre-allotted time slot. Heather's conduct communicated confidence in her work, simultaneously illustrating subtle insider knowledge of how to navigate the UN human rights apparatus's icelike inner contours to make an impact. Her behavior at the NGO hearing demonstrated the needed know-how to push the border demarcating inclusion from exclusion in her favor while maneuvering opportunistically through the UN human rights apparatus to advance her cause.

The Nostalgic Old-Timer

A few days later, before the formal session began, I found a chance to discuss the events of the closed NGO session with Heather as we moved to our seats at the back of the Palais Wilson's conference room. She recounted the point she was trying to make and shared her frustration that the Committee members—and the international community more generally—failed to see the severity of the issue. She noted, with aggravation, that people tended to nod sympathetically and then overlook what she was saying. This overlooking, to her, was what makes the issue so compelling.

When I asked her how she felt about the hearing, she said it did not go particularly well. With visible disdain, she stated that she understood Sir Nigel wished to give grassroots NGOs more time than her, a representative of a prominent international NGO, and thus she received a shorter slot than she wanted. I refrained from mentioning that the slots were assigned not by Sir Nigel but by the CCPR Center, and thus, the decision to give her a shorter slot was made by the Center staff who put together the schedule. To Heather, these details hold little significance: she had less time than she desired, ran out of time, and remained frustrated that she could not make her point heard.

At present, she said, it looks very unlikely that the issue would be picked up in the Concluding Observations. I asked whether the recommendations she tried to share in her oral intervention were in the NGO's shadow report. She responded that they are, but that she doubted they would travel further beyond the report. Should this be the outcome, it would, to her, evidently form a failure: an instance in which professional goals were not met, and the issues lobbied for did not move forward in the desired manner within the UN human rights apparatus.

Importantly, so I soon learned, her efforts were not in vain. After the NGO session, she shared, Sir Nigel indicated which member might be the right contact on the issue. She wondered aloud during our discussion whether there might be other opportunities to engage with this member, then sprung to her feet and approached the member in the Palais Wilson entryway while the member waited for the formal session to continue. A moment later, she returned—joyous—stating the member had heard her and promised to look into the issue.

As the session began at 10:00 a.m., I shared Heather's anticipation about whether her personal intervention bore fruit. We first listened as the state answered the questions the Committee posed the previous day, when the Constructive Dialogue on the given state had commenced. Then Sir Nigel, chairing the session, opened the floor for follow-up questions by the members. The member Heather had approached took the floor. Would they mention the issue? The member spoke at length about a number of different matters. I began to doubt that Heather's issue would come up at all, but finally, before concluding, the member addressed it directly.

When the session adjourned for a fifteen-minute break to allow the state delegation time to prepare its responses, I asked Heather if she was happy with the outcome. She was divided: yes, the member mentioned the issue, but it still could have been made clearer. I asked whether she thought that her impromptu verbal intervention before the session made an impact. She considered that it is possible, and shared that she followed up with an email to the member during the session, in which she had summarized her concerns around three very specific issues. She was still uncertain whether this issue would find its way to the Concluding Observations, but she remained hopeful.

Heather's response confirms her insider knowledge over the format information needs to take in the Committee's sessions: verbal interventions are often too complex and unstructured to assist members during the Constructive Dialogue. By organizing her concerns around three specific issues in an email, she transformed them into a form that is practical and usable for a member in the middle of an oral exchange. Further, by following up during the session, Heather received an additional opportunity to underscore the issue's gravity, increasing the chance that it would move forward into the Constructive Dialogue and, ideally, into the Concluding Observations.

This instance exemplifies the subtle lobbying opportunities that the Committee's sessions offer NGO delegates. For these opportunities to reveal themselves, NGO delegates need a combination of insider knowledge, boldness, opportunism, and good luck, as well as fortuitous timing. Such moments form individual pieces in longer ongoing chains of engagement that together constitute what I call movement in the rights direction.

In all of this I am surprised by Heather's tense emotions. Everything in her demeanor suggests that she has been involved in this work for quite a while. Thus, one might expect her to be aware of the need to conform to the rules of the game and the expectations of ceremony, including the importance of sticking to specific time limits. Likewise, one might expect that the sense of urgency in her work would have become toned down over the years. At the same time, her emotions—disappointment, frustration, and joy of success—remained intense, communicating that despite her lengthy professional path, she is continually affectively engaged in her work.

As the session paused, we moved to have coffee, and I asked her just how she got involved with her issue. She said that, of course, it was a "very [NGO] cause," and thus focus on it is quite expected. I asked her how long she had been working for the large INGO, expecting it to have been a while, and I was right: she had been involved for thirty-two years. I expressed my enthusiasm, noting how rare it was to find people who have been engaged in international advocacy for so long, as most NGO delegates joining the Committee's session were quite junior. I added that experienced NGO delegates embody an "institutional memory" of international advocacy's progress. She laughed: "I embody that all right."

Heather then described how the NGO space had changed over the decades, noting with a hint of nostalgia that it felt as if INGOs were no longer needed because local NGOs had become so professional and organized: they knew whom to contact to secure funds to attend the sessions and how to frame their issues in the human rights vernacular. I was surprised by this nostalgia, I shared, as I would have imagined this to be a great sign of success: proof of movement in the rights direction, embodied by skilled local mobilization where people on the grassroots level can do it themselves without needing aid from international representatives. Heather agreed, but said: "It's a great thing for human rights, but a sad thing for me personally."

The sense of nostalgia remained as she described past activism at UN meetings. When she started, "There was hardly anyone there"; circles were really small and few people attended. I suggested that she must have known most everyone who participated at the time. She said this was certainly true for people within her own INGO, and perhaps more generally. I described my own sentiments of feeling intimidated by the group of young, bright, highly educated, fluent, professionally clad, target-oriented NGO delegates who now frequent the proceedings at a steady flow and for whom activist work appears an attractive career option.

Heather echoed my sentiments, noting that there was now a distinct group of people who have INGOs as their professional target. She noted that, for her, this had never been the case. I asked whether she felt a sense of alienation or has difficulty relating to this new generation of activists. She did not think so. Clearly, she saw them as having a different set of interests, but this did not mean that she disapproved of their work or thought their engagement had adverse consequences for the human rights cause per se.

Heather's example illustrates numerous key elements of NGO advocacy at UN human rights bodies in general, and the Human Rights Committee in specific. First, successful lobbying in the highly competitive NGO field requires skill and boldness, backed by the conviction that the causes one represents truly matter—perhaps a little bit more than the causes that others represent. It demands perseverance in the face of obstacles and setbacks, such as running out of time at a hearing, and determination to find alternative opportunities to make impact, such as approaching individual Committee members in person.

Successful lobbying necessitates awareness of the formal rules governing advocacy opportunities, as well as the guts and ingenuity to overstep their borders and seize impromptu moments under the guise of the UN human rights apparatus's opaque transparency. Together, all of the above forms the kind of knowledge that newcomers to UN human rights mechanisms will lack—and this knowledge is not available in the formal guidelines for UN human rights sessions. Rather, it is implicit knowledge gained from experience that intermediaries and facilitators hold, and it is knowledge that, over time, transforms an inexperienced NGO delegate into an established member of the community of practice of the Guardians of Vision.

Furthermore, as Heather summarizes, the NGO field has changed over the past decades. Her experience suggests that the field has become truly globalized, with grassroots NGOs around the world now possessing the competencies needed to make interventions—rendering international NGOs partly unnecessary. The increased competence among local NGOs does not arise solely from grassroots mobilization in various parts of the world. Rather, it is supported by facilitative NGOs such as the CCPR Center, which trains NGOs in the needed skills for successful advocacy and seeks funding to secure their participation.

Increased activeness of grassroots NGOs is undoubtedly seen by human rights insiders as embodying greater universality of human rights advocacy. Nevertheless, the crucial role of facilitative NGOs in instigating and sustaining global flows of people, expertise, and lobbying tactics between diverse local contexts and the Human Rights Committee's sessions in Geneva complexifies this outcome. As the CCPR Center's example illustrates, facilitation is carried out from the Global North with funding from Northern funders, thus reproducing historical patterns of North-South relations in international collaboration. On a personal level, as Heather's story shows, grassroots NGOs' growing engagement may evoke nostalgia among experienced NGO delegates who find themselves questioning the continuing need and justification for their advocacy work.

Conclusion: "This Is Not the End, It's the Beginning"

"Thanks to all of you for the discipline you have shown, and renewed apologies to those whom I had to cut short on flow. It was necessary to ensure that everyone got the opportunity to speak. Let me assure you, this is not the end, it's the beginning. You have helped take our work forward." Sir Nigel concludes the NGO session and the crowd begins to exit the room.

This chapter has discussed the Human Rights Committee's sessions from the viewpoint of NGOs. Rather than taking the customary approach of focusing on the issues that NGOs represent, I have focused on *how* NGOs represent themselves—and the underlying structures, patterns, and networks of collaboration that enable their representations. I have paid particular attention to the tacit insider knowledge required for successful lobbying in the Committee's sessions and to the insiders and intermediaries who possess this knowledge, simultaneously becoming integral participants in the community of practice of the Guardians of Vision.

I have traced how insiders solicit participation in the Committee's sessions, concomitantly generating a type of embodied universalism with NGO delegates' presence. This universalism is supported by facilitative NGOs—most notably, in the Committee's case, the CCPR Center—which encourages grassroots organizations from around the world to participate while reproducing earlier patterns of North-South relations in international collaboration.

As this chapter illustrates, a crucial part of insider knowledge concerns the forms that lobbying must take, whether providing statistics and personal narratives for shadow reports and NGO lunchtime briefings, or delivering two-minute interventions that stand out among thirty similar interventions at a hearing. NGOs operate in a competitive humanitarian market in which impact increasingly equals attention. To succeed at this competition, NGO delegates need to be insightful, organized, and, at times, somewhat pushy.

Further, NGO operations have changed over the past decades. Whereas the early years of the Committee's sessions saw few NGO representatives, their number has grown exponentially. In the same time frame, NGO delegates have become increasingly professionalized, with many aspiring professionals now viewing work at NGOs and INGOs as a prospective career path. Even so, activist commitment remains visible in the Palais Wilson's corridors—embodied in frustrations over failed attempts to secure attention or in sentiments of triumph when particular concerns appear in the Concluding Observations.

Using examples from Finnish NGOs, I have explored why many NGOs may choose not to join UN treaty body sessions. This exploration revealed that participation may rank low as an organizational priority, due in part to limited resources but, more significantly, to the low impact that UN treaty bodies, the Human Rights Committee included, are seen to have. Instead of joining treaty body sessions, many NGOs prioritize the UPR.

Finally, this chapter has illustrated how the continuously growing role of NGOs within the UN human rights framework—particularly from the 1990s onward—has been enabled by the subtle, ongoing maneuvering of the Guardians of Vision within the UN human rights apparatus's opaque transparency. This maneuvering has significantly expanded and strengthened NGOs' input, despite the lack of a clear Covenant-based mandate for this role.

Today, NGOs' significance in international human rights work is increasingly recognized by the UN and its treaty bodies. NGO staff form an integral part of the community of practice of the Guardians of Vision, and NGO experience is increasingly common for UN staff and Committee members. As the OHCHR has concluded, the UN treaty body framework would not be operational without NGOs' continued input. Simultaneously, the finding that treaty body proceedings may rank low in NGOs' lobbying priorities challenges the idea that the future will be marked by continually greater NGO participation for UN treaty. Rather, the future remains uncertain, with possibilities of "movement in the other direction" as NGOs' organizational preferences change.

CHAPTER 8

Movement in the Rights Direction

"I would like to welcome the excellent delegation to the session, and thank you for the diligence with which you have answered our questions. However, some issues remain, and I would like to start engaging with them by posing questions on Issues 4 and 5." The member continued his intervention with the familiar litany of specific legislative changes, action plans, policies, and their shortcomings in realizing Covenant provisions. The "international" was again convened at the Palais Wilson, in full swing, to address global wrongs and improve the world with increased realization of the ICCPR.

In the past weeks, a steady stream of state delegations had continued to arrive at and depart from the Palais Wilson, taking turns at the podium to share their views regarding how their governments had implemented Covenant provisions. NGO delegates had followed suit, generating a sustained flow of hundreds of people traveling back and forth between Geneva and their places of origin. The interventions of state delegations, embedded in a fluent tale of societal improvement, became enmeshed in a steady narrative of progress. The details of individual interventions began to vanish, becoming both too specific and, ironically, general, echoing what one UN insider noted: "It's always the same groups addressed: women, girls, minorities, Indigenous peoples."

Details also started to blur in the ethnographer's observations. The Committee's sessions felt increasingly indistinguishable from one another. The ethnographer realized she could carry on a meaningful lunchtime conversation about an earlier Committee session without remembering which state was under review. As her fieldwork trips multiplied, travel to Geneva started to lose its distinctiveness, and the once-special commute through Geneva airport and Cornavin railway station became routine and uniform. The scenery, both of the city and the UN, which once felt exotic and particular, began to appear commonplace and mundane.

Things that previously seemed surprising became familiar—the once seemingly inaccessible ceremony that accompanied the Human Rights Committee's sessions; the jargon and documentary aesthetics; the face of the Geneva-based NGO delegate who remained at the Palais Wilson week after week while every other NGO representative around him changed, and the lady in the Palais Wilson cafeteria who—to the ethnographer's amazement—still remembered her months after her previous visit. The ethnographer's gaze shifted from details and the specific toward the session's underlying dynamics: the nonstop movement of documents, people, and expertise, as well as the meanings this movement acquired in our current world order.

Furthermore, she was increasingly struck by the elements that did not move or change, but remained constant: the small group of Guardians of Vision who stayed put—either geographically in Geneva or as integral participants in human rights monitoring cycles with international or local affiliations—if not permanently, at least for longer than others. Other constants included the unchanging nature of the ceremony, regardless of the participants' origins, the standardization of documentation, and, of course, the unvarying physical venues in which the Committee carries out its work.

What consequences do UN treaty body proceedings have? What follows from these elaborate reporting cycles, with all the documents and personal lobbying that accompany them? In existing scholarship, answers to these questions are often sought outside the monitoring mechanisms: scholars trace impact by examining how Concluding Observations surface in parliamentary debates, action plans, civil-society lobbying, court cases, and legislative initiatives.[1]

While such efforts are illuminating in many ways, they remain fraught with uncertainty, as Chapter 5 showed in its analysis of Finland's seven documentary cycles. Scholars acknowledge that chains of causality are long and complex, and thus establishing definitive links between specific documents and distinct outcomes is difficult.[2] In cases of legislative changes, their sources are manifold, and if UN treaty body Concluding Observations or Views on individual communications play a role, that influence is typically embedded in a broader matrix of inputs—such as domestic pressure, political debate, and other international obligations, including decisions by the European Court of Human Rights.

In this final chapter, I offer an answer to the question of impact from the viewpoint of movement by considering both the elements that move nonstop as a consequence of the Committee's operations and those that remain constant. This approach makes a novel contribution to the ongoing debate, as existing scholarship has paid limited attention to the consequences of the continuous circulation of documents, people, and expertise generated by the operations of UN human rights treaty bodies and similar institutions.

Moreover, virtually no attention has been paid to the elements that remain constant—both the people involved in the work and its physical localities as well as material forms, including document aesthetics. When noted at all, movement has been cast as an insignificant side effect—or even an impediment—to the *real* work that such bodies should be doing.[3] My analysis suggests a different approach: that sustaining movement—which is accompanied by the elements that remain static—*is* the work of the Human Rights Committee and the other treaty bodies. In this final chapter I draw on ethnographic material to elaborate this argument, as well as to discuss its conclusions.

Movement as Life

Close observation suggests that members of the Guardians of Vision community of practice are fully aware of the difficulties of achieving change with Concluding Observations. In discussions, many emphasize the complementary nature of different monitoring mechanisms, including the review of state reports, individual communications, the UPR, and different regional and local courts. Committee insiders emphasize the need for patient, long-view approaches, reflected in the frequent use of movement metaphors.

When members describe human rights work, as this book has also shared in different chapters, they may talk of "movement" as being "slow but still happening." During the Constructive Dialogues, when asking states about progress toward Covenant obligations, they may request elaboration on legislative and other "steps" taken to realize specific rights, or commend states on the steps already taken. In addition, steps serve as a metaphor for the complex dynamics of human rights improvement: that things can move "a few steps forward, a few steps backward."

Sir Nigel's concluding remarks during Ukraine's seventh Constructive Dialogue in July 2013 illustrate these tendencies. He noted: "There have clearly been *a lot of moves* in protecting the rights of individuals. If there are rights problems of impunity, certainly a lot of measures have been put in place to prevent such abuses. Still, there is always room for non-preventive approaches. One hopes that the *moves* that were urged by the Committee already last time will be a fait accompli by the next time. Advocacy for homosexuality is likely to see the light of day. Certainly, it would be politically *a step back* if it did not receive international [recognition]."[4]

The metaphor "to keep the ball rolling" is another example. Ironically, this metaphor is moreover a critique of UN treaty bodies: a member of the Finnish Parliament who joined Finland's Constructive Dialogue in July 2013 criticized the Committee for being out of sync with the temporality of everyday politics, characterizing its work in a follow-up interview as "bouncing the same old tired ball." Another movement metaphor—used to describe both the Committee's work and human rights work more generally—was shared by an experienced Finnish state delegate who, in the opening remarks for Finland's Constructive Dialogue in July 2013, described human rights work as "forming an upward spiral that is all the time moving forward, making the realization of rights better and better."[5]

Another time, a Finnish civil servant described the Committee as "operating like a steady train that keeps on moving forward with diligent consideration and no sudden moves." In discussions, interlocutors paired movement with the outcomes of human rights work, with one Committee member summarizing: "I suppose that in the human rights context one could describe success as change—however, not just any change, but change in a certain direction; an improvement."[6] Movement metaphors emerge also from writings. In their obituary of Sir Nigel, Roberts and Crewe note how he "had no illusions about the snail's pace of achieving compliance with international law standards: he would talk about "the slow, nagging effect of my work." Carraro quotes in her study an interviewee summarizing how "you cannot come and talk of promoting human rights for women in a country where a woman still doesn't have an ID, so you have to come *step by step, movement by movement*."[7]

This emphasis on movement relates to the underlying operational logic of treaty bodies as compared to courts. One overarching goal of court proceedings is their singularity: by the ideals of *deterrence* and *rehabilitation*, the goal—even if not often realized—is for a wrongdoer to appear before a court only once, face the consequences of their misdeeds, and undergo personal improvement, with the outcome that the encounter is never repeated.[8]

The purpose of treaty body proceedings is the exact opposite: to create a lasting relationship of progressive rights realization, embodied in a sustained dialogue between states and the Committee, representing universal humanity.[9] This relationship derives its raison d'être from an underlying sentiment associated with the Committee's operations: the idea that all the human rights in the

Covenant will realistically never be fully realized. States will continue to lag in meeting their obligations, and the world will continually change, prompting new interpretations of what the ICCPR's provisions mean. Thus, rather than generating action that begins and ends at a particular moment in time, the movement sustained by the Human Rights Committee and the other UN treaty bodies is envisaged as nonstop, never reaching completion or an endpoint.

The idea that continuing movement comprises the raison d'être of UN treaty bodies is communicated directly by a graph of the UN OHCHR, which shows how human rights reporting creates an ongoing cycle. The graph depicts six phases that follow one another to form a seamless, never-ending circle in which the last step of the previous cycle immediately connects to the first step of the next.[10] Each step derives importance and validation from its link to the preceding and following ones, which together create movement that generates its own legitimation. The world may move *in the rights direction* with sustained human rights work, but it will never reach a point where no further improvement is needed, making further movement around human rights redundant. Thus, in order to remain in existence—alive—human rights action must remain infinitely in motion.

The minute details that characterize the Human Rights Committee's operations help sustain ongoing movement. The example of Finland in Chapter 6 illustrates how government ministries dedicate personnel specifically to attending to the state's Covenant-bound obligations. This dedicated staff contributes to intensifying movement by, for example, informing civil society organizations of upcoming hearings and funding civil society delegates' participation in the Committee's sessions. Additionally, such centrally positioned actors as the CCPR Center, the Geneva-based facilitating NGO discussed in Chapter 7, support ongoing movement by mobilizing civil-society participation globally, thereby generating additional momentum for the Committee's work.

To develop this analytical line of thought further, Ingold's observations are helpful. As he notes, "Wherever there is life there is movement."[11] Ingold adds that this insight prompts a decisive analytical shift "to replace the end-directed or teleonomic conception of the life-process with a recognition of life's capacity continually to overtake the destinations that are thrown up in its course." He continues, "It is of the essence of life that it does not begin here or end there, or connect a point of origin with a final destination, but rather that it keeps on going, finding a way through the myriad of things that form, persist and break up in its currents."[12]

Applied to the Committee's operations, this perspective cast them as constituting "a wayfarer [that remains] continually on the move." More strictly, the wayfarer "is his movement . . . [and] has no final destination, for wherever he is, and so long as life goes on, there is somewhere further he can go."[13] Approaching human rights action as ongoing movement captures the progressive forward-looking ethos of much human rights scholarship that sees the future as an improved version of today to be attained with increased human rights consciousness.[14]

Furthermore, it offers a novel lens for reflecting on what constitutes success or failure in the Committee's operations: as long as there is movement in the desired direction, for the actors themselves human rights work can be framed as being successful. From this perspective, the inability to realize certain rights today appears as a temporary setback, to be remedied by sustained movement toward future improvement—and failure, by contrast, would be if the movement stopped all together.

Movement Sustained by Hope

This analysis leaves open a pivotal question: What motivates participants to continue joining the ongoing movement that the Human Rights Committee's sessions sustain? This study suggests that the uncertain consequences of the Committee's cycles are well known to many human rights actors and largely anticipated in advance. These sentiments were illustrated by Sámi activists Susan and Jonas, featured in Chapter 6. When we discussed their motivations for and expectations of the proceedings, it quickly became clear what meaning they attached to them and what outcomes they expected: *nothing*. Plain and simple. Both Susan and Jonas said they knew with absolute certainty what Finland would say in response to Sámi issues, and that it would do absolutely nothing regarding the issues that the Committee raised in the Constructive Dialogue or the Concluding Observations.[15]

Jonas expressed doubt about the treaty body system as a whole, noting that it suffers from a lack of credibility. He contrasted the treaty body framework with the UPR and mentioned that for the Sámi, that is the prime focus of activism, resonating with the views of many other Finnish NGOs discussed in Chapter 7. He characterized the UPR as generating real engagement, zeal, enthusiasm, and action, whereas the Committee felt quite different, he summarized. Similar sentiments surfaced in numerous discussions during research for this book.

Why, then, if Susan and Jonas expected disappointing—or rather, *no*—outcomes, did they continue participating in the Committee's sessions? Jonas's response combined skepticism with a sense of hope: perhaps something might happen in the end anyway, even though he considered it unlikely. Our discussion clarified how the Committee, and treaty bodies more generally, connect in the long chain of activism in which both Susan and Jonas are engaged. Perhaps it was possible that, at some point, all this orchestrated activism would result in tangible changes, even if none followed individual instances of lobbying.

This exchange illustrates how human rights work is sustained by both hope and belief that, as long as there is movement—in the rights direction—the world will become a better place. Taken together, these notions align with the widely discussed view that human rights are ultimately articles of faith—a secular religion grounded in belief.[16] Hope and belief have profound implications for temporality: movement today remains meaningful only as long as it is sustained by hope and belief in future improvements.[17]

Hope becomes thus cast as a "cultural accelerator," to use Urban's terminology,[18] providing momentum for sustained movement in human rights work. In maintaining this hope, different moments of engagement connect: disappointment at treaty body hearings may be compensated by small victories at the national level, offering renewed motivation to join future Committee sessions. Collective experiences of commitment likewise matter: when a topic has strong civil society support, this can "speed up the issue,"[19] strengthening individual hope in continued change. By contrast, recurring disappointment can lead to disengagement, cynicism, and loss of belief.[20]

The significance of hope and belief as crucial cultural accelerators is illustrated in instances where the Committee "has a dialogue with itself." This occurred in July 2013 regarding Belize's nonexistent state report.[21] Sir Nigel opened the session by noting: "We're going to have a hearing on Belize in the absence of a report. . . . Essentially, the role of the Committee is to review states' periodic reports. Because for a number of countries there were no reports at all, the Committee adopted a rule of procedure whereby it is permitted to consider a situation in the absence of a report."

It was an irregular session in that the seats customarily occupied by state representatives in the Palais Wilson's main conference room were empty. In all other respects, the stage was fully set for a Constructive Dialogue: members were sitting in their assigned places and ready for action, the interpreters were at their glass booths, members of the UN Secretariat were there, as were UN Conference service representatives and a number of NGO staff, interns, and other observers. Press secretaries were ready to record the events, and the webcam operated by the CCPR Center was prepared to start broadcasting the event to the world. Only the lead character in the scene—the state—remained conspicuous by its absence.

What happened at this moment when there was, in fact, no dialogue at all—no human face on which to place blame for concrete human rights violations or to pin hope for change? Instead, there was only a soundscape of monologues as various Committee members shared their frustrations over the absence of Belize's delegation. What sense can it possibly make to have a *dialogue with oneself*? Sir Nigel explained the reasons for the session, invoking ideas of movement and hope: "[Processing reports in the absence of a state party,] it is hoped, will lead to the production of a report. In fact, as often as not, it does. But sometimes it doesn't. And then the Committee has to deal with whether or not the state sends a response to the List of Issues and/or a delegation. As often as not, we get both. But this time we have the responses but not the delegation, which is why we're going to be having the Constructive Dialogue with ourselves."

Sir Nigel thus summarized how the Guardians of Vision had maneuvered—once again creatively interpreting the Committee's Rules of Procedure[22]—to introduce this new procedure in the hope it would improve the Committee's ability to monitor and secure the ICCPR's realization. As a result, the Committee initiated movement on its own in a session where, instead of dialogue with the state party, members offered monologues. This was prompted by the hope that the session would motivate the state party to join in, transforming one-sided movement into a two-sided dialogue. In effect, the session was an attempt by the Committee to bring the Constructive Dialogue to life by unilaterally jump-starting it for a state whose monitoring cycle remained inactive—"dead"—due to a lack of participation. The Committee has since incorporated this practice into its operations and routinely conducts reviews in the absence of states parties.

Movement That Is Just Right

At the same time, movement accompanying the Committee's sessions cannot occur at just any rate. Rather, just as movement accompanying the Human

Rights Committee's sessions needs to occur *in the rights direction*, it needs to occur *at the right pace* to keep the sessions meaningful, legitimate, and impactful. Movement that is either too slow or too fast is detrimental to the Committee's operations, compromising hope for and belief in future improvement.

The Committee's operations are most significantly slowed by the backlogs that it faces, a recurring topic among Committee insiders, with a familiar cause that has been discussed throughout this book: a lack of resources. Today, the Committee's backlog primarily concerns individual communications, driven by the high number of submissions it receives when compared to the other treaty bodies—reflecting its authoritative status—even though the number remains only a fraction of the more than fifty thousand annual submissions to the European Court of Human Rights.[23] By 2013, the Committee's backlog was estimated at around 160 communications, rising to over 700 by 2018, and surpassing 1,000 by 2022.[24] The result has been prolonged processing times, averaging between three years and nearly five. Committee members are understandably concerned about the unreasonable wait for complainants and how processing outdated information undermines the monitoring mechanisms' overall relevance.

In a public discussion on the topic, one member stated, "If a state has to wait two or three years for a report to be processed, it is not such a big problem. However, regarding individual cases, which already take years and years, we are becoming really irrelevant. . . . We know from regional courts that once you have a certain backlog, it becomes impossible to catch up." Another echoed these sentiments, stating, "If we do not do something to shorten time, we will lose credibility," adding, "It seems that we are sitting on a crisis."

These statements underscore the threat that members perceive delayed or halted movement to pose to the Committee's relevance, credibility, and legitimacy: if movement becomes too slow, the Committee's operations lose value as a redress mechanism for applicants. The threat of irrelevance the Committee faces is similar to that of many other monitoring bodies. Nevertheless, the Committee's nature as an authoritative, quasi-legal expert body may render it particularly vulnerable to such delays, as Chapter 4 discussed, which may bolster the belief that its impact is limited.

Movement that is excessively rapid likewise poses a threat to the Committee's continued operations. The "burned-out bureaucrat" in Chapter 6—the Finnish civil servant who had participated in different international hearings for more than two decades—clearly articulated the consequences of an accelerated pace. Even before I posed my question, she blurted out: "I remember nothing at all of this entire hearing!" referring to Finland's Constructive Dialogue that had taken place some eighteen months prior. During her tenure, Finland's reporting obligations, like those of most other states, had proliferated exponentially so that Finland now submits reports to a dozen different international committees at the UN and Council of Europe.

Although not all these reporting obligations entail in-person hearings like those related to principal UN human rights treaties, for individual civil servants handling these responsibilities the end result is evident: a massive amount of work and a series of distinct, formally defined tasks generating vast quantities of movement. As the "burned-out bureaucrat" stated, "reporting fluff" had increased, embodied by the follow-up phase discussed with regard to Finland's Sixth Concluding Observations. This "fluff" expanded civil servant responsibilities and accelerated the rhythm of documentary preparation and movement.

The feeling of "nothingness" she described captures the danger that, as volume and movement continually increase—making human rights work in Latour's terms "too mobile,"[25] and in Eriksen's terms, "overheated"[26]—monitoring generates reporting fatigue.[27] This alienates the individuals who carry out practical labor, rendering belief in human rights "too unstable."[28] This accelerated pace distances such work from commitment to human rights values, hope, and belief, reducing reporting into an internally hollow "bullshit job."[29] If such sentiments continue to spread, the result will be a paradoxical sense of failure: despite movement continuing, its content will become increasingly meaningless to those sustaining it, making human rights work "just like any other job."[30]

In many ways, this paradox results from the tremendous "human rights triumph"[31] of the post–World War II era, and particularly the post–Cold War period: human rights have been increasingly mainstreamed into bureaucratic and legal decision-making processes such as treaty body documentary cycles. In the process, they have lost their distinctiveness, becoming an obligation for civil servants instead of a passion. Creating endless formalized practices—rather than connecting people to human rights ideology, thus strengthening commitment—can alienate people. At its most extreme, it reduces participants to mechanical actors who merely go through the motions, feeling and—to quote the "burned-out bureaucrat"—remembering "nothing at all" after the fact.

The Power of Legal Technicalities and Aesthetics

The last element I will explore that sheds light on the role of both movement and immobility in the Committee's operations is legal aesthetics: just as movement must occur *in the right direction* and *at the right pace*, it needs to be accompanied by the right formats in order to contribute to movement in the rights direction. Distinct legal aesthetics form—just as the centrality of the state as an institution—in Latour's terms an "immutable mobile," a constant, in the Committee's operations, forming distinct "pathways" for related documentary flows. The importance of legal aesthetics in document drafting—as well as the knowledge practices needed to meet these aesthetics—was illustrated in my discussion with Maria, the UN staff member tasked with drafting the Committee's Concluding Observations on Finland's sixth state report.

I was able to track Maria down in the Palais Wilson cafeteria to ask how she was doing with the document. She said she was busy as she had to complete this List of Issues for another state in the next few minutes. She sat down for a quick lunch. I joined her and watched her eat her quiche and salad at a brisk pace. Despite her evident rush, she seemed calm and composed. The job may be stressful on occasion, but, her demeanor suggested, she need not be. I asked if she had a lot of work in her position. She agreed, but said that she knew to expect this: she had previously worked with Individual Communications for a year and, before that, at a local OHCHR office for two years. She is thus well versed in the work despite being new to her current position.

We discussed Finland's Concluding Observations. I told her that the Finnish media had picked them up, with the result that they became one of the most-read news stories the previous night—after midnight, I added, but still. She seemed genuinely impressed. I explained that, curiously, the media focused almost exclusively on gender inequality and violence against women, which dominated headlines. She seemed surprised, and we both noted that this was by no means the only issue in the report, nor, in our view, the most important. Maria wondered whether it was even among the three issues the Committee selected for follow-up on, but then said she believed that was the case.

She asks what I considered the most important issue in the Observations, and I mentioned pre-trial detention. She agreed, noting a genuine problem: the Committee expects a person to be brought before a judge within forty-eight hours, whereas in Finland, the maximum is still ninety-six hours. She says that, although drafting the Observations was straightforward in other respects, this part was tricky because she received additional information from the state within the allotted forty-eight-hour window after the hearing clarifying aspects of Finnish law. Maria recounted, "The situation is confusing as there is detention, arrest, and still something else." After consideration, her conclusion remained the same: ninety-six hours is too long. I recall having heard of this issue before and thought it was one of the "staple" matters on which Finland receives regular recommendations.

We moved on to the drafting process for the Concluding Observation and the role of legal aesthetics in it. Maria described the task as relatively straightforward: Committee members only had a few comments about the first version. I asked whether this made her feel she had authored the document, recalling staff remarks that the Secretariat does most of the work while the Committee assumes the glory. To her, however, this was not how things appeared.

"How do you draft documents, concretely?" I asked. She hesitated, searching for the right words. I suggested that the work is not like starting with a blank page and going from paragraph one to the end. She agreed: "That is definitely not the case." By contrast, she continued, the work resembled drafting any other document in UN human rights monitoring: she began with the materials circulated during Finland's review, including the List of Issues and NGO reports.[32] She then copied and pasted things, reworked segments, shifted their order, added a word here, deleted another there.[33] At the end, the text was neither a copy-pasted version of any previous document, nor, she noted, authored from scratch—a workflow that echoes how Finland's state report was compiled, as discussed in Chapter 5.

Maria concluded that the finalized document replicates the logic and structure of case law: it is closely tied to previous documents and serves as merely the last link in these longer chains. At the same time, the new document inherits the legalistic aesthetics of its predecessors. I suggested that this might be an area where the law comes in. She agreed, noting that she had not really thought about it because, as a lawyer, this is "rather self-evident." She finished her quiche and we said goodbye as she rushed back to her duties.

This glimpse into Maria's drafting work illustrates the importance of tangible forms—embedded in distinct legal aesthetics—that accompany the Committee's documents. In the Committee's reporting cycles, these formats function as immutable mobiles that forge the pathways that transform texts from artifacts of "real reality" into tangible contributions in "UN reality." This transformation concerns expectations on how the documents' wording should be structured and how the issues are formatted, thereby conferring on the documents authority and legitimacy.

From Means to Ends: Movement, Cultural Forms, and Agency

Tsing reminds us of the "importance of interaction in defining movement, cultural form, and agency,"[34] while Latour emphasizes that "without something that moves, there is no transportation of information, no accumulation of knowledge, no domination, no power."[35]

These insights help conclude the analysis of the Committee's reporting cycles. I have shown how the elements that move are documents, to an extent the issues addressed in the Constructive Dialogues, and people—and that such movement needs to occur at the right pace and along distinct legal aesthetics to constitute movement in the rights direction. Legal aesthetics, in turn, form constants, in Latour's terms, "immutable mobiles," that shape and constrain the movement accompanying the Committee's operations. Additional immutable mobiles include shared expert practices, educational and geographic backgrounds of the Guardians of Vision, and the Committee's emphasis on state-based rule of law.

What significance do these findings hold globally? One tangible consequence of the incessant movement of documents is a flurry of never-ending activity: at any moment, around the world, hundreds, even thousands of individuals—civil servants, experts, and NGO delegates like Maria, Sam, Jonas, Heather, Susan, and the burned-out bureaucrat—are engaged in drafting and analyzing human rights documents. One empirically observable consequence of the Committee's operations, along with other treaty bodies and similar "lawlike" mechanisms in the UN and other IOs, is the elevation of such documents—and their distinct legal aesthetics—into central reference points for bureaucratic engagement as "standards for a better world."[36]

From this perspective, the legal traditions underlying the Committee's operations become less relevant—namely, that the Committee prioritizes modern state-based rule of law as I have previously argued.[37] Instead, more central becomes how legal technicalities accompanying the Committee's operations have, over the Committee's existence, spread worldwide, subsequently becoming globalized, even universalized. This echoes Riles's observation on what makes the law global: its technical elements, as a consequence of which a lawyer will approach the documents along a "similar set of routinized pathways,"[38] no matter where in the world they work.

This finding raises pivotal questions on the consequences of human rights practices: Is this ongoing movement, paired with immutable mobiles, ultimately emancipatory or restrictive? Scholars have posed this question, often in the language of universality versus cultural relativism/particularity, since the outset of the contemporary human rights movement.[39] Almost without exception, these questions have been directed at the ideological content of human rights: Are they genuinely universal notions found worldwide or cultural imposition originating in Western ideals? By extension, the answer to this question is taken to determine whether human rights are fundamentally emancipatory or restrictive.[40]

The question takes on a different tenor when linked to the movement and immutable mobiles that accompany human rights reporting. In this analytical approach, the core ideological content that human rights documents entail becomes secondary, while the importance of the cultural forms accompanying these documents' movement intensifies. In his analysis of global flows, Appadurai notes that "the globalization of culture is not the same as its homogenization, but globalization involves the use of a variety of instruments of homogenization (armaments, advertising techniques, language hegemonies, and clothing styles) that are absorbed into local political and cultural economies."[41]

This applies beyond a doubt to human rights practices: whatever their ideological origins, since World War II, the movement of documents, artifacts, and expertise from the international human rights centers to localities around the world—in this book catalyzed by the Human Rights Committee's monitoring cycles—has contributed to the global homogenization of bureaucratic and legal practices by universalizing a distinct jargon and legal aesthetics. Simultaneously, this movement has disseminated a set of knowledge practices, exactly as Riles observes of the "international" nature of the law. The outcome has rendered civil society actors, to borrow Englund's phrase, "prisoners of freedom": they must frame their activities according to these legal aesthetics and knowledge practices in order for them to become visible and existent in UN monitoring mechanisms, often also accommodating funders' expectations.[42]

Thus one consequence of the flows the Human Rights Committee's operations generate has been to prioritize distinct legal and bureaucratic competence over other forms of knowledge, while intensifying the agency of individuals fluent in these practices—such as Maria drafting Finland's

Concluding Observations, or Heather lobbying for distinct issues as an NGO delegate in Chapter 7. Rather than irrelevant side effects of human rights protection, these outcomes play a crucial role in constituting what human rights practices are and produce today. These knowledge practices and aesthetics become synonymous with world improvement that human rights practices introduce. In Obregón's words, together with the notion of law embedded in modern states, they come to be seen as "the ultimate product of civilization, making it into a utopian ideal of a transnational organized legal system that would bring progress and peace to the world";[43] they become what movement in the rights direction means in practice.

The idea of a "standard of civilization"—often treated as being contingent on meeting metrics set by human rights reporting obligations and quantified indicators—aligns with Mbembe's account of postcolonial power. He argues that power operates "in its minute details," by means of "principles of assemblage" that generate their own efficacy and spawn institutions, knowledges, norms, and practices.[44] The increasing centrality of legal aesthetics acquires a similar function: it organizes attention and authority, codifies what counts as credible, and thereby naturalizes distinct distributions of power.

Movement, States, and Current World Order

The massive flows of documents inherent to the Human Rights Committee's operations also contribute to another kind of global homogenization. This regards strengthening the state's role as the central reference point in international collaboration and diplomacy, supported by the Committee's view that state-based rule of law is the ideal setting for realizing civil and political rights.

From this perspective, rather than celebrating the diversity of human societies and their varied social and legal orders, UN human rights monitoring has contributed to marginalizing diverse political and legal institutions in favor of the singular model of the state. One can further argue that robust statehood is a direct goal of much human rights action, which sees weak—or even "failed"—states as the key source of rights violations.[45] As the different chapters illustrate, in the Committee's operations, the state is both the mandated point of reference and the institution deemed ideal for guaranteeing the realization of civil and political rights. Beyond Kant and Hobbes, this view resonates with Bentham's claim that rights are "nonsense upon stilts" without a functioning political and legal system—ideally, a state—to back them up.[46] Thus, the movement instigated by the Human Rights Committee's sessions, like the other UN treaty bodies, is cast essentially as a global state-building project.

The Committee's focus on statehood in today's interdependent world has manifold consequences. It ruptures the causal chains between human rights violations and their root causes in the prevailing unequal world order—a legacy of colonialism. In practice, this translates into the Committee frequently identifying violations such as prison overcrowding or shortage of police officers, courts, and schools—symptoms that may stem from resource constraints due to state poverty rooted in historic structural injustices. This outcome is characteristic of human rights practices more generally as Marks notes how "the systemic context of abuses and vulnerabilities is largely removed from view. Despite, or rather, because of, attempts to explain them, human rights violations are made to seem random, accidental or arbitrary."[47]

Resource scarcity may explain why some states refrain from joining the Committee's monitoring cycles. As this book has shown, participation requires personnel with the right competences, ample working time to prepare documentation, coordination between different government offices, and travel to Geneva—all of which demand significant resources that may be unavailable for economically marginalized states. From this viewpoint, active participation in international human rights reporting is possible particularly for prosperous states, casting these practices as elitist. One may even question whether poverty-affected states *should* allocate such resources to documentary practices of uncertain outcomes when hospitals, schools, and basic infrastructure require support. Joining these cycles may be a legal responsibility for ICCPR states parties, but that does not guarantee it is the legitimate choice.

At the Human Rights Committee, discussions of economic viability are remarkably scarce. Whereas some states mention dire financial situations to explain failures to realize Covenant obligations, the Committee does not treat this as a mitigating factor—even when poverty is rooted in the structural inequalities of the colonial era. Discussion of Global South debt and its economic consequences is likewise conspicuous by its absence, reflecting how the Committee ultimately operates within "UN reality," where such issues of "real reality" do not become central. Moyn has underscored how problematic this omission is, arguing that precisely because economic and structural considerations are absent, human rights are "not enough."[48] Alston, in turn, describes how lack of engagement with economic inequality is "a cause of shame on the part of the international human rights movement."[49]

The same gap applies to discussions on human rights violations by multinational corporations whose supply chains rely on legally independent subcontractors, for example, in the textile or electronics sectors. Consumer demand and corporate headquarters may be located in one country—often in the Global North—while subcontractors and laborers are in another—often in the Global South. Subcontractors may impose working conditions and contracts that violate human rights by depriving laborers of an adequate standard of living, under pressure from their contracting companies. Simultaneously, because those contracting companies are located in a different state from the subcontractors, the Committee cannot assign responsibility to the appropriate party; instead, it addresses only the state in which the subcontractors are based.[50]

The Committee's inability to address cross-border chains stems from its Covenant-based mandates, as Chapter 4 discussed. This mandate was set during the drafting of the Covenant between 1948 and 1966, and it is anchored in the post–World War II order that, for the first time, made the state the primary organizing unit, embodied in the UN's organizing principle of formal sovereign equality of states instead of empires.[51] Thus, also the UN treaty body framework and the Committee's mandate reflect an earlier era, when today's global flows of goods and cross-border supply chains were far less prevalent. This historical perspective clarifies the limits of what the Human Rights Committee and the other UN treaty bodies can achieve. A monitoring model premised on the continual movement of people, expertise, and documents—while structured around geographically immobile states—is ill equipped to a world order in which flows of capital and consumer demand routinely transcend national borders.

This world order may, nevertheless, be changing, as suggested by the imposition of high tariffs by President Trump at the outset of his second presidential term, followed in 2026 by broad US disengagement from international organizations, including UN human rights bodies. Whyte argued recently, drawing on her long-term analysis of human rights as the post–World War II "morals of the market" underpinning global neoliberal policies,[52] that Trump's tariffs mark the end of the world order structured around the facilitated flow of capital and goods.[53] For now, we do not know how long-term and pervasive the effects of these actions will be. Yet these developments could profoundly affect the post–World War II foundations of multilateralism, and future research will therefore shed significant new light on them.

As Chapter 1 noted, a sense of perennial crisis has accompanied the UN treaty body framework since the bodies' inception, marked by numerous reform proposals. The future will likely bring further proposals to streamline treaty body operations amid shrinking resources. Simultaneously, one may expect novel suggestions on ways to secure the bodies' funding base, including allowing states to earmark financial contributions.[54] Scarcity of funds may offer states that have long resisted international oversight new opportunities to downplay the treaty bodies' role. Limited resources can reduce the bodies' capacity to examine state reports and prolong processing times for individual communications. Such slowing of pace would compromise the Committee's relevance and legitimacy.

Despite such perils, developments far more dramatic than those seen today would be required to halt the sustained movement, around both the Human Rights Committee and the treaty body framework, and let their momentum die. This book has shown how, despite their fragility, the treaty bodies demonstrate remarkable resilience. This is rooted in the bodies' treaty-based mandates, which make them difficult to dismantle while setting limits to the scope of institutional reform. In this respect, the treaty bodies rest on a notably stronger institutional foundation than the political side of UN human rights monitoring—exemplified by the 2006 restructuring of the former Commission on Human Rights into the Human Rights Council.

Momentum, around both the Human Rights Committee and treaty bodies more generally, is integrally sustained by the Guardians of Vision. Human rights work has ever since the adoption of the UDHR been a combination of paid labor and calling, with many insiders working excessive hours to meet its demands, sometimes without remuneration. While problematic from the standpoint of labor law and organizational culture, this finding helps explain how momentum can remain alive even when resources decline. To summarize, the international human rights framework is facing urgent challenges, and we may be approaching a radical shift in our current world order, accompanied by declining resources and states adverse to international human rights oversight. At the same time we are far from the day when all the movement around UN treaty bodies would cease and the system would die. By contrast, political resistance around human rights—for example, the global backlash against LGBTIQ+ rights—may strengthen advocate commitment, as is visible in the Committee's operations.[55]

Conclusion: Completing the Full Cycle

This chapter brings together the analytical angles of previous chapters and concludes this book's analysis of the Human Rights Committee's operations from the vantage point of movement. It opened by connecting with current scholarship on UN treaty bodies, which remains embedded in a normative framework and often assesses the Committee's and other treaty bodies' operations from the viewpoint of impact and effectiveness, or challenges thereto. This chapter contributes to this scholarship by broadening the scope of consequences beyond a normative framework, highlighting such developments as the growing salience of human rights language in legislation and policymaking in bureaucracies around the world as tangible outcomes.

The chapter then turned to the theme of movement. Building on Ingold's notion of movement as life, the analysis shows how Committee insiders frequently use movement metaphors to describe the Committee's work—and how these metaphors correspond to the UN's graphical depiction of treaty bodies' operations as forming a nonstop cycle. This movement, nevertheless, endures only as long as the Committee, and the UN human rights apparatus as a whole, continues to generate hope, belief, and commitment within the Guardians of Vision community of practice. Only engagement based on these sentiments transforms the cycle from a graph on a UN website into something tangible in "real reality."

This analysis further showcased the profound implications hope and belief have for temporality, arguing how movement today remains meaningful only insofar as it is sustained by hope and belief in future improvements. Furthermore, given the contested nature of tangible outcomes, movement backed by belief *alone* can suffice to cast present action as successful to engaged actors, regardless of tangible consequences—as when Finland overlooks the Committee's Concluding Observations decade after decade in its legislation and policymaking. From this perspective, the final arbiter of success is not time, but hope and belief: as long as there is faith in the changes to come, ongoing movement alone—in the rights direction—suffices to justify continued action *and* to determine whether that movement is deemed successful and impactful.

Using the example of the Committee "having a dialogue with itself," I described instances in which the Committee unilaterally jump-starts movement in the hope of prompting states to join the dialogue. The chapter then showed how, for movement to continually connect to sentiments of hope and belief, it needs to proceed at the right pace—neither so slow that it causes backlogs threatening the Committee's legitimacy and relevance, nor so accelerated that it alienates those doing the work, destabilizing belief.

In the third part, I examined the channels through which movement occurs, highlighting the knowledge practices and legal aesthetics that accompany the documents UN staff prepare for the Committee's operations, denoting these documents in Latour's terms as "immutable mobiles." I then linked this discussion to Tsing's notion of "friction" to show how the specific features of the Committee's documentary flows translate abstract human rights ideals into tangible material realities—enabling certain cultural forms and agency, while marginalizing others. Finally, I noted that, paradoxically, the nonstop movement of documents, people, and expertise solidifies and legitimizes our current world order structured around static states.

Together, these elements form what I call movement in the rights direction. It is a nonstop dynamic that the Guardians of Vision skillfully steer to continually expand the Human Rights Committee's mandate, and thereby the influence of human rights, both within the ice-like, partially opaque UN human rights apparatus and beyond. Guardians maneuver from multifaceted positions: as Committee members and UN Secretariat staff, as state civil servants implementing reporting obligations and acting as intermediaries to facilitate civil society participation, and as NGO delegates. Although everyone rotates in the treaty bodies' operations—members serve for four-year terms before possible re-election, and UN staff change positions every so often—some insiders stay put longer than others, thereby increasing these Guardians' subtle impact on the Committee's operations.

As discussed in Chapter 6, Constructive Dialogue sessions are pivotal in sustaining hope and belief in the Committee's work. Particularly significant are members' expertise and the sense they have prepared appropriately—that they have "done their homework." The Dialogues provide a human interface to cycles that would otherwise constitute essentially an elaborate mailing system. Personal participation elicits warmth and generates affective sparks that thaw the icy surface of the UN human rights apparatus, bringing the monitoring mechanism to life and providing additional momentum to its cycles. Thus the "cultural accelerator" for the Human Rights Committee's operations and other UN treaty bodies emerges from a combination of hope and belief, animated by the human encounters of the hearings.

At the surface level, movement in the rights direction occurs at the Committee's sessions via the submission of state reports and their processing in the public Constructive Dialogues. Yet it likewise occurs "in the shadows," as

Chapter 7 detailed in its analysis of civil society participation, hinging on the direct personal relations and indirect connections that unite members of the Guardians of Vision community of practice across the categories of expert member, UN staff, state delegate, and NGO representative.

This movement has a paradoxical relationship with the state: in the UN treaty body framework, the state is cast as the primary violator of human rights—since only states are parties to the ICCPR and other UN human rights treaties. In response, much human rights advocacy seeks to curb the state's role. This analysis shows, unexpectedly, how the Committee's reporting cycles increase the state's salience as the central political and legal reference point globally. The story of the Human Rights Committee and the movement accompanying its operations is thus, to a large extent, the story of the state, both historically and today.

This outcome appears natural when connecting it to the civilizing mission of international law, which sees humanity as progressing from "savage" anarchy and lawlessness to modern states with established rule of law. This viewpoint shows how the Committee's operations do not encourage reflections on alternative societal models, but instead replicate familiar hierarchies from much human rights and international law scholarship that privilege modern states over other governance arrangements such as municipalities, chieftainships, provinces, and clans.

Chapter 4 showed that the Committee has an unexpectedly complex relationship to law: undoubtedly the Committee forms a legalistic professional space that confers high status as the UN's most authoritative and lawlike human rights monitoring mechanism. Concurrently, in practice the law is something that members both seek and set aside when rights protection can be more effectively realized by other means. This regards both the threat of "excessive legality" governing the Committee's operations, as well as the members' ambivalence toward transparency, a core component of the rule of law, when they construe that the realization of the rights enlisted in the ICCPR could be better advanced by other means. Thus, although the Committee remains dedicated to a world order organized around human rights and law, in the Committee's own operations law ultimately functions as a means rather than an end—the ultimate goal being the continually greater realization of human rights.

Finally, this chapter shows that—despite uncertain impact given complex chains of causality—the Committee's operations yield undisputed consequences. One is the specificity of channels—the pathways—by which the

Committee's monitoring cycles occur. These pathways transform abstract human rights ideals into tangible materialities that both enable and constrain different viewpoints and actors. Over recent decades, the Committee's cycles have rendered these materialities, including document aesthetics and distinct knowledge practices, increasingly universalized.

This suggests that realizing human rights entails distinct homogenizing elements. Thus—much like the focus on the state—rather than preserving ever greater space for human diversity, from this perspective movement in the rights direction fundamentally engenders global sameness. This outcome undermines the idea of human rights as tools for safeguarding human diversity, casting homogenization as an endlessly unfinished project, since the world is never ready and all human rights will never be fully realized.

Over the past few years, the UN human rights framework, and multilateralism more generally, have faced profound challenges, from direct political attacks as well as state withdrawals from international organizations and agreements to dramatic funding cuts. These pressures have compromised the effective functioning of treaty bodies, which have consistently pursued the realization of their mandates with insufficient resources. The current challenges for the Human Rights Committee and the treaty bodies raise questions of their continued relevance and legitimacy. These questions are sharpened by the fact that the treaty body framework was designed for a different, state-centric post–World War II order, and is thus ill equipped to address today's realities of cross-border supply chains and the resulting rights violations that transcend state borders.

This book nevertheless argues that the Human Rights Committee's operations and the treaty body framework more generally entail numerous features that make them resilient to such external challenges. At the core are their treaty-based mandates, which would require dramatic events for these bodies to be dismantled. Additionally, as this book has shown, resilience is generated by the sustained hope and belief in a better world held by the Guardians of Vision, a belief that inspires continued movement around the bodies.

My arguments draw on a broad array of data and materials that have been grounded in ethnography. My participant observation has been prolonged and layered, opening up avenues for novel insights also for documentary analysis. Crucially, this approach has resulted in a holistic analytical stance: in the book's different chapters the Committee is viewed as a community of practice rather than its eighteen expert members. This comprehensive approach has enabled situating the Committee within broader UN bureaucracies and tracing interactions between localized action occurring in Geneva and related activity around the world.

A holistic perspective has enabled connecting minute details of the Committee's operations to such underlying themes as state challenges to the Committee's legitimacy, as well as how the community of practice as a whole—including active collaboration from Guardians working as state civil servants—combats these challenges. My aim has been to bring the Committee's operations—and their participants—to life, capturing their most crucial component. For all the elaborate proceedings and formal documents, the Human Rights Committee, like the UN treaty bodies more generally, ultimately consists of the people who participate in them; without them we would be left with an automated mailing center, devoid of affect, hope, and belief. Ultimately, with all its challenges and obstacles, the *movement in the rights direction* continues as long as it is sustained by people who deem it worthwhile.

NOTES

Chapter 1

1. On the Committee's operations, see K. Young (2002), *The Law and Process of the UN Human Rights Committee* (Leiden: Brill); Y. Tyagi (2011), *The UN Human Rights Committee: Practice and Procedure* (Cambridge: Cambridge University Press); P. M. Taylor (2020), *A Commentary on the International Covenant on Civil and Political Rights: The UN Human Rights Committee's Monitoring of ICCPR Rights* (Cambridge: Cambridge University Press).

2. UN OHCHR (2012), *The United Nations Human Rights Treaty System: Fact Sheet No. 30/ Rev. 1.*

3. For example, Martin Scheinin concludes, "My view that [the Human Rights Committee] is the closest we now have, to a future World Court of Human Rights, has served as a major intellectual beacon for the evolution of my project [to create a template for a World Court]." M. Scheinin (2009), "Towards a World Court of Human Rights," Agenda for Human Rights, https://enlazandoalternativas.org/IMG/pdf/hrCourt_scheinin0609.pdf.

4. J. Connors (2000), "An Analysis and Evaluation of the System of State Reporting," in *The UN Human Rights System in the 21st Century*, ed. A. F. Bayefsky (The Hague: Kluwer Law International), 4–21.

5. J. Crawford (2000), "The UN Human Rights Treaty System: A System in Crisis?," in *The Future of UN Human Rights Treaty Monitoring*, ed. P. Alston and J. Crawford (Cambridge: Cambridge University Press), 1–13; Bayefsky (2000), *The UN Human Rights System in the 21st Century*. On UN human rights treaty bodies and the future of the UN human rights regulatory framework, see S. Egan (2011), *The UN Human Rights Treaty System: Law and Procedure* (New York: Bloomsbury Professional); H. Keller and G. Ulfstein, eds. (2012), *UN Human Rights Treaty Bodies: Law and Legitimacy* (Cambridge: Cambridge University Press).

6. "Predictable Review Cycle," UN OHCHR, https://www.ohchr.org/en/treaty-bodies/ccpr/predictable-review-cycle.

7. Article 36 of the ICCPR states: "The Secretary-General of the United Nations shall provide the necessary staff and facilities for the effective performance of the functions of the Committee under the present Covenant." Article 39, paragraph 2 clarifies that "The Committee shall establish its own rules of procedure, but these rules shall provide, inter alia, that (a) Twelve members shall constitute a quorum; (b) Decisions of the Committee shall be made by a majority vote of the members present."

8. See, for example, A. Neier (2013), *The International Human Rights Movement: A History* (Princeton, NJ: Princeton University Press); D. Kennedy (2002b), "International Human Rights Movement: Part of the Problem?," *Harvard Human Rights Journal* 15, 101–126; H. J. Steiner and P. Alston (2002), *International Human Rights in Context: Law, Politics, Morals* (Oxford: Oxford

University Press); A. W. B. Simpson (2001), *Human Rights and the End of Empire: Britain and the Genesis of the European Convention* (Oxford: Oxford University Press); K. Sellars (2002), *The Rise and Rise of Human Rights* (Phoenix Mill, UK: Sutton); M. Mutua (2002), *Human Rights: A Political and Cultural Critique* (Philadelphia: University of Pennsylvania Press).

9. A. Appadurai (1996), *Modernity at Large: Cultural Dimension of Globalization* (Minneapolis: University of Minnesota Press); A. Ong and S. J. Collier, eds. (2007), *Global Assemblages: Technology, Politics, and Ethics as Anthropological Problems* (Hoboken, NJ: Blackwell).

10. A. Tsing (2005), *Friction: An Ethnography of Global Connection* (Princeton, NJ: Princeton University Press).

11. T. Ingold (2011), *Being Alive: Essays on Movement, Knowledge and Description* (London: Routledge).

12. T. H. Eriksen (2016), *Overheating: An Anthropology of Accelerated Change* (New York: Pluto Press).

13. B. Latour (1987), *Science in Action: How to Follow Scientists and Engineers Through Society* (Cambridge, MA: Harvard University Press); B. Latour (1999), *Pandora's Hope: Essays on the Reality of Science Studies* (Cambridge: Cambridge University Press).

14. Tsing (2005), 6.

15. G. W. Bush, "Address to a Joint Session of Congress and the American People" (September 20, 2001), White House, https://georgewbush-whitehouse.archives.gov/news/releases/2001/09/20010920-8.html. President Trump has echoed President Bush's language use, for example, by calling distinct individuals "bad people." For summary, see "A Look into Trump's Recent Rhetoric Focusing on Revenge and Threats," NPR, 21 October 2024, https://www.npr.org/transcripts/1211597189.

16. See, for example, D. M. Crane (2020), "The Wrong Side of History: The United States and the International Criminal Court," *Jurist*, 13 June 2020, https://www.jurist.org/commentary/2020/06/david-crane-wrong-history-icc/.

17. M. Saez (2019), "In the Right Direction: Family Diversity in the Inter-American System of Human Rights," *North Carolina Journal of International Law* 44(2), 317–352.

18. United Nations Archives, SOA 317/1/01 D, 1955, italics added. Eckel notes how in the 1950s and the early 1960s, "None of the proposals brought forward at the United Nations, such as an international court, a high commissioner, or a system of individual petitions, was adopted during this period." J. Eckel (2013), "The International League for the Rights of Man, Amnesty International, and the Changing Fate of Human Rights Activism from the 1940s through the 1970s," *Humanity: An International Journal of Human Rights, Humanitarianism, and Development* 4(2), 183–214, quotation on 188.

19. M. Halme-Tuomisaari and P. Slotte (2015), "Revisiting the History of Human Rights: Introduction," in *Revisiting the Origins of Human Rights*, ed. P. Slotte and M. Halme-Tuomisaari (Cambridge: Cambridge University Press), 1–36.

20. On translation, see S. Gal (2015), "Politics of Translation," *Annual Review of Anthropology* 44, 225–240; E. Babül (2017), *Bureaucratic Intimacies: Translating Human Rights in Turkey* (Stanford, CA: Stanford University Press); T. Kelly (2011), *This Side of Silence: Human Rights, Torture, and the Recognition of Cruelty* (Philadelphia: University of Pennsylvania Press); A. Ballestro (2014), "What Is in a Percentage? Calculations as the Poetic Translation of Human Rights," in *Indiana Journal of Global Legal Studies* 24(1), 27–53; H. Englund (2006), *Prisoners of Freedom: Human Rights and the African Poor* (Berkeley: University of California Press); S. Merry (2006), *Human Rights and Gender Violence: Translating International Law into Local Justice* (Chicago:

University of Chicago Press); G. Sarfaty (2012), *Values in Translation: Human Rights and the Culture of the World Bank* (Stanford, CA: Stanford University Press); N. Mathur (2012), *Paper Tiger: Law, Bureaucracy and the Developmental State* (Cambridge: Cambridge University Press).

21. T. Hobbes (1651/1996), *Leviathan*, ed. R. Tuck (Cambridge: Cambridge University Press); I. Kant (1795/1991), "Perpetual Peace: A Philosophical Sketch," in *Kant: Political Writings*, ed. H. S. Reiss (Cambridge: Cambridge University Press), 93–115.

22. L. Obregón (2012), "The Civilized and the Uncivilized," in *The Oxford Handbook of the History of International Law*, ed. B. Fassbender and A. Peters (Oxford: Oxford University Press), 917–940. See also R. Parfitt (2019), *The Process of International Legal Reproduction: Inequality, Historiography, Resistance* (Cambridge: Cambridge University Press); D. P. Fidler (2001), "Return of the Standard of Civilization: The International Human Rights Law in Practice," *Chicago Journal of International Law* 2, 137–157; A. Anghie (2005), *Imperialism, Sovereignty, and the Making of International Law* (Cambridge: Cambridge University Press).

23. For an introduction to the Committee, see "Human Rights Committee," UN OHCHR, https://www.ohchr.org/en/treaty-bodies/ccpr.

24. See UN Human Rights Committee (2021), *Rules of Procedure*, Chapter XI, par. 60–62.

25. See UN OHCHR (2021), *Reporting Under the International Covenant on Civil and Political Rights: Training Guide*, https://www.ohchr.org/en/publications/training-and-education-publications/reporting-under-international-covenant-civil-and.

26. As Chapter 4 discusses, Constructive Dialogue, despite being utilized consistently in the Committee's operations, has no clear-cut definition and is mentioned only in passing in Rule 73 of the Committee's Rules of Procedure. UN Human Rights Committee (2021), *Rules of Procedure*; W. Kälin (2012), "Examination of State Reports," in Keller and Ulfstein, 16–72; M. O'Flaherty and P. Tsai (2011), "Periodic Reporting: The Backbone of the UN Treaty Body Review Procedures," in *New Challenges for the UN Human Rights Machinery: What Future for the UN Treaty Body System and the Human Rights Council Procedures?*, ed. M. C. Bassiouni and W. A. Schabas (Portland, OR: Intersentia), 37–56.

27. See "Sessions for CCPR—International Covenant on Civil and Political Rights," UN Treaty Body Database, https://tbinternet.ohchr.org/_layouts/15/TreatyBodyExternal/SessionsList.aspx?Treaty=CCPR.

28. See UN Human Rights Committee, Rules of Procedure and Working Methods, CCPR/C/3/Rev. 11, https://www.ohchr.org/en/treaty-bodies/ccpr/rules-procedure-and-working-methods. The Committee operates under unanimity; see Rules 69 and 74.

29. M. O'Flaherty (2006), "The Concluding Observations of United Nations Human Rights Treaty Bodies," *Human Rights Law Review* 6(1), 27–52.

30. The Council was founded in 2006 to replace the UN Human Rights Commission, a body that long faced charges of promoting state politics in place of human rights concerns. See E. Tistounet (2020), *The UN Human Rights Council: A Practical Anatomy* (Cheltenham, UK: Edward Elgar); H. Charlesworth and E. Larking, eds. (2014), *Human Rights and the Universal Periodic Review: Rituals and Ritualism* (Cambridge: Cambridge University Press).

31. ICCPR, Article 40, https://www.ohchr.org/en/instruments-mechanisms/instruments/international-covenant-civil-and-political-rights.

32. On ratification of the ICCPR's first optional protocol, see "Status of Ratification Interactive Dashboard," UN OHCHR, https://indicators.ohchr.org.

33. Currently, eight UN human rights treaty bodies receive and consider individual petitions under certain conditions, most commonly via stipulations in optional covenant protocols

to which states parties have become parties. See "Complaints About Human Rights Violations," UN OHCHR, https://www.ohchr.org/EN/HRBodies/TBPetitions/Pages/HRTBPetitions.aspx#individualcomm. For the current situation of UN human rights covenant ratifications and reservations, see "Status of Ratification Interactive Dashboard." For ratifications of the ICCPR, see "International Covenant on Civil and Political Rights," https://www.ohchr.org/Documents/HRBodies/CCPR/OHCHR_Map_ICCPR.pdf; for ratifications of its first optional protocol, see "Optional Protocol to the International Covenant on Civil and Political Rights," https://www.ohchr.org/Documents/HRBodies/CCPR/OHCHR_Map_ICCPR-OP1.pdf.

34. H. Keller and L. Grover (2012), "General Comments of the Human Rights Committee and Their Legitimacy," in Keller and Ulfstein, 116–94; "General Comments," UN OHCHR, https://www.ohchr.org/en/treaty-bodies/general-comments.

35. See OHCHR Juris Database, https://juris.ohchr.org.

36. Civil and political rights can be described as freedoms that project individuals against intrusions by the state, whereas economic, social, and cultural rights are defined as positive rights that—in order to be realized—create obligations to states. See E. Riedel, G. Giacca, and C. Golay, eds. (2014), *Economic, Social, and Cultural Rights in International Law: Contemporary Issues and Challenges* (Oxford: Oxford University Press).

37. See F. Mégret and P. Alston (2020), *The United Nations and Human Rights: A Critical Appraisal* (Oxford: Oxford University Press); G. Alfredsson, J. Grimheden, B. Ramcharan, and A. Zayas, eds. (2009), *International Human Rights Monitoring Mechanisms: Essays in Honour of Jakob Th. Möller* (Leiden: Brill).

38. "OHCHR Organizational Chart," UN OHCHR, https://www.ohchr.org/sites/default/files/Documents/AboutUs/OHCHR_orgchart_2014.pdf. The UN human rights system also includes Special Procedures.

39. "OHCHR's Funding and Budget," UN OHCHR, https://www.ohchr.org/en/about-us/funding-and-budget.

40. Ibid.

41. As of 2022, the European Commission and Sweden are the main voluntary contributors with contributions of $30 million and $25 million, respectively. Sweden donates almost double the Netherlands' $14 million contribution. Finland is in fourth place at $6 million. "Voluntary Contributions to OHCHR in 2022," UN OHCHR, https://www.ohchr.org/sites/default/files/2022-02/VoluntaryContributions2022.pdf.

42. Ibid.; "OHCHR's Funding and Budget"; "Funding Trends," UN OHCHR, https://www.ohchr.org/en/about-us/funding-and-budget/funding-trends.

43. "UN Budget Shortfalls Seriously Undermine the Work of UN Human Rights Treaty Bodies," press release, 17 May 2019, https://www.ohchr.org/en/press-releases/2019/05/un-budget-shortfalls-seriously-undermine-work-human-rights-treaty-bodies; N. Cumming-Bruce, "Budget Cuts May Undercut the U.N.'s Human Rights Committees," *New York Times*, 24 May 2019, https://www.nytimes.com/2019/05/24/world/un-budget-cuts-human-rights.html.

44. "UN Budget Shortfalls."

45. "NGO Open Letter on Critical Funding Gap Affecting Human Rights," Global Initiative for Economic, Social and Cultural Rights, 28 May 2019, https://www.gi-escr.org/latest-news/open-letter-ngos-regarding-critical-funding-gap-affecting-un-human-rights-mechanisms-ohchr.

46. Quoted in N. Cumming-Bruce, "Budget Cuts," italics added.

47. M. Halme-Tuomisaari (2017), "Meeting 'the World' at the Palais Wilson: Embodied Universalism at the UN Human Rights Committee," in *Palaces of Hope: Anthropology of the*

United Nations, ed. R. Niezen and M. Sapignoli (Cambridge: Cambridge University Press), 127–151.

48. Information on the Committee's sessions including which states have been reviewed and the documents that have accompanied these reviews are found at "Human Rights Committee," https://www.ohchr.org/en/treaty-bodies/ccpr.

49. "Human Rights Committee Holds Emergency Meeting with States Parties as the United Nations' Financial Crisis Threatens Its Survival," UN OHCHR, 10 July 2025, https://www.ohchr.org/en/meeting-summaries/2025/07/human-rights-committee-holds-emergency-meeting-states-parties-united.

50. "UN Faces Deepening Financial Crisis, Urges Members to Pay Up," UN News, 19 May 2025, https://news.un.org/en/story/2025/05/1163436.

51. The COVID-19 pandemic intensified the situation with the OHCHR estimating in its 2022 *Human Rights Report* that "As of 30 June 2022, 426 State reports and 1,868 communications were pending review by the relevant Committees." UN OHCHR (2022), *United Nations Human Rights Report 2022*, https://www.ohchr.org/sites/default/files/documents/publications/ohchr-reports/ohchr-report-2022.pdf.

52. UN OHCHR (2017), *UN Human Rights Report 2017*, 155, https://www2.ohchr.org/english/OHCHRreport2017/allegati/Downloads/1_Whole_Report_2017.pdf.

53. J. Cowan (2007), "The Success of Failure? Minority Supervision at the League of Nations," in *Paths to International Justice: Social and Legal Perspectives*, ed. M.-B. Dembour and T. Kelly (Cambridge: Cambridge University Press), 29–56.

54. The CESCR Committee was founded by ECOSOC Resolution 1985/17 of 28 May 1985.

55. UN General Assembly (2006), Resolution 60/251 (3 April 2006), UN Doc A/RES/60/251. See discussion at J. Cowan (2014), "The Universal Periodic Review as Public Audit Ritual: An Anthropological Perspective on Emerging Practices in the Global Governance of Human Rights," in *Human Rights and the Universal Periodic Review: Rituals and Ritualism*, ed. H. Charlesworth and E. Larkin (Cambridge: Cambridge University Press), 42–62; see also M. Strathern (2000a), *Audit Cultures: Anthropological Studies in Accountability, Ethics and the Academy* (London: Routledge); C. Shore and S. Wright (2015), "Audit Culture Revisited: Rankings, Ratings, and the Reassembling of Society," *Current Anthropology* 56, 421–444.

56. Bassiouni and Schabas (2011).

57. Philip Alston was appointed as an independent expert to study the issue and propose policy outcomes. See P. Alston (1989), "Initial Report on Enhancing the Long-Term Effectiveness of the United Nations Human Rights Treaty System," UN Doc. A/44/668; P. Alston (1993), "Interim Report on Updated Study," UN Doc. E/CN.4/1997/74; P. Alston (1997), 'Final Report on Enhancing the Long-Term Effectiveness of the United Nations Human Rights Treaty System," UN Doc. E/CN.4/1997/74; "Treaty Body Strengthening," UN OHCHR, https://www.ohchr.org/en/treaty-bodies/treaty-body-strengthening. For discussion, see also P. Alston and J. Crawford, eds. (2000), *The Future of UN Human Rights Treaty Monitoring* (Cambridge: Cambridge University Press); Bayefsky (2000).

58. UN Concept Paper on the High Commissioner's Proposal for a Unified Standing Treaty Body, 22 March 2006, HRI/MC/2006/2.

59. N. Pillay (2012), *Strengthening the United Nations Human Rights Treaty Body System: A Report by the United Nations High Commissioner for Human Rights*, Report A/66/; UN General Assembly, "Resolution Adopted by the General Assembly on 9 April 2014," 68/268,

21 April 2014, https://www.ohchr.org/sites/default/files/Documents/HRBodies/TB/HRTD/A-RES-68-268_E.pdf.

60. "Presentation of the Annual Report of the United Nations High Commissioner for Human Rights," UN OHCHR, 13 October 2022, https://www.ohchr.org/en/statements-and-speeches/2022/10/presentation-annual-report-united-nations-high-commissioner-human.

61. See discussion in S. Egan (2020), "Transforming the UN Human Rights Treaty System: A Realistic Appraisal," *Human Rights Quarterly* 42(4), 762–789.

62. See P. Alston (2014), "Against a World Court of Human Rights," *Ethics and International Affairs* 28(4), 197–212; I. de la Rasilla (2019), "The World Court of Human Rights: Rise, Fall and Revival?," *Human Rights Law Review* 19, 585–603.

63. In the 1990s, for example, the CESCR was ratified by the Former Yugoslav Republic of Macedonia, Turkmenistan, Uzbekistan, Slovakia, Slovenia, Moldova, Georgia, Czech Republic, Croatia, Bosnia and Herzegovina, and Armenia, as well as all the Baltic countries. By the end of the 1990s the Covenant had fifty new ratifications, which made the decade almost as active in ratifications as the 1970s. In terms of ratified treaties, former socialist states have rapidly become some of the most active participants in the human rights phenomenon: by 2010 two of them had ratified all twelve principal UN human rights treaties—a record held by only three other states—and a supplementary eight had ratified all but one.

64. See M. Halme-Tuomisaari (2010a), *Human Rights in Action: Learning Expert Knowledge* (Leiden: Brill).

65. See M. Kirby (2020), "Multilateralism, Pushback, and Prospects for Global Engagement?," *Indiana Journal of Global Legal Studies* 27(2), 1–32.

66. See R. Chipaike, N. Tshuma, and S. Hofisi (2019), "African Move to Withdraw from the ICC: Assessment of Issues and Implications," *India Quarterly* 75(3), 334–350; S. J. Tilden (2018), "Africa's Conflict with the International Criminal Court: The African Court of Justice and Human and Peoples' Right as an Alternative to the ICC," *Tulane Journal of International and Comparative Law* 27, 201.

67. See A. Riles (2017), "Outputs: The Promises and Perils of Ethnographic Engagement After the Loss of Faith in Transnational Dialogue," *Journal of the Royal Anthropological Society* 23 (S1), 182–197; S. V. Scott (2018), "The Decline of International Law as a Normative Ideal," *Victoria University of Wellington Law Review* 49(4), 627–644; D. Guilfoyle (2019), "The Future of International Law in an Authoritarian World," *European Journal of International Law* TALK!, 3, June 2019, https://www.ejiltalk.org/the-future-of-international-law-in-an-authoritarian-world/; A. Bianchi (2018), "The Unbearable Lightness of International Law," *London Review of International Law* 6(3), 335–359.

68. S. Hopgood (2013), *The Endtimes of Human Rights* (Ithaca, NY: Cornell University Press); L. Allen (2013), *The Rise and Fall of Human Rights Cynicism and Politics in Occupied Palestine* (Stanford, CA: Stanford University Press). These sentiments emerged also in the PoLAR Virtual Edition on human rights: in their afterwords all authors appeared more pessimistic toward human rights when compared to their original articles written some decades earlier. See J. Clark and M. Halme-Tuomisaari, eds. (2016), "Virtual Edition: Human Rights," https://polarjournal.org/2016-virtual-edition-human-rights/.

69. J.-M. Barreto, ed. (2013), *Human Rights from a Third World Perspective* (Cambridge: Cambridge Scholars); S. Madhok (2021), *Vernacular Rights Cultures: The Politics of Origins, Human Rights and Gendered Struggles for Justice* (Cambridge: Cambridge University Press).

70. Anghie (2005); L. Eslava (2015), *Local Space, Global Life: The Everyday Operations of International Law and Development* (Cambridge: Cambridge University Press).

71. A. Grear (2018), "Human Rights and New Horizons? Thoughts Toward a New Juridical Ontology," *Science, Technology, and Human Values* 43(1), 129–145; A. Grear (2021), "International Law, Legal Anthropocentrism and Facing the Planetary," in *The Handbook of International Law and Anthropocentrism*, ed. V. Chapaux, F. Mégret, and N. Usha (New York: Routledge), 165–182; D. Celermajer and A. Lefebre, eds. (2020), *The Subject of Human Rights* (Stanford, CA: Stanford University Press).

72. S. Moyn (2018), *Not Enough: Human Rights in an Unequal World* (Cambridge, MA: Harvard University Press).

73. M. Halme-Tuomisaari (2019), "Consultancy, Confidentiality and Scholarly Responsibility: Glimpses from the UN OHCHR," *Humanity Journal Blog*, 5 September 2019, http://humanityjournal.org/blog/consultancy-confidentiality/.

74. One example is Amnesty International's increasing shift toward sustainability, a new concern in the field of human rights. "Sustainable Development Goals: A Practical Guide for National Action and Accountability," Amnesty International, 28 September 2016, https://www.amnesty.org/en/documents/act10/4699/2016/en/.

75. See, for example, G. L. Neuman (2018a), "Human Rights, Treaties, and International Legitimacy," in *Human Rights, Democracy, and Legitimacy in a World of Disorder*, ed. S. Voeneky and G. L. Neuman (Cambridge: Cambridge University Press), 51–72; A. Seibert-Fohr (2018), "The UN Human Rights Committee," in *International Human Rights Institutions, Tribunals, and Courts*, ed. G. Oberleitner (Leiden: Springer), 1–25.

76. M. O'Flaherty and G. Ulrich, eds. (2010), *The Professional Identity of the Human Rights Field Officer* (London: Ashgate).

77. B. S. Chimney (1999), "Marxism and International Law: A Contemporary Analysis," *Economic and Political Weekly* 34(6), 337–349.

78. See discussions in J. Krommendijk (2012), "The (Non) Implementation of Recommendations of the Committee on the Elimination of Racial Discrimination in the Netherlands Explained," *Perspectives on European Politics and Society* 13(4), 462–479; W. M. Cole (2015), "Mind the Gap: State Capacity and the Implementation of Human Rights Treaties," *International Organization* 69(2), 405–441; C. Heyns and F. Viljoen (2002), *The Impact of the United Nations Human Rights Treaties on the Domestic Level* (The Hague: Kluwer Law International); B. Simmons (2009), *Mobilizing for Human Rights: International Law in Domestic Politics* (Cambridge: Cambridge University Press).

79. See, for example, J. Crawford (2013), "The 'Compliance Gap' and the Efficacy of International Human Rights Institutions," in *The Persistent Power of Human Rights: From Commitment to Compliance*, ed. T. Risse, S. Ropp, and K. Sikkink (Cambridge: Cambridge University Press), 85–102.

80. In his analysis of treaty body effectiveness in Finland, the Netherlands, and New Zealand, Jasper Krommendijk found that the Concluding Observations had not been considered at all in parliamentary debate or decision-making. J. Krommendijk (2015a), "The Domestic Effectiveness of International Human Rights Monitoring in Established Democracies: The Case of the UN Human Rights Treaty Bodies," *Review of International Organizations* 10(4), 489–512.

81. R. Niezen and M. Sapignoli (2016), "Introduction," in Niezen and Sapignoli, *Palaces of Hope*, 1–57, quotation on 1.

82. J. Klabbers and G. F. Sinclair (2020), "On Theorizing International Organizations Law: Editors' Introduction," *European Journal of International Law* 31(2), 489–496, quotation on 490.

83. H. Moore (2004), "Global Anxieties: Concept-Metaphors and Pre-Theoretical Commitments in Anthropology," *Anthropological Theory* 4(1), 71–88.

84. Niezen and Sapignoli (2016), "Introduction," 3.

85. B. Müller, ed. (2013), *Gloss of Harmony: The Politics of Policy Making in Multilateral Organizations* (London: Pluto Press), 2.

86. J. Billaud and J. Cowan (2020), "The Bureaucratisation of Utopia: Ethics, Affects and Subjectivities in International Governance Processes," *Social Anthropology / Anthropologie Sociale* 28(1), 6–16, quotation on 12.

87. M. Foucault (1972), *The Archaeology of Knowledge and the Discourse on Language* (New York: Pantheon Books).

88. J. Lave and E. Wenger (1991), *Situated Learning: Legitimate Peripheral Participant* (Cambridge: Cambridge University Press). See also discussions on epistemic communities in Chapter 3.

89. P. Lauren (2003), *The Evolution of International Human Rights: Visions Seen* (Philadelphia: University of Pennsylvania Press). For criticism and discussion, see R. Afshari (2007), "On Historiography of Human Rights: Reflections on Paul Gordon Lauren's *The Evolution of International Human Rights*: Visions Seen," *Human Rights Quarterly* 29(1), 1–67. The language of guardians is also utilized by Susan Pedersen to discuss the operations of the League of Nations. See S. Pedersen (2015), *The Guardians: The League of Nations and the Crisis of Empire* (Oxford: Oxford University Press).

90. See discussion in G. Frankenberg (2014), "Human Rights and the Belief in a Just World," *International Journal of Constitutional Law* (12)1, 35–60; M.-B. Dembour (2006), *Who Believes in Human Rights? Reflections on the European Convention* (Cambridge: Cambridge University Press).

91. J. Cowan, M.-B. Dembour, and R. Wilson, eds. (2001), *Culture and Rights: Anthropological Perspectives* (Cambridge: Cambridge University Press); M. Goodale and S. Merry, eds. (2007), *The Practice of Human Rights: Tracking the Law Between the Local and the Global* (Cambridge: Cambridge University Press).

92. M. Abélès (2011), *Des anthropologues à l'OMC: scènes de la gouvernance mondiale* (Paris: CNRS); H. Deeb and G. Marcus (2011), "In the Green Room: An Experiment in Ethnographic Method at the WTO," *PoLAR: Political and Legal Anthropology Review* 34(1), 51–76; I. Schulte-Tenckhoff and A. H. Khan (2011), "The Permanent Quest for a Mandate: Assessing the UN Permanent Forum on Indigenous Issues," *Griffith Law Review* 20(3), 673–701.

93. A. Riles (2021), "Introduction to the Symposium on the Anthropology of International Law," *AJIL Unbound* 115, 283–272.

94. M. Sapignoli (2018), *Hunting Justice: Displacement, Law and Activism in the Kalahari* (Cambridge: Cambridge University Press).

95. A. Cubucku (2018), *For the Love of Humanity: The World Tribunal on Iraq* (Philadelphia: University of Pennsylvania Press).

96. Dembour (2006); J. Greenberg (2025), *Justice in the Balance: Democracy, Rule of Law, and the European Court of Human Rights* (Stanford, CA: Stanford University Press).

97. K. Clark (2019), *Affective Justice: The International Criminal Court and the Pan-Africanist Pushback* (Durham, NC: Duke University Press); J. Bens (2022), *The Sentimental Court: The Affective Life of International Criminal Justice* (Cambridge: Cambridge University Press).

98. R. Wilson (2001), *The Politics of Truth and Reconciliation in South Africa* (Cambridge: Cambridge University Press).

99. Cowan (2014).

100. Merry (2006).

101. Kelly (2011).

102. J. Clark (2016), "The Global Fight Against Racial Discrimination: Human Rights Assessment and the Making of Obligation in Costa Rica and at the United Nations," PhD diss., University of California, Irvine.

103. S. Merry (2016), *Seduction of Quantification* (Chicago: University of Chicago Press).

104. L. Bear and N. Mathur (2015), special issue: "Remaking the Public Good: A New Anthropology of Bureaucracy," *Cambridge Journal of Anthropology* 33(1); A. Riles, ed. (2005), *Documents: Artefacts of Modern Knowledge* (Ann Arbor: University of Michigan Press); M. S. Hull (2012a), *Government of Paper: The Materiality of Bureaucracy in Urban Pakistan* (Berkeley: University of California Press); K. Hetherington (2011), *Guerrilla Auditors: The Politics of Transparency in Neoliberal Paraguay* (Durham, NC: Duke University Press).

105. G. Feldman (2011), "If Ethnography Is More Than Participant-Observation, Then Relations Are More Than Connections: The Case for Nonlocal Ethnography in a World of Apparatuses," *Anthropological Theory* 11(4), 375–395.

106. A. Littoz-Monet (2021), *Governing Through Expertise* (Cambridge: Cambridge University Press); M. E. Keck and K. Sikkink (1998), *Activists Beyond Borders: Advocacy Networks in International Politics* (Ithaca, NY: Cornell University Press).

107. T. Piccone (2012), *Catalysts for Change: How the U.N.'s Independent Experts Promote Human Rights* (Washington, DC: Brookings Institution Press).

108. N. Reiners (2021), *Transnational Law-making Coalitions for Human Rights* (Cambridge: Cambridge University Press).

109. P. Leino-Sandberg (2021), *The Politics of Legal Expertise in EU Policy-Making* (Cambridge: Cambridge University Press).

110. J. Pauwelyn, R. Wessel, and J. Wouters, eds. (2012), *Informal International Lawmaking* (Oxford: Oxford University Press).

111. S. Hopgood (2016), "Law and Lawyers in a World After Virtue," *London Review of International Law* 4(3), 451–466.

112. G. Simpson (2015), "The Sentimental Life of International Law," *London Review of International Law* 3(3), 3–29; Bianchi (2018).

113. H. Y. Kang and S. Kendall (2019), "Legal Materiality," *Oxford Handbooks Online*, https://www.oxfordhandbooks.com/view/10.1093/oxfordhb/9780190695620.001.0001/oxfordhb-9780190695620-e-9#oxfordhb-9780190695620-e-9-bibliography-2.

114. N. Krisch, ed. (2021), *Entangled Legalities Beyond the State* (Cambridge: Cambridge University Press).

115. Feldman (2011); P. Rabinow, G. E. Marcus, and J. D. Faubion (2008), *Designs for an Anthropology of the Contemporary* (Durham, NC: Duke University Press); D. Holmes and G. Marcus (2005), "Cultures of Expertise and the Management of Globalization: Toward the Re-functioning of Ethnography," in *Global Assemblages*, ed. A. Ong and S. J. Collier (Oxford: Blackwell, 235–252); G. Marcus (1995), "Ethnography in/of the World System: The Emergence of Multi-sited Ethnography," *Annual Review of Anthropology* 24, 95–117.

116. R. Higgins (2009), *Themes and Theories: Selected Essays, Speeches, and Writings in International Law* (Oxford: Oxford University Press), 588. On the role of human rights in

Finnish society, see J. Lavapuro, T. Ojanen, and M. Scheinin (2016), "Intermediate Constitutional Review in Finland: Promising in Theory, Problematic in Practice," in *Rights-Based Constitutional Review: Constitutional Courts in a Changing Landscape*, ed. J. Bell and M.-L. Paris (London: Edward Elgar); T. Ojanen and J. Salminen (2019), "Finland: European Integration and International Human Rights Treaties as Source of Domestic Constitution Change and Dynamism," in *National Constitutions in European and Global Governance: Democracy, Rights, the Rule of Law*, ed. A. Albi and S. Bardutzky (The Hague: Asser Press), 359–404; A. Björk, J.-M. Paavola, T. Strik, I. Tanhua, and A. Vainio (2019), *Finland in the International Human Rights System* (Helsinki: Publications of the Government's Analysis, Assessment and Research Activities), 50. For critical takes, see L. Näre (2020), "'Finland Kills with a Pen'—Asylum Seekers' Protest Against Bureaucratic Violence as Politics of Human Rights," *Citizenship Studies* 24(8), 979–993; T. Kasa, M. Rautiainen, M. Malama, and A. Kallioniemi (2021), "'Human Rights and Democracy Are Not Self-Evident': Finnish Student Teachers' Perceptions on Democracy and Human Rights Education," *Human Rights Education Review* 4(2), 69–84.

117. This does not suggest that such states as Finland are without societal problems or human rights violations, as has been repeatedly noted by different treaty bodies, including the UN Human Rights Committee, for example, on Finland's treatment of the Sámi people, as Chapter 5 discusses. Despite being repeatedly celebrated as the home of the "happiest people of the world," Finland is plagued by some of the highest suicide rates in the world. "Finland Tops World Happiness Report for Fifth Time in a Row, . . ." This Is Finland, 2022, https://finland.fi/life-society/happinessreport2022/; T. Partonen et al. (2022), "Suicides from 2016 to 2020 in Finland and the Effect of the COVID-19 Pandemic," *British Journal of Psychiatry* 220(1), 38–40. Violence against women is also prevalent, as Chapter 5 also discusses. For criticism toward the Orpo government program, see "Hallitusohjelmassa on vakavia puutteita ihmisoikeuksien kannalta," Ihmisoikeusliitto, 20 June 2023, https://ihmisoikeusliitto.fi/hallitusohjelmassa-vakavia-puutteita-ihmisoikeuksien-kannalta/; "Hallitusohjelma ihmisoikeuksien näkökulmasta heikko ja ristiriitainen," Amnesty, 21 June 2023, https://www.amnesty.fi/amnesty-hallitusohjelma-ihmisoikeuksien-nakokulmasta-heikko-ja-ristiriitainen/.

118. Krommendijk echoes these sentiments in his comparative study of Finland, the Netherlands, and New Zealand, naming Finland most likely to illustrate the effectiveness of treaty body Concluding Observations. J. Krommendijk (2014), "Finnish Exceptionalism at Play? The Effectiveness of the Recommendations of UN Human Rights Treaty Bodies in Finland," *Nordic Journal of Human Rights* 32(1), 18–43.

119. M. Halme-Tuomisaari (2018), "Methodologically Blonde at the UN in a Tactical Quest for Inclusion," *Social Anthropology / Anthropologie Sociale* 26(4), 456–470.

120. I. Jean-Klein and A. Riles (2005), "Introducing Discipline: Anthropology and Human Rights Administrations," *PoLAR: Political and Legal Anthropology Review* 28(2), 173–202.

121. L. Nader (1974), "Up the Anthropologist––Perspectives Gained from Studying Up," in *Reinventing Anthropology*, ed. Dell Hymes (New York: Vintage Books), 284–311.

122. For discussion on the use of pseudonyms in anthropology, see E. Weiss and C. McGranahan (2021), "Rethinking Pseudonyms in Ethnography: An Introduction," and M. Halme-Tuomisaari (2021), "Between Organizational Narratives and Individual Stories: Pseudonyms Revisited," in *Rethinking Pseudonyms in Ethnography*, ed. C. McGranahan and E. Weiss, American Ethnologist website, 13 December 2021, https://americanethnologist.org/features/collections/rethinking-pseudonyms-in-ethnography.

123. Hugh Gusterson has observed this doing fieldwork in elite contexts in the US. See H. Gusterson (1997), "Studying Up Revisited," *Political and Legal Anthropological Review* 20(1), 114–119, esp. 116.

Chapter 2

1. Nader (1974).

2. See also Halme-Tuomisaari (2018).

3. The role of interns has also been discussed in J. Billaud (2014), "Keepers of the 'Truth': Producing 'Transparent' Documents for the Universal Periodic Review," in *Human Rights and the Universal Periodic Review: Ritual and Ritualism*, ed. H. Charlesworth and E. Larkin (Cambridge: Cambridge University Press), 63–84; M. Sapignoli (2017), "A Kaleidoscopic Institutional Form: Expertise and Transformation in the UN Permanent Forum on Indigenous Issues," in Niezen and Sapignoli, *Palaces of Hope*, 78–105.

4. «Palais Wilson,» UN OHCHR, https://www.ohchr.org/en/about-us/where-we-work/geneva-headquarters.

5. For discussion on the Palais Wilson's history, see J. Kuntz (2016), *International Geneva: 100 Years of Architecture*, trans. V. Lowe, esp. Chapter 2, "Palais Wilson, the Memory and Hostage of Geneva," Genève internationale, https://www.geneve-int.ch/chapter-2-palais-wilson-memory-and-hostage-geneva.

6. «Palais des Nations,» United Nations, https://www.ungeneva.org/en/about/palais-des-nations.

7. "Accreditation to Attend Treaty Body Sessions," UN OHCHR, https://www.ohchr.org/en/treaty-bodies/accreditation. The UN introduced a digital ID system in 2024. It was gradually implemented across different bodies and meetings within the organization, also for the Human Rights Committee's sessions, and is now used consistently. "UN Digital ID," UN System Chief Executives Board for Coordination, https://unsceb.org/topics/un-digital-id?utm.

8. For example, ten days prior to the opening of the Human Rights Committee's 136th session (10 October–4 November 2022), there was neither information available on accreditations for the session nor an accreditations form located online. UN OHCHR: Human Rights Committee.

9. UN guidelines for entry in treaty body sessions in New York mention the "NGO doorway at the Visitor's entrance at 46th Street and First Avenue." This leaves room for error as it is possible that the NGO doorway is not clearly marked, making it difficult for those visiting the premises for the first time to identify it. A search via Google Maps offers a general location for this address, but no information about an NGO doorway. UN premises are often large, meaning that distances one must cover to track down a particular doorway may likewise be large. "Access to the United Nations: How to Get the Right Badge/Pass," United Nations, https://www.un.org/esa/coordination/ngo/passes.htm. For UN treaty bodies, the website of the OHCHR mentions that accreditations are to be picked up from the Pregny Gate, with the website offering the general address of 8–14 Avenue de la Paix. Here, one needs to check the location of the Pregny Gate on an online map as this address alone is insufficient. The Pregny Gate is about half a kilometer's distance from the UN's main entrance. "Accreditation to Attend Treaty Body Sessions."

10. See "Types of Accreditations," UN Media Accreditation and Liaison Unit, https://www.un.org/en/media/accreditation/types.shtml.

11. On center-periphery dynamics in our current world order, see I. Wallerstein (2004), *World-Systems Analysis: An Introduction* (Durham, NC: Duke University Press). Hannerz

connects the center-periphery dynamic to the flow of meanings. U. Hannerz (1992), *Cultural Complexity: Studies in the Social Organization of Meaning* (New York: Columbia University Press). This connects with Appadurai's (1996) notion of ideascapes and global flows.

12. Feldman (2011), 378.

13. Ibid.

14. M. Foucault (1980 [1977]), "The Confessions of the Flesh," in *Power/Knowledge: Selected Interviews and Other Writings*, ed. C. Gordon (New York: Pantheon Books), 194–228.

15. P. Bourdieu (1990), *In Other Words: Essays Toward a Reflexive Sociology* (Stanford, CA: Stanford University Press), 62–63; see also P. Bourdieu (1977), *Outline of a Theory of Practice* (Cambridge: Cambridge University Press), 81–82.

16. A. Bianchi (2013), "On Power and Illusion: The Concept of Transparency in International Law," in *Transparency in International Law*, ed. A. Bianchi and A. Peters (Cambridge: Cambridge University Press), 1–20, quotation on 1.

17. C. Hood (2006), "Transparency in Historical Perspective," in *Transparency: The Key to Better Governance?*, ed. C. Hood and D. Heald (Oxford: Oxford University Press), 3–23, quotation on 4; see also A. Boyle and K. McCall-Smith (2013), "Transparency in International Lawmaking," in Bianchi and Peters, *Transparency in International Law*, 419–435, esp. 419; I. Koivisto (2022), *The Transparency Paradox* (Oxford: Oxford University Press).

18. Bianchi (2013), 1.

19. D. Berliner (2014), "The Political Origins of Transparency," *Journal of Politics* 76(2), 479–491.

20. C. Garsten and M. Lindh de Montoya (2008), "Introduction: Examining the Politics of Transparency," in *Transparency in a New Global Order: Unveiling Organizational Visions*, ed. C. Garsten and M. Lindh de Montoya (Cheltenham, UK: Edward Elgar), 1–21, quotation on 4.

21. A. Peters (2015), "The Transparency Turn of International Law," *Chinese Journal of Global Governance* 1(1), 3–15.

22. C. Garsten and M. Lindh de Montoya (2008), "Introduction," 1.

23. E. Alloa and D. Thomä, eds. (2018), *Transparency, Society and Subjectivity: Critical Perspectives* (Cham, Switzerland: Springer), 2.

24. Bianchi (2013), 2.

25. J. Fox (2007), "The Uncertain Relationship Between Transparency and Accountability," *Development in Practice* 17(4–5), 663–671.

26. A. Ballestro (2018), "Transparency," in *The International Encyclopedia of Anthropology*, Wiley Online Library, https://onlinelibrary.wiley.com/doi/abs/10.1002/9781118924396.wbiea1505; R. Adams (2020), *Transparency: New Trajectories in Law* (London: Routledge).

27. M. Strathern (2000b), "The Tyranny of Transparency," *British Educational Research Journal* 26(3), 309–321.

28. See C. Garsten and M. Lindh de Montoya (2008), "Introduction," 7.

29. Bianchi (2013), 4.

30. Peters (2015).

31. A. Peters (2013), "Towards Transparency as a Global Norm," in Bianchi and Peters, *Transparency in International Law*, 534–607, quotations on 541, 542.

32. Bianchi (2013), 4; see also U. Soirila (2021), *The Law of Humanity: A Story of International Law Reform and State Making* (London: Hart).

33. Feldman (2011).

34. This is not to suggest that existing connections and relations are integral for a scholar's access. Research contexts are different, and some contexts may have greater openness from the outset. For an experience of doing research as an "innocuous ethnographer," see J. Clark (2016).

35. P. Shipton (2003), "Legalism and Loyalism: European, African, and Human 'Rights,'" in *At the Risk of Being Heard: Identity, Indigenous Rights, and Postcolonial States*, ed. B. Dean and J. Levi (Ann Arbor: University of Michigan Press), 45–79, quotation on 67; D. W. Cohen and E. S. Atieno Odhiambo (1989), *Siaya: The Historical Anthropology of an African Landscape* (London: James Currey), 27.

36. See Tsing (2005).

37. Jean-Klein and Riles (2005).

38. Merry (2006).

39. Considering the prevalence and importance of often unpaid intern labor, surprisingly little scholarship exists on the topic.

40. See "Internship Programme," United Nations, https://www.un.org/en/academic-impact/page/internships?utm; on UN Careers, see https://careers.un.org/lbw/home.aspx?viewtype=ip.

41. In addition, almost all NGOs who frequented the Palais Wilson had interns, the total number of which is difficult to estimate but would likely be several dozen annually.

42. J. K. Cowan and J. Billaud (2017), "The 'Public' Character of the Universal Periodic Review: Contested Concept and Methodological Challenge," in Niezen and Sapignoli, *Palaces of Hope*, 106–126.

43. See UN Human Rights Committee (2021), *Rules of Procedure*. See also discussion on the selection process in Chapter 3.

44. UN System Chief Executives Board for Coordination (1982), *Report on Conditions of Service of Field Staff*, ACC/1982/5, Annex IV, in *UN System Chief Executives Board for Coordination: Staff Mobility*, https://digitallibrary.un.org/record/31493/files/ACC_1982_PER_33-EN.pdf?utm; see also UN General Assembly (1991), *Rotation of Staff within the United Nations—Note by the Secretary General*, A746/326, 29 July 1991, and UN Joint Inspection Unit (1991), *Report on the Rotation of Staff within the United Nations*, JIU/REF/91/3, Geneva, June 1991, both available at https://www.unjiu.org/sites/www.unjiu.org/files/jiu_document_files/products/en/reports-notes/JIU%20Products/JIU_REP_1991_3_English.pdf. There is very little discussion in UN publications or existing scholarship of the consequences of and motivations for staff mobility from an organizational viewpoint.

45. UN Development Program, 1, https://popp.undp.org/document/721/view.

46. In a UN staff survey from 2010, building on an earlier source, "Job rotation is defined as 'the planned movement of men from one position to another for the basic purpose of encouraging and stimulating the growth of the individual.'" United Nations Staff Union (2010), *Mobility in the United Nations Secretariat: A Survey of Staff*, June 2010, https://staffunion.unov.org/docs/trail_SMCC_31_mobility_staff_by_UNSU_Vienna.pdf, 1.

47. Many other IOs have similar practices, among them UNICEF. See "Requirements for the International Professional Staff Category," UNICEF, https://www.unicef.org/careers/sites/unicef.org.careers/files/2019-08/Detailed_requirements_for_IP_Staff.pdf.

48. UN HR Portal (2015), Staff Rules; Rule 3.13 Mobility Incentive, https://policy.un.org/en/salaries-and-related-allowances#Rule3.13.

49. See also UN Development Program.

50. A full list of all current Committee members with their tenure is available at "Membership, Human Rights Committee," UN OHCHR, https://www.ohchr.org/en/node/33623/membership.

51. United Nations Staff Union (2010).

52. Bourdieu (1990); on transparency as an ideal in policymaking and legislation, see Adams (2020); Alloa and Thomä (2018); Bianchi (2013). See also discussion in Chapter 7.

53. In their work, Cowan and Billaud (2017) show how, in the Human Rights Council, this included the complex ways in which concrete information about session times and accessibility are shared on relevant UN websites.

54. See discussion in Chapter 7.

Chapter 3

1. "Summary Record of the 3,000th Meeting, Held at the Palais de Nations, Geneva, on Monday, 22 July 2013, Human Rights Committee, 108th session," 3:00–6:00 p.m., United Nations, https://digitallibrary.un.org/record/767309?ln=en. All citations are from interviews, conversations, or the Committee's public sessions. See Chapter 1 for more elaboration, and the acknowledgments for the full list of interviewees.

2. Optional Protocol to the ICCPR, Article 5, par. 2(b) provides that the Committee "shall not consider" the case unless "the individual has exhausted all available remedies." However, this requirement does not apply if "the application of the remedies is unreasonably prolonged." The Committee interprets the term "unreasonably" as covering cases where a judicial remedy would be available in a country but the court or other body that can be approached is not able or obliged to correct the decision by a lower court even if it is clear that the law has been violated. In such cases, the Committee considers that the domestic proceedings would be "unreasonably prolonged" because the remedy is not effective. In the case of Belarus, the government rejected this interpretation. On individual communications, see V. Shikhelman (2019), "Implementing Decisions of International Human Rights Institutions—Evidence from the United Nations Human Rights Committee," *European Journal of International Law* 30(3), 753–777; M. Halme-Tuomisaari and R. Toivanen (forthcoming), "The Dangers of Distant Evidence: The UN Human Rights Committee's Individual Communications, 512,000 Potential New Sámi Voters and Other 'Objective' Facts." In *UN Evidentiary Regimes*, ed. D. Casalin, M.-B. Dembour, and C. Klocker. Cambridge: Cambridge University Press.

3. Intergovernmental Process of the General Assembly on Strengthening and Enhancing the Effective Functioning of the Human Rights Treaty Body System, G.A. Res. 66/254, U.N. Doc. A/66/254, 15 May 2012, https://docs.un.org/en/A/RES/66/254. On the voting record, see also "66 States Abstain on GA Resolution Creating Treaty Body Strengthening Process," International Service for Human Rights, 24 February 2012, http://www.ishr.ch/news/66-states-abstain-ga-resolution-creating-treaty-body-strengthening-process.

4. These controversies have continued to the present day, illustrated by Belarus's withdrawal from the Human Rights Committee's individual complaint procedure in November 2022. "Belarus' Withdrawal from Individual Complaints Procedure a Serious Setback for Human Rights Protection, UN Human Rights Committee Says," UN OHCHR, 25 November 2022, https://www.ohchr.org/en/press-releases/2022/11/belarus-withdrawal-individual-complaints-procedure-serious-setback-human.

5. Interventions were also made by Switzerland addressing the issue of reprisals against NGOs submitting shadow reports, Uzbekistan on the Committee's interpretation of the death penalty, and South Korea concerning the lengthy time frame for introducing interim measures.

6. Piccone (2012); Merry (2016).

7. See, for example, Littoz-Monet (2021); Keck and Sikkink (1998); W. Korey (2001), *The UDHR and NGOs: A Curious Grapevine* (New York: Palgrave Macmillan).

8. P. Haas (1992), "Introduction: Epistemic Communities and International Policy Coordination," *International Organization* 46(1), 1–35; see also P. Haas (2012), "Epistemic Communities," in *The Oxford Handbook of International Environmental Law*, ed. D. Bodansky, J. Brunnée, and H. Hey (Oxford: Oxford University Press), 792; P. Haas (2014), "Ideas, Experts and Governance," in *The Role of "Experts" in International and European Decision-Making Processes: Advisors, Decision Makers or Irrelevant Actors?*, ed. M. Ambrus et al. (Cambridge: Cambridge University Press), 19–43; M. Cross (2013), "Rethinking Epistemic Communities Twenty Years Later," *Review of International Studies* 39(1), 137–160; A. Bianchi (2019), "Epistemic Communities," in *Concepts for International Law*, ed. J. d'Aspremont and S. Sing (Cheltenham, UK: Edward Elgar), 251–266.

9. Bianchi (2019); W. G. Werner (2014), "The Politics of Expertise: Applying Paradoxes of Scientific Expertise to International Law," in Ambrus et al., *The Role of "Experts,"* 44–62, esp. 60–62.

10. Haas (1992); see also D. J. Galbreath and J. McEvoy (2013), "How Epistemic Communities Drive International Regimes: The Case of Minority Rights in Europe," *Journal of European Integration* 35(2), 169–186; F. Amahazion (2016), "Epistemic Communities, Human Rights, and the Global Diffusion of Legislation Against the Organ Trade," *Social Sciences* 5(4), 69.

11. J. K. Cowan (2021), "Modes of Acting Virtuously at the Universal Periodic Review," in *Ethical Leadership in International Organizations: Concepts, Narratives, Judgment, and Assessment*, ed. G. Vilaça and M. Varaki (Cambridge: Cambridge University Press), 176–202.

12. See Lave and Wenger (1991); E. Wenger (1998), *Communities of Practice: Learning, Meaning, and Identity* (Cambridge: Cambridge University Press).

13. See J. Beckett (2022), "The Divisible College: A Day in the Lives of Public International Lawyers," *German Law Journal* 23(9), 1159–1192; see also J. A. Orange (2016), "Translating Law into Practice: Museums and a Human Rights Community of Practice," *Human Rights Quarterly* 38(3), 706–735.

14. See S. Ortner (2006), *Anthropology and Social Theory: Culture, Power, and the Acting Subject* (Durham, NC: Duke University Press).

15. Feldman (2011).

16. Riles (2015), 258.

17. Fourteen out of seventeen members of the Committee on Economic, Social, and Cultural Rights mention having a background in law in their treaty body member profiles; for the Human Rights Committee, the number is seventeen out of eighteen members. "Membership: Committee on Economic, Social and Cultural Rights," UN OHCHR, https://www.ohchr.org/en/treaty-bodies/cescr/membership; "Membership: Human Rights Committee," UN OHCHR, https://www.ohchr.org/en/treaty-bodies/ccpr/membership. In other bodies, such as the Committee on the Elimination of Discrimination Against Women, legal emphasis is less common as expertise is more varied. See "Membership: Committee on the Elimination of Discrimination Against Women," UN OHCHR, https://www.ohchr.org/en/treaty-bodies/cedaw/membership.

18. "Human Rights Treaties Division," *UN Human Rights Report 2017*, https://www2.ohchr.org/english/OHCHRreport2017/allegati/17_Human_Rights_Treaties_Division_2017.pdf.

19. O. Schachter (1977), "The Invisible College of International Lawyers," *Northwestern University Law Review* 72(2), 217–226.

20. Babul (2017); Halme-Tuomisaari (2010a).

21. UN Human Rights Council (2014), "Composition of the Staff of the Office of the United Nations High Commissioner for Human Rights," 18 June 2014, A/HRC/27/18.

22. For statistics on world populations, see "Regions in the World by Population," Worldometers, https://www.worldometers.info/world-population/population-by-region/; "World Population Dashboard," United Nations Populations Fund, https://www.unfpa.org/data/world-population-dashboard.

23. UN Human Rights Council (2014), 8.

24. UN Human Rights Council (2020), "Composition of the Staff of the Office of the United Nations High Commissioner for Human Rights," 25 September 2020, A/HRC/45/4.

25. Figures in this section are based on an analysis of biographical member information available at the Human Rights Committee's website. "Membership: Human Rights Committee," UN OHCHR.

26. It is important to note that besides China (18 percent of the world population), other countries with large populations, including Myanmar and Malaysia, have not ratified the Covenant and thus cannot have Committee members. Furthermore, with nineteen countries not being states parties to the Covenant, the Asia-Pacific is the region with the biggest ratification gaps, which diminishes its voting power during elections. The region accounts for 23 percent of all state ratifications of UN human rights treaties. Area divisions are based on the UN's own categorization and contrasted to those of Worldometers.

27. Tsing (2005), 6.

28. On the Committee members' role, see G. Neuman (2018b), "Giving Meaning and Effect to Human Rights: The Contributions of Human Rights Committee Members," in *The Human Rights Covenants at 50: Their Past, Present, and Future*, ed. D. Moeckli, H. Keller, and C. Heri (Cambridge: Cambridge University Press), 31–47; P. Slotte and M. Scheinin (2011), "Captain, Fire Brigade or Icebreaker? Political Legitimacy as a Rationale in Human Rights Adjudication," in *Legitimacy: The Treasure of Politics*, ed. T. Kurtén and L. Hertzberg (Lausanne: Peter Lang), 89–128.

29. In 2015, a year after this interview, the OHCHR published a handbook for members: *Handbook for Human Rights Treaty Body Members*, https://www.ohchr.org/sites/default/files/Documents/Publications/HR_PUB_15_2_TB_Handbook_EN.pdf.

30. UN Human Rights Committee, *Rules of Procedure*, Rules 16, 17.

31. By comparison, CEDAW Committee members are usually of more advanced age. See member profiles at "Membership: CEDAW."

32. UN OHCHR formal criteria describe experts as "persons of high moral character and recognized competence in the field of human rights." "Membership: Human Rights Committee."

33. For membership profiles, see "Membership: Human Rights Committee."

34. The list of nominated state candidates is drafted and published several months prior to elections. During this time frame, campaign support from the state's permanent mission in New York is pivotal. See V. Carraro (2019a), "Electing the Experts: Expertise and Independence in the UN Human Rights Treaty Bodies," *European Journal of International Relations* 25(3), 826–851.

35. For example, Dame Rosalyn Higgins became a judge at the International Court of Justice, later becoming also the Court's president; Iulia Motoc became a judge at the European Court of Human Rights; Martin Scheinin became the UN special rapporteur on Human Rights and Counter-terrorism; Walter Kälin became the representative of the UN Secretary-General on

the Human Rights of Internally Displaced Persons, and Michael O'Flaherty became the director of the European Union Agency for Fundamental Rights.

36. This emerged also in an interview study of treaty bodies and their elections. Carraro (2019a).

37. "Professor Sir Nigel Rodley Obituary," University of Essex, 22 March 2017, https://www.essex.ac.uk/news/2017/03/22/professor-sir-nigel-rodley-obituary; "Human Rights Community Mourns Passing of Sir Nigel Rodley, Former UN Rights Expert," UN News, 27 January 2017, https://news.un.org/en/story/2017/01/550332.

38. "Nigel Rodley, Former Special Rapporteur on Torture (1993–2000)," United Nations, https://www.ohchr.org/en/special-procedures/sr-torture/nigel-rodley-former-special-rapportuer-torture-1993-2001.

39. "The ICJ Mourns Its President Professor Sir Nigel Rodley," International Commission of Jurists, 25 January 2017, https://www.icj.org/the-icj-mourns-its-president-professor-sir-nigel-rodley/; B. Çali (2017), "In Memoriam: Professor Sir Nigel Rodley," *EJIL: Talk!* (blog), 2 February 2017, https://www.ejiltalk.org/in-memoriam-professor-sir-nigel-rodley/.

40. "Human Rights Committee—Members: Nigel Rodley," UN OHCHR, https://www2.ohchr.org/english/bodies/hrc/membersCVs/rodley.htm; "Human Rights Community Mourns"; B. Çali (2017); "Professor Sir Nigel Rodley Obituary."

41. "Professor Sir Nigel Rodley Obituary"; G. Robertson with Ivor Crewe (2017), "Sir Nigel Rodley Obituary," *Guardian*, 2 February 2017, https://www.theguardian.com/law/2017/feb/02/sir-nigel-rodley-obituary.

42. "ICJ Mourns Its President."

43. "Nigel Rodley 1941–2017," Amnesty International, 26 January 2017, https://www.amnesty.org/en/latest/news/2017/01/nigel-rodley-1941-2017/.

44. Ibid.; G. Robertson with I. Crewe (2017).

45. "Nigel Rodley, Former Special Rapporteur on Torture."

46. "Professor Sir Nigel Rodley Obituary."

47. G. van Bueren (2016), "Obituary: Professor Sir Nigel Rodley," *Queen Mary Human Rights Review* 3(1).

48. Human Rights Committee, opening of the 107th session, 11 March 2013, Palais Wilson.

49. His contribution was often highlighted by state delegates who appeared in front of the Committee under his chairmanship. After Finland's Constructive Dialogue in July 2013, his contribution to the Committee was highlighted both by Finnish civil servants and the member of Parliament who joined the delegation. Carraro also shares how Rodley was mentioned as a notable example. Carraro (2019a).

50. "Professor Sir Nigel Rodley Obituary."

51. See discussion on fuzzy logic in Chapter 2.

52. In the Committee's operations, members are recognized as state nationals. For example, when treaty body members are enlisted, their name is consistently accompanied by the name of their state.

53. See V. Carraro (2019a).

54. This was likewise revealed in Carraro's study. Interviewees highlighted some members' lack of knowledge of specific country situations accompanied by lack of political expertise. Ibid.

55. In other studies of UN treaty bodies, advanced age and lacking "the capacity to concentrate (and remain awake) have been identified as sources of inadequate performance." An

interviewee in Carraro's study notes candidly that Committee members appeared "so old and frail that they would hardly be awake during the meeting. If you [had gone] to the meetings of the [Committee] in the afternoon, you would [have seen] in the whole right branch everyone sleeping. It looked like a nursing home, really, sometimes." Ibid.

56. "Human Rights Treaties Division"; "About UN Human Rights," United Nations, https://www.ohchr.org/en/about-us/where-we-work/un-human-rights-our-organization. Both the division and the OHCHR have their roots in the 1940s when the UN's Human Rights Division, then located in New York, was formed to oversee drafting the UDHR in 1946–1948. The division also assumed responsibility for drafting the UN's main human rights treaties, including the ICCPR and the ICESCR, and oversaw the activities of the Human Rights Commission. Later, the division moved to Geneva. In the 1980s, it was upgraded into the Centre for Human Rights. On 20 December 1993, after extensive lobbying by the international human rights community and a recommendation by the Vienna Declaration and Program of Action in June 1993, the General Assembly established the post of high commissioner for human rights to spearhead the UN's human rights efforts.

57. See M. Di Nunzio (2018), "Anthropology of Infrastructure," *LSE Cities, Governing Infrastructure Interfaces—Research Note* 1, 1–4; B. Larkin (2013), "The Politics and Poetics of Infrastructure," *Annual Review of Anthropology* 42, 327–343.

58. B. Latour (2009), "Scientific Objects and Legal Objectivity," in *Law, Anthropology, and the Constitution of the Social: Making Persons and Things*, ed. A. Pottage and M. Mundy (Cambridge: Cambridge University Press), 73–114; Halme-Tuomisaari (2010a).

59. On the use of pseudonyms, see Weiss and McGranahan (2021).

60. UN Human Rights Council, Composition of the Staff of the Office of the United Nations High Commissioner for Human Rights, 25 September 2020, A/HRC/45/4.

61. Billaud (2014).

62. Human Rights Committee, 107th session, 25 March 2013, 10:00 a.m., Palais Wilson.

63. Cowan's analysis of the League of Nations shows how the League similarly left discretion to sections (e.g., the Minority Section) to come up with their procedures. Cowan also emphasizes the significance of the Secretariat, normally neglected in analysis of the League of Nation's history. See J. K. Cowan (2020), "'The Feeling of Pursuing an Ideal': A League of Nations Civil Servant Reflects on His Work," *Social Anthropology / Anthropologie Sociale* 28(1), 17–34; Cowan (2007). For a nuanced history of the League of Nations drawing attention to its personnel, see C. Biltoft (2021), *A Violent Peace: Media, Truth, and Power at the League of Nations* (Chicago: University of Chicago Press).

64. Carraro (2019a).

65. This issue was discussed, for example, in the Human Rights Committee's session on 13 March 2013 on Methods of Work, 4:00–5:15 p.m., Palais Wilson.

66. Committee on Migrant Workers, Committee on the Rights of Persons with Disabilities, Sub-Committee on Prevention of Torture, Committee on Enforced Disappearances, in "Human Rights Treaties Division."

67. Ibid. Committee members may echo these sentiments. One member stated, "I would not say that the treaty body system is in crisis, but rather that there is no system to begin with," highlighting as the biggest problem "the absolute lack of coordination between the different treaty bodies." The member elaborated that, paradoxically, "states blame the treaty bodies for this lack of coordination, although it is the states themselves that have created the current

situation." The member likewise emphasized that there are simply not enough resources to sustain the current system.

68. D. Giauque, S. Anderfuhren-Biget, and F. Varone (2019), "Stress and Turnover Intents in International Organizations: Social Support and Work-Life Balance as Resources," *International Journal of Resource Management* 30(5), 879–901; T. Bruno-van Vijfeijken (2019), "'Culture Is What You See When Compliance Is Not in the Room': Organizational Culture as an Explanatory Factor in Analyzing Recent INGO Scandals," *Nonprofit Policy Forum*, 8 November 2019, https://www.degruyter.com/document/doi/10.1515/npf-2019-0031/html.

69. K. Avula, L. McKay, and S. Galland, *Amnesty International Staff Wellbeing Review*, 31 January 2019, https://www.amnesty.org/en/documents/org60/9763/2019/en/.

70. I. Seiderman (2019), "The UN High Commissioner for Human Rights in the Age of Global Backlash," *Netherlands Quarterly of Human Rights* 37(1), 5–13.

71. M. O'Flaherty (2010), "The Professionalization of Human Rights Field Work," *Journal of Human Rights Practice* 2(1), 1–27, quotations on 8; see also Hopgood (2013).

72. See discussion in Larkin (2013).

73. In 2013 a Committee insider denoted the per diem at 550 USD. UN Office of Human Resources (2025), "Policy Guideline—Fee Ranges for International Consultants and Individual Contractors," OHR/PG/2025/2, 17 January 2025, https://policy.un.org/sites/default/files/2025-01/OHR_PG_2025_2_consultant_contractor_fee_range.pdf. Treaty body members receive a per diem as UN external experts. In addition, they receive remuneration for their travel. However, they do not receive any additional compensation for preparatory work done outside the sessions. They are also required to cover all accommodation and living costs from this per diem, which at Geneva prices amounts to a significant sum. In addition to this per diem, many Committee members have salaries from their primary positions, as, for example, university professors.

74. UN salaries are competitive when compared to most government salaries. Salaries are also usually tax-exempt. The annual salaries for entry-level professionals requiring up to five years of work experience (P1–P3) is $37,000–$80,000. For mid-career professionals with a minimum of seven and ten years of work experience (P4–P5), salaries are $67,000–$106,000, respectively. For senior-level professionals with more than fifteen years of work experience (D1–D2), the range is $95,000–$123,000. These salaries are adjusted according to the cost of living in the duty station, which, in the case of Geneva, means an upgrade of 65.7 percent. "UN Careers: Pay and Benefits," https://careers.un.org/lbw/home.aspx?viewtype=sal&lang=en-US, see extracted document also at https://www.ids.ac.uk/download.php?file=wp-content/uploads/2024/10/Handbook_on_UN_careers.pdf&utm_.

75. UN Human Rights Council (2020), Composition of the Staff.

76. "Human Rights Treaties Division."

77. News reports suggest that the UN struggles to address sexual harassment, with staff reluctant to speak out under their own names due to UN rules that preclude staff from speaking and for fear of retaliation. R. Ratcliffe (2018), "Sexual Harassment and Assault Rife at United Nations, Staff Claim," *Guardian*, 18 January 2018, https://www.theguardian.com/global-development/2018/jan/18/sexual-assault-and-harassment-rife-at-united-nations-staff-claim; L. Rickard-Martin (2018), "The UN and #MeToo: All Forms of Abuse Must End Now," PassBlue, 9 May 2018, http://www.passblue.com/2018/05/09/the-un-and-metoo-the-saga-of-abuse-must-end-once-and-for-all/; L. Kirkpatrick (2017), "Sexual Harassment at the UN Is Alive

and Persistent," PassBlue, 22 December 2017, https://www.passblue.com/2017/12/22/sexual-harassment-at-the-un-is-alive-and-persistent/.

78. For similar findings on the male dominance within human rights expert positions, see Halme-Tuomisaari (2010a).

79. See discussion also in Cowan (2021).

Chapter 4

1. The subsequent section is based on fieldnotes from the following Human Rights Committee public sessions: 107th Session, Palais Wilson, 52 Rue des Paquis, 21 March 2013, 2967th session, 11:00 a.m., General Comment 9; 107th Session, 26 March 2013, 2973th session, 10:00 a.m., General Comment 9—continued; 108th session—23 July 2013, 3,001st session, 10:00 a.m.–1:00 p.m.; 108th session—25 July 2013, 3,005th session, 10 a.m.–1:00 p.m., draft General Comment on Article 9; 109th session—17 October 2013, (session information not available), 3:00 p.m., General Comment 9; 109th session—25 October 2013, 3,025th session, 11:00 a.m.–1:00 p.m.

2. General Comments address individual articles of the ICCPR and, in light of the Committee's "jurisprudence" and "case law," offer an elaborated understanding of the article's scope and significance. See Keller and Grover (2012); see also M. Halme-Tuomisaari (2020), "Guarding Utopia: Law, Vulnerability and Frustration at the UN Human Rights Committee," *Social Anthropology / Anthropologie Sociale* 28(1), 35–49. The Human Rights Committee began adopting General Comments in 1982. The above discussion referenced General Comment No. 35 of 2014 on Article 9 on the Liberty and Security of Persons that the Committee adopted on 23 October 2014. The length of this General Comment document alone testifies to the level of detail involved in drafting it: whereas the entire ICCPR is circa 7,700 words, General Comment No. 35 is almost double that length. UN OHCHR (2014), General Comment No. 35 on Article 9, Liberty and Security of Persons, CCPR/C/GC/35.

3. Shipton (2003).

4. The final text of General Comment No. 35, par. 3, reads: "Article 9 guarantees those rights to everyone. 'Everyone' includes, among others, girls and boys, soldiers, persons with disabilities, lesbian, gay, bisexual and transgender persons, aliens, refugees and asylum seekers, stateless persons, migrant workers, persons convicted of crime, and persons who have engaged in terrorist activity." UN OHCHR (2014), General Comment No. 35.

5. On legal indeterminacy, see M. Koskenniemi (1989/2009), *From Apology to Utopia: The Structure of International Legal Argument* (Cambridge: Cambridge University Press); D. Kennedy (2002a), "The Critique of Rights," in *Left Legalism / Left Critique*, ed. W. Brown and J. Halley (Durham, NC: Duke University Press), 178–228; M. Tushnet (1984), "An Essay on Rights," *Texas Law Review* 62(8), 1363–1403; J. Boyle (1985), "Ideals and Things: International Legal Scholarship and the Prison-House Language," *Harvard International Law Journal* 26(1), 327–359; N. Onuf (1985), "Do Rules Say What They Do? From Ordinary Language to International Law," *Harvard International Law Journal* 26(2), 385–410.

See, for example, M. Bódig (2017), "Soft Law, Doctrinal Development, and the General Comments of the UN Committee on Economic, Social and Cultural Rights," in *Tracing the Roles of Soft Law in Human Rights*, ed. S. Lagoutte, T. Gammeltoft-Hansen, and J. Cerone (Oxford: Oxford University Press) 69–88.

6. See, for example, Kälin (2012), 51.

7. A. T. Guzman and T. L. Meyer (2010), "International Soft Law," *Journal of Legal Analysis* 2(1), 171–225; S. Lagoutte et al. (2016), *Tracing the Roles of Soft Law in Human Rights*; see also M. Goldmann (2012), "We Need to Cut Off the Head of the King: Past, Present, and Future Approaches to International Soft Law," *Leiden Journal of International Law* 25(2), 335–368.

8. Guzman and Meyer (2010), 172.

9. J. Klabbers (1998), "The Undesirability of Soft Law," *Nordic Journal of International Law* 67(4), 381–391; J. Klabbers (1996), "The Redundancy of Soft Law," *Nordic Journal of International Law* 65(2), 167–182.

10. Guzman and Meyer (2010), 171.

11. J. Ellis (2012), "Shades of Grey: Soft Law and the Validity of Public International Law," *Leiden Journal of International Law* 25(2), 313–334.

12. Guzman and Meyer (2010), 172; see also Goldmann (2012). This approach links up with discussion on legal aesthetics; see A. Riles (2015), "Afterword: A Method More Than a Subject," in *Exploring the "Legal" in Socio-legal Studies*, ed. D. Cowan and D. Wincott (London: Palgrave Macmillan), and discussion in Chapter 8.

13. K. McCall-Smith (2017), "Interpreting International Human Rights Standards: Treaty Body General Comments as a Chisel or a Hammer," in Lagoutte et al., *Tracing the Roles of Soft Law in Human Rights*, 27–46, esp. 33–34.

14. Ibid.

15. See Kennedy (2002a).

16. OHCHR Juris Database, https://juris.ohchr.org.

17. H. Brown, A. Reed, and T. Yarrow (2017), "Introduction: Towards an Ethnography of Meeting," *Journal of the Royal Anthropological Institute* 23(1), 10–27, quotation on 10.

18. Riles (2015), 259. These insights resonate with an aesthetic theory of law, which means that, as Philippopoulos-Mihalopoulos notes, law employs certain aesthetic practices "in order to prove itself socially relevant" and construct distinct "legal magic." A. Philippopoulos-Mihalopoulos (2019), "Law Is a Stage: From Aesthetics to Affective Aestheses," in *Research Handbook on Critical Legal Theory*, ed. E. Christodoulidis, R. Dukes, and M. Goldoni (London: Routledge), 201–222; see also A. Fischer-Lescano (2020), "Sociological Aesthetics of Law," *Law, Culture and the Humanities* 16(2), 268–293; P. Heritier (2014), "Legal Liturgies: The Aesthetic Foundation of Positive Law," *Pólemos* 8(1), 137–152; see also P. Heritier (2023), "Aesthetics of Law as 'Iconic Legal Theology': Legendre, Schmitt and Vico," *International Journal for the Semiotics of Law* 36, 477–508.

19. See Scheinin (2009).

20. See Cowan (2014); Strathern (2000a); Shore and Wright (2015).

21. See G. Neuman (2018a).

22. See discussion in Halme-Tuomisaari (2010a); see also C. Gearty and C. Douzinas, eds. (2012), *The Cambridge Companion to Human Rights Law* (Cambridge: Cambridge University Press); M. T. Kamminga and M. Scheinin, eds. (2009), *The Impact of Human Rights Law on General International Law* (Oxford: Oxford University Press).

23. J. Donnelly (2003), *Universal Human Rights in Theory and Practice*, 2nd ed. (Ithaca, NY: Cornell University Press), 1. See also Kennedy (2002), 187; O. Harris, ed. (1996), *Inside and Outside the Law* (London: Routledge), 185.

24. M. Mazower (2004), "The Strange Triumph of Human Rights, 1933–1950," *Historical Journal* 47(2), 379–398, quotation on 397.

25. UN Information Centre (2006), "Rapid Entry into Force of International Criminal Court Statute 'a Great Victory for Justice, and for World Order,' Secretary-General Says," https://press.un.org/en/2002/l3007.doc.htm?utm.

26. Tomkins noted when the UK's Human Rights Act was adopted in 1998, "Nowhere were the celebrations more pronounced or more intense than among communities of lawyers." A. Tomkins (2001), "Introduction: On Being Sceptical About Human Rights," in *Sceptical Essays on Human Rights*, ed. K. D. Ewing and A. Tomkins (Oxford: Oxford University Press), 1–11, quotation on 1.

27. P. Alston (1988), "Making Space for New Human Rights: The Case of the Right to Development," *Harvard Human Rights Yearbook* 1(3), 3–40.

28. J. Klabbers, A. Peters, and G. Ulfstein (2011), *The Constitutionalization of International Law* (New York: Oxford University Press); J. Dunoff and J. Trachtman (2009), "A Functional Approach to International Constitutionalization," in *Ruling the World?: Constitutionalism, International Law, and Global Governance*, ed. J. Dunoff and J. Trachtman (Cambridge: Cambridge University Press), 3–35; see also D. Shelton, ed. (2011), *International Law and Domestic Legal Systems: Incorporation, Transformation, and Persuasion* (Oxford: Oxford University Press). On the fragmentation of international law, see M. Koskenniemi (2006), *Fragmentation of International Law: Difficulties Arising from the Diversification and Expansion of International Law*, Report of the Study Group of the International Law Commission, A/CN.4/L.682.

29. S. Meckled-Garcia and B. Çali (2007), eds. (2007), *The Legalization of Human Rights: Multidisciplinary Perspectives on Human Rights and Human Rights Law* (London: Routledge), 1.

30. For discussion, see A. Sarat and W. Felstiner (1995), *Divorce Lawyers and Their Clients: Power and Meaning in the Legal Process* (Oxford: Oxford University Press).

31. A. Cohen (2017), "ADR and Some Thoughts on 'the Social' in Contemporary Legal Thought," in *Searching for Contemporary Legal Thought*, ed. J. Desautels-Stein and C. Tomlins (Cambridge: Cambridge University Press), 454–464; Riles (2017), 179, 183–84.

32. Scott (2018), 627; Guilfoyle (2019).

33. P. Goodrich (2008), "On the Relational Aesthetics of International Law: Philosophy of International Law," *Journal of the History of International Law* 10, 321–341.

34. For broader discussion on the role of education in the contemporary human rights phenomenon, see Halme-Tuomisaari (2010a); see also Babül (2017).

35. Fidler (2001); G. Simpson (2004), *Great Powers and Outlaw States: Unequal Sovereigns in the International Legal Order* (Cambridge: Cambridge University Press); J. Donnelly (1998), "Human Rights: A New Standard of Civilization?" *International Affairs* 74(1), 1–23.

36. See UN Human Rights Committee (2004), "General Comment No. 32, Article 14, Right to Equality Before Courts and Tribunals and to Fair Trial," CCPR/C/GC/32, https://www.refworld.org/docid/478b2b2f2.html.

37. See M. Koskenniemi (2001), *The Gentle Civilizer of Nations: The Rise and Fall of International Law, 1870–1960* (Cambridge: Cambridge University Press); Obregón (2012); Simpson (2004).

38. For discussion on "real reality" and "UN reality," see Chapter 5.

39. See discussion also at G. Dancy and C. J. Fariss (2017), "Rescuing Human Rights Law from International Legalism and Its Critics," *Human Rights Quarterly* 39(1), 1–36.

40. UN OHCHR, *Individual Complaint Procedures Under the United Nations Human Rights Treaties*, Fact Sheet No. 7, Rev. 2, 1, https://www.ohchr.org/sites/default/files/Documents/Publications/FactSheet7Rev.2.pdf; see also Halme-Tuomisaari and Toivanen (forthcoming).

41. A. Iriye, P. Goedde, and W. I. Hitchcock, eds. (2012), *The Human Rights Revolution: An International History* (New York: Oxford University Press); S.-L. Hoffmann, ed. (2010), *Human Rights in the Twentieth Century* (Cambridge: Cambridge University Press); J. Morsink (2000), *The Universal Declaration of Human Rights: Origins, Drafting, and Intent* (Philadelphia: University of Pennsylvania Press); W. Schabas, ed. (2013), *The Universal Declaration of Human Rights: The Travaux Préparatoires* (Cambridge: Cambridge University Press).

42. See American Law Institute (1998), *Statement of Essential Human Rights*, American Law Institute, Seventy-Fifth Anniversary, 1923–1998 (Philadelphia: American Law Institute); S. A. Seo (2007), "A Shattered Dream: The American Law Institute and the Drafting of the International Bill of Rights," *Thomas Jefferson Law Review* 30, 179–196.

43. J. P. Humphrey (1983), "The Memoirs of John P. Humphrey, the First Director of the United Nations Division of Human Rights," *Human Rights Quarterly* 5(4), 387–439; J. P. Humphrey (1984), *The Great Adventure: Human Rights and the United Nations* (New York: Transnational); J. P. Humphrey (1976), "The International Bill of Rights: Scope and Implementation," *William and Mary Law Review* 17(3), 527–541.

44. Billaud and Cowan (2020).

45. T. Hoopes and D. Brinkley (2000), *FDR and the Creation of the UN* (New Haven, CT: Yale University Press); E. Borgwardt (2007), *A New Deal for the World: America's Vision for Human Rights* (Cambridge: Belknap Press); Mazower (2004); M. Halme-Tuomisaari (2015), "Lobbying for Relevance: US Internationalists, French Civil Libertarians and the UDHR," in *Revisiting the Origins of Human Rights*, ed. P. Slotte and M. Halme-Tuomisaari (Cambridge: Cambridge University Press), 330–361.

46. Simpson (2001); M. Duranti (2017), *The Conservative Human Rights Revolution: European Identity, Transnational Politics and the Origins of the European Convention* (Oxford: Oxford University Press).

47. A. Prost and J. M. Winter (2013), *René Cassin and Human Rights: From the Great War to the Universal Declaration* (Cambridge: Cambridge University Press); S. Jensen (2016), *The Making of International Human Rights: The 1960s, Decolonization, and the Reconstruction of Global Values* (Cambridge: Cambridge University Press); Hoffmann (2010).

48. A. J. Hobbins (2001), "Humphrey and the High Commissioner: The Genesis of the Office of the UN High Commissioner for Human Rights," *Journal of the History of International Law* 3(1), 38–74.

49. A. D. Moses, M. Duranti, and R. Burke, eds. (2020), *Decolonization, Self-Determination, and the Rise of Global Human Rights Politics* (Cambridge: Cambridge University Press).

50. United Nations Archives, SOA 317/1/01 D, 1955; Eckel (2013), 188.

51. On the process of signature and ratification, see "What Is the Difference Between Signing, Ratification and Accession of UN treaties?," Dag Hammarskjöld Library, https://ask.un.org/faq/14594. See also discussion on the Covenants' development in Humphrey (1976).

52. S. Moyn (2010), *The Last Utopia: Human Rights in History* (Cambridge, MA: Harvard University Press); J. Eckel and S. Moyn (2014), *The Breakthrough: Human Rights in the 1970s* (Philadelphia: University of Pennsylvania Press).

53. United Nations Archives, SO 221 9 (1-3-5), Roger Baldwin to Egon Schelb of the UN Human Rights Division, 22 September 1959.

54. For a recent summary of these arguments, see M. Nowak (2018), "A World Court of Human Rights," in *International Human Rights Institutions, Tribunals, and Courts*, ed. G. Obertleinter (The Hague: Springer), 271–290.

55. Klabbers et al. (2011); I. Hurd (2015), "The International Rule of Law and the Domestic Analogy," *Global Constitutionalism* 4(3), 365–395; Soirila (2021).

56. Halme-Tuomisaari and Slotte (2015).

57. F. Fukuyama (1992), *The End of History and the Last Man* (New York: Free Press).

58. See also A. Cassese, ed. (2012), *Realizing Utopia: The Future of International Law* (Oxford: Oxford University Press).

59. See also discussion in Keller and Grover (2012).

60. Scholarship echoes this finding. From this viewpoint General Comments are "non-binding rules that have legal consequences because they shape states' expectations as to what constitutes compliant behavior." Guzman and Meyer (2010), 175.

61. These statements connect with Soave's analysis of legal norms according to which their meaning "cannot be discovered, but only created." T. Soave (2022), *The Everyday Makers of International Law: From Great Halls to Back Rooms* (Cambridge: Cambridge University Press), 227.

62. Kennedy (2002).

63. See Halme-Tuomisaari (2020).

64. Ibid.; see also L. Oette (2018), "The UN Human Rights Treaty Bodies: Impact and Future," in Oberleitner, *International Human Rights Institutions*, 95–116.

65. Koskenniemi (1989/2009).

66. Halme-Tuomisaari (2017).

67. "UN Human Rights Committee Regrets Burundi's Withdrawal from Public Dialogue," UN OHCHR, 3 July 2023, https://www.ohchr.org/en/press-releases/2023/07/un-human-rights-Committee-regrets-burundis-withdrawal-public-dialogue.

68. In the press release the Committee stated, "We deeply regret that the delegation decided to withdraw, rather than present the State's position on the improvements, challenges and critical issues that we are mandated to discuss with them." Further, the press release emphasized that "by doing so, the Government of Burundi has deprived itself of the opportunity to engage with the Committee and provide further information on the issues raised." Simultaneously, the Committee stressed that the delegation of Burundi retains the possibility of submitting responses to the questions posed by Committee members within forty-eight hours. Ibid.

69. Human Rights Committee, 107th Session, Palais Wilson, 52 Rue des Paquis, 19 March 2013, Macau, China, Initial Report, 10:00 a.m., day two.

70. For example, the year 2001 was named the UN Year of Dialogue Among Civilizations. UNGA (1998), "United Nations Year of Dialogue Among Civilizations," A/RES/53/22, 4 November 1998; UNGA (2001), "Global Agenda for Dialogue Among Civilizations," A/RES/56/6, 9 November 2001. As Chapter 8 discusses, a central goal of treaty body proceedings is to establish ongoing dialogue.

71. A. Riles (1998), "Infinity Within the Brackets," *American Ethnologist* 25(3), 378–398.

72. Human Rights Committee, 107th Session, Palais Wilson, 52 Rue des Paquis, 19 March 2013, 3:00 p.m., Peru I.

73. UN Human Rights Committee, 108th session, 9 July 2013 (public), 3:00 p.m., Seventh report of Ukraine, CCPR/C/UKR/7.

74. Sir Nigel was referring to the intergovernmental treaty body process that had appointed representatives from Indonesia and Iceland as co-chairs. UNGA (2002), "Intergovernmental Process of the General Assembly on Strengthening and Enhancing the Effective Functioning of the Human Rights Treaty Body System," GA Resolution 66/254, 23 February 2012.

75. UN Human Rights Committee, 108th session, 10 July 2013 (public), 2984th session, 15h 00 Initial report of Indonesia (CCPR/C/IND/1) (public); see discussion on the similar use of compliments at CERD in Clark (2016).

76. E. Domínguez-Redondo (2012), "The Universal Periodic Review—Is There Life Beyond Naming and Shaming in Human Rights Implementation?," *New Zealand Law Review* 4, 673–706; J. K. Cowan (2024), "Recommendations in Words and Numbers: Thinking with Sally Engle Merry at the Universal Periodic Review," in *The Complexity of Human Rights: From Vernacularization to Quantification*, ed. P. Alston (Oxford: Hart), 203–228. However, Cowan and Billaud note how, by contrast, interventions at the Human Rights Council were occasionally direct and accusatory. See J. K. Cowan and J. Billaud (2015), "Between Learning and Schooling: The Politics of Human Rights Monitoring at the Universal Periodic Review," *Third World Quarterly*, 36(6), 1175–1190.

77. Bens (2022), 30–31, 7.

78. Ibid., 7.

79. UN Human Rights Committee, 2,978th session, 28 March 2013 (public), 4:00 p.m., Methods of Work and announcement of bureau decisions. In recent years sessions where the Committee discusses its working methods have been closed from external observers.

80. The bureau includes the chair and the Committee's three vice chairs. See Human Rights Committee, *Rules of Procedure*.

81. The Human Rights Committee (2011), General Comment No. 34 on art, 19 CCPR, Freedoms of Opinion and Expression, 12 September 2011, CCPR/C/GC/34, italics added.

82. M. Halme-Tuomisaari (2013), "Contested Representation: Exploring China's State Report," *Journal of Legal Anthropology* 1(3), 333–359.

83. Consensus is the dominant approach in the Committee's work, with the exception of final views under the optional protocol, where separate and dissenting opinions can be voiced. See "Rules of Procedure and Working Methods," CCPR/C/3/Rev. 11, https://www.ohchr.org/en/treaty-bodies/ccpr/rules-procedure-and-working-methods.

84. This policy has since been changed, and today the rapporteur is identified by a placard posted by their name during the sessions.

85. Peters (2013), 547.

86. J. K. Cowan (2013), "Before Audit Culture: Towards a Genealogy of International Oversight of Rights," in *The Gloss of Harmony: The Politics of Policy Making in Multilateral Organisations*, ed. B. Müller (London: Pluto Press), 103–133.

87. Ibid., 125.

Chapter 5

1. UN Human Rights Committee: Constructive Dialogue on Finland, 108th session, 2,987th and 2,998th sessions, 12 July 2013, 10:00 a.m.–1:00 p.m. and 3:00–6:00 p.m., Palais Wilson.

2. After the COVID-19 pandemic in 2020–2021, the setup changed. Today, the Palais Wilson conference room is equipped with screens that allow observers seated in the back to see the faces of those speaking.

3. Scholars, including anthropologists, have long debated whether any notion of "real reality" exists, as well as how one might define or ascertain its content. This section does not engage with these discussions nor aspire to propose a definition of "real reality." Instead, in this and subsequent chapters, I use this expression to capture the idea visible in Committee

proceedings that something empirically and objectively observable constituting a stable condition of "real reality" might exist.

4. On the multifaceted processes of policy translation, see Gal (2015); Babül (2017); Kelly (2011); Ballestro (2014); Englund (2006); Merry (2006); Sarfaty (2012); Tsing (2005); Mathur (2015); T. Kelly (2009), "The UN Committee Against Torture: Human Rights Monitoring and the Legal Recognition of Cruelty," *Human Rights Quarterly* 31(3), 777–800.

5. Information provided by states parties to complement state reports in other languages may be overlooked as resources will not permit the translation of all material. Merry has discussed how in the CEDAW committee proceedings, draft documents as well as suggested alternative wordings are presented in English. Thus, a person who has not mastered the language "would have a great deal of difficulty assessing the implications and innuendos of different phrases and sentences." Merry (2006), 44. The same applies to the Human Rights Committee's operations. This choice of language is neither always voluntary nor neutral: for example, NGO caucuses are typically held in English only because NGOs cannot afford interpreters. Shortage of resources reproduces the privileged position of the powerful English-speaking actors, emphasizing their elitist nature. Thus UN reality both reflects and strengthens the dominance of English as the lingua franca, reproducing the privileges and exclusions linked to its competence among different groups of actors participating in the sessions of the Human Rights Committee and the other UN treaty bodies.

6. Hull (2012a), 254; see also Riles (2005); C. Moon (2012), "What One Sees and How One Files Seeing: Human Rights Reporting, Representation and Action," *Sociology* 46(5), 876–890.

7. Hull (2012a), 17; see also Riles (2015); Brown et al. (2017).

8. Halme-Tuomisaari (2013).

9. Cowan (2021) has discussed the same regarding the UPR, noting how the monitoring mechanisms' temporality may even prevent addressing ongoing conflicts.

10. Hull (2012a), 40.

11. Müller (2013), 9.

12. Hull (2012a), 32.

13. Babul (2017), 10.

14. A. Riles (2004), "Real Time: Unwinding Technocratic and Anthropological Knowledge," *American Ethnologist* 31(3), 392–405, quotation on 402; L. Clarke (1999), *Mission Improbable: Using Fantasy Documents to Tame Disaster* (Chicago: University of Chicago Press).

15. T. Osborne (1994), "Bureaucracy as a Vocation: Governmentality and Administration in Nineteenth-Century Britain," *Sociology Lens* 7(3), 289–313; see also Billaud (2014).

16. M. Weber (1978), "Bureaucracy," in *Economy and Society*, vol. 2, ed. G. Roth and C. Wittich (Berkeley: University of California Press), 956–1005.

17. M. Hull (2012b), "Documents and Bureaucracy," *Annual Review of Anthropology* 41, 251–267, quotation on 251.

18. J. C. Scott (1998), *Seeing Like a State: How Certain Schemes to Improve the Human Condition Have Failed* (New Haven, CT: Yale University Press).

19. On the "illegibility of the state," see also C. Hoag (2010), "The Magic of the Populace: An Ethnography of Illegibility in the South African Immigration Bureaucracy," *Political and Legal Anthropology Review* 33(1), 6–25.

20. Finland: *Sixth Periodic Reports* [*sic*] *of States Parties* (hereafter *Sixth State Report*), CCPR/C/FIN/6, 12 September 2011, https://tbinternet.ohchr.org/_layouts/15/treatybodyexternal/Download.aspx?symbolno=CCPR%2FC%2FFIN%2F6&Lang=en.

21. See Riles (1998); see also A. Riles (2000), *The Network Inside Out* (Ann Arbor: University of Michigan Press), 78.

22. "Unit for Human Rights Courts and Conventions," Ministry for Foreign Affairs of Finland, https://um.fi/unit-for-human-rights-courts-and-conventions. See also *Finland 2021 Human Rights Report*, Executive Summary, https://www.state.gov/wp-content/uploads/2022/02/313615_FINLAND-2021-HUMAN-RIGHTS-REPORT.pdf.

23. *Sixth State Report*, 3.

24. Ibid., 3–10.

25. Riles (1998), 380.

26. UN (2009), *International Human Rights Instruments: Compilation of Guidelines on the Form and Content of Reports to Be Submitted by States Parties to the International Human Rights Treaties*, HRI/GEN/2/Rev.6, 3 June 2009, https://digitallibrary.un.org/record/445470?v=pdf.

27. Merry (2006).

28. M. Halme-Tuomisaari (2012), "'The State Is One': Examining What 'Fact' Means in the Compilation of a Human Rights Report," *Suomen Antropologi: Journal of the Finnish Anthropological Society* 37(1), 22–30.

29. UN General Assembly (2014), Resolution 68/268, 21 April 2014, https://www.ohchr.org/sites/default/files/Documents/HRBodies/TB/HRTD/A-RES-68-268_E.pdf.

30. Alternately the Unit's staff solicits statements from different ministries and on the basis of these statement updates the document.

31. Hull (2012a), 13; see also K. Webb (1997), *Signs of Recognition: Powers and Hazards of Representation in an Indonesian Society* (Chicago: University of Chicago Press), 96.

32. Hull (2012b), 53, 54.

33. Mathur (2012), 5.

34. The report utilizes capital letters to refer to these.

35. United Nations (2009), Treaty Body Database: Common Core Documents, https://tbinternet.ohchr.org/_layouts/15/TreatyBodyExternal/CoreDocuments.aspx; see also UN (2009), *International Human Rights Instruments.*

36. Finland (2020), Common Core Document Forming Part of the Reports of States Parties, 17 March 2020, HRI/CORE/FIN/2020, p. 20, sec. h, par. 138, italics added.

37. Ibid., p. 21, sec. h, par. 140, 142.

38. Scott (1998), 183.

39. Ong and Collier (2007), 12.

40. Fieldnotes on UN Human Rights Committee, 108th session, 2,984th session, Initial Report of Indonesia, CCPR/C/IND/1, 10 July 2013, 3:00 p.m. (public).

41. Clark (2016), 256.

42. Moon (2012), 877.

43. Hull (2012a), 119.

44. B. Frohmann (2008), "Documentary Ethics, Ontology, and Politics," in *Archival Science* 8(3), 165–180; Hull (2012a), 259.

45. Hull (2012a), 260.

46. Kelly (2009).

47. See J. Ferguson and A. Gupta (2002), "Spatializing States: Toward an Ethnography of Neoliberal Governmentality," *American Ethnologist* 29(4), 981–1002; see also M.-R. Trouillot (2001), "The Anthropology of the State in the Age of Globalization," *Current Anthropology* 42(1), 125–138.

48. Mathur (2012), 2.

49. Latour (1987), 227.

50. Niezen and Sapignoli (2016), "Introduction," 1.

51. UN Human Rights Committee (2011), *Finland: Consideration of Reports Submitted by States Parties Under Article 40 of the Covenant*, CCPR/C/FIN/6, 8 August 2011.

52. United Nations (1998), Finland: Core Document Forming a Part of the Reports of States Parties, 29 June 1998, HRI/CORE/1/Add.59/Rev.2.

53. UN Human Rights Committee (2012), List of Issues, Finland, CCPR/C/FIN/Q/6, 23 November 2012.

54. UN Human Rights Committee (2012), List of Issues, Replies of Finland to the List of Issues, CCPR/C/FIN/Q/6/Add.1.

55. Additional information is not titled or given a documentary number. Documents available at UN Treaty Bodies: CCPR—Civil and Political Rights, 108th session (8–26 July 2013), https://tbinternet.ohchr.org/_layouts/15/treatybodyexternal/SessionDetails1.aspx?SessionID=623&Lang=en.

56. UN Human Rights Committee (2013), *Concluding Observations on the Sixth Periodic Report of Finland*, CCPR/C/FIN/CO/6, August 22, 2013.

57. UN Human Rights Committee (2014), *Concluding Observations on the Sixth Periodic Report of Finland, Addendum: Information Received from Finland on Follow-up to Concluding Observations*, CCPR/C/FIN/CO/6/Add.1, document distributed on 13 August 2014.

58. UN OHCHR, reference KF/fup-11, 13 April 2015, https://tbinternet.ohchr.org/_layouts/15/treatybodyexternal/Download.aspx?symbolno=INT%2FCCPR%2FFUL%2FFIN%2F22486&Lang=en.

59. UN Human Rights Committee (2014), *Concluding Observations on the Sixth Periodic Report of Finland, Addendum: Information Received from Finland on Follow-up to Concluding Observations*, CCPR/C/FIN/CO/6/Add.2. Document distributed on 13 August 2014.

60. In December 2015 the Committee published its twenty-seven-page follow-up report, which included follow-up views on the Committee's sessions 105 to 111. UN Human Rights Committee (2015), *Report on Follow-up to the Concluding Observations of the Human Rights Committee*, CCPR/C/115/2, 21 December 2015. The report also included follow-up views on Finland's report and a summary of Finland's additional information (pp. 14–18).

61. UN Human Rights Committee (2016), Concluding Observations, information provided by the Government of Finland on its follow-up to recommendations contained in paragraphs 10, 11, and 16, 11 April 2016. Document available at UN Treaty Bodies: CCPR—Civil and Political Rights, 108th session (8–26 July 2013), https://tbinternet.ohchr.org/_layouts/15/treatybodyexternal/Download.aspx?symbolno=INT%2FCCPR%2FAST%2FFIN%2F25246&Lang=en.

62. UN OHCHR (2013), Reference: GH/fup-120, document available at UN Treaty Bodies: CCPR—Civil and Political Rights, 108th session (8–26 July 2013), https://tbinternet.ohchr.org/_layouts/15/treatybodyexternal/Download.aspx?symbolno=INT%2FCCPR%2FFUT%2FFIN%2F28397&Lang=en.

63. UN Treaty Bodies (2013), CCPR—Civil and Political Rights, 108th session (8–26 July 2013).

64. For comparison, these figures are slightly higher than those from 2019, when Finland submitted its next state report, reviewed in 2021: the Committee examined thirteen state reports accompanied by 174 NGO shadow reports, adopted eight Lists of Issues, and issued

views on 137 individual communications. See UN Treaty Body Database: Sessions for CCPR—International Covenant on Civil and Political Rights, https://tbinternet.ohchr.org/_layouts/15/TreatyBodyExternal/SessionsList.aspx?Treaty=CCPR.

65. In addition to these documents, Committee members process Lists of Issues, General Comments, and documents related to individual communications.

66. UN General Assembly (2014), *Strengthening and Enhancing the Effective Functioning of the Human Rights Treaty Body System*, Resolution adopted by the General Assembly on 9 April 2014, A/RES/68/268.

67. J. Krommendijk (2020), "Less Is More: Proposals for How UN Human Rights Treaty Bodies Can Be More Selective," *Netherlands Quarterly of Human Rights* 38(1), 5–11.

68. United Nations General Assembly (1977), *Report of the Human Rights Committee, Thirty-Second Session, Supplement No. 44* (A/32/44), pp. 26–28, par. 123–126. The initial report submitted by Finland under article 40 of the Covenant was considered by the Committee at its 30th meeting on 18 August 1977, p. 26, par. 123, 125a.

69. Ibid., p. 27, par. 125d.

70. UN General Assembly (1991). *Report of the Human Rights Committee, Forty-Sixth Session* (A/46/40), par. 164–225. Finland's report processed on 22 October 1990.

71. Ibid., p. 26, par. 104.

72. Chapter 8 elaborates the issue of impact and effect.

73. UN Human Rights Committee (1998), *Concluding Observations on the Third Periodic Report of Finland, Sixty-Second Session*, CCPR/c/79/Add.91, 8 April 1998, p. 37, par. 180.

74. UN Human Rights Committee (2004), *Concluding Observations on the Fifth Report of Finland*, CCPR/CO/82/FIN, 2 December 2004, p. 2, par. 3c, 9. The Committee repeats its concern in the Sixth Concluding Observations (p. 2, par. 6).

75. Non-Discrimination Act (No. 1325/2014), adopted in 2014, accompanied by the setting up of the Non-Discrimination Ombudsman and the National Non-Discrimination and Equality Tribunal. The Committee also highlights a recent Amendment (No. 1329/2014) to the Act on Equality Between Women and Men from 2014. UN Human Rights Committee (2021), *Concluding Observations on Finland*, CCPR/C/FIN/CO/7, 3 May 2021, p. 1, par. 3. Despite recognizing these positive developments, the Committee notes with concern how "the Non-Discrimination Act is not yet widely known among the public, and victims of discrimination thus tend to seek remedies through varying and sometimes confusing channels." UN Human Rights Committee (2021), *Concluding Observations on the Seventh Periodic Report of Finland*, CCPR/C/FIN/CO/7, 3 May 2021, pp. 3–4, par. 12.

76. Tasa-arvoasiain neuvottelukunta (2023), "#Tasa-arvovaalit: Naisten ja miesten eläke-erot ovat ansiotasoissa ja perhevapaiden jakautumisessa," 12 March 2023, https://tane.fi/-/-tasaarvovaalit-naisten-ja-miesten-elake-eron-takana-ovat-erot-ansiotasoissa-ja-perhevapaiden-jakautumisessa.

77. "Naisten palkkapäivä muistuttaa tasa-arvon heikosta tilasta," Akava, 4 April 2022, https://akava.fi/blogit/naisten-palkkapaiva-muistuttaa-tasa-arvon-heikosta-tilasta/; "Naisten ja miesten palkkaero ennallaan, ratkaisu voisi olla palkka-avoimmuuden lisääminen," STTK, 4 November 2022, https://www.sttk.fi/2022/11/04/sttk-naisten-ja-miesten-valinen-palkkaero-ennallaan-ratkaisu-voisi-olla-palkka-avoimuuden-lisaaminen/.

78. The paragraph states, "No one shall be liable to be tried or punished again for an offence for which he has already been finally convicted or acquitted in accordance with the law and

penal procedure of each country." International Covenant on Civil and Political Rights, Adopted and opened for signature, ratification and accession by General Assembly resolution 2200A (XXI) of 16 December 1966, entry into force 23 March 1976, in accordance with Article 49, https://www.ohchr.org/en/instruments-mechanisms/instruments/international-covenant-civil-and-political-rights.

79. First Concluding Observations, par. 125(l).

80. UN General Assembly (1977), *Report of the Human Rights Committee, Thirty-Second Session, Supplement No. 44 (A/32/44)*, Finland on pp. 26–28, par. 123–146; UN General Assembly (1986), *Report of the Human Rights Committee, Official Records: Forty-First Session, Supplement No. 40* (AI4114O), Finland on pp. 34–47, par. 164–225; UN General Assembly (1991), *Report of the Human Rights Committee, Forty-Sixth Session* (A/46/40); UN Human Rights Committee, *Concluding Observations on Finland, Sixty-Second Session*, CCPR/c/79/Add.91, 8 April 1998; UN Human Rights Committee (2004), *Concluding Observations on Finland*, CCPR/CO/82/FIN, 2 December 2004; UN Human Rights Committee (2013), *Concluding Observations on Finland*, CCPR/C/FIN/CO/6, 22 August 2013; UN Human Rights Committee (2021), *Concluding Observations on Finland*, CCPR/C/FIN/CO/7, 3 May 2021.

81. In the third reporting cycle Finland declared, "The Government did *not intend to withdraw the reservation* to article 14 (7) of the Covenant since the paragraph in question did not appear to be in conformity with the spirit of Nordic law, and the present legislation was not contrary to the principle on which article 14 (7) of the Covenant was based." UN General Assembly (1991), *Report of the Human Rights Committee, Forty-Sixth Session* (A/46/40), p. 32, par. 125, italics added.

82. See *Second Concluding Observations*, p. 44, par. 213; *Third Concluding Observations*, p. 26, par. 104; *Fourth Concluding Observations*, p. 6, par. 21; *Fifth Concluding Observations*, p. 3, par. 14; *Sixth Concluding Observations*, p. 4, par. 14.

83. UN General Assembly (1986), *Report of the Human Rights Committee*, 213.

84. *Seventh Concluding Observations*, p. 8, par. 36.

85. For background on the position of the Sámi in Finland, see R. Toivanen (2003), "Saami People and the Nordic Civil Societies," in *Civil Society in the Baltic Sea Region*, ed. N. Götz and J. Heckmann (Aldershot, UK: Ashgate), 205–16. On the Sámi in international advocacy, see R. Toivanen (2019), "European Fantasy of the Arctic Region and the Rise of Indigenous Sámi Voices in the Global Arena," in *Arctic Triumph*, ed. N. Sellheim, Y. Zaika, and I. Kelman (Cham, Switzerland: Springer Polar Sciences).

86. *Second Concluding Observations*, p. 46, par. 222.

87. This resonates with the broader state of Indigenous rights, which had not yet cemented their status as an uncontroversial part of the human rights movement within the UN. See Shipton (2001).

88. *Third Concluding Observations*, p. 33, par. 136.

89. In the issue the Committee's views become more positive, and in the Fourth Concluding Observations "the Committee notes with appreciation Finland's actions to develop their language and culture." *Fourth Concluding Observations*, p. 2, par. 5.

90. *Third Concluding Observations*, p. 33, par. 136.

91. In the *Fourth Concluding Observations* the Committee notes how "the proposed Sámi Act, by which forests within the Sámi homeland would be turned into commons owned by the Sámi Villages, have not passed the Parliament and that the issue of land rights of the Sámi have

not been resolved." *Fourth Concluding Observations*, p. 4, par. 11. In the *Fifth Concluding Observations* the Committee "regrets that it has not received a clear answer concerning the rights of the Sámi as an indigenous people (Constitution, sect. 17, subsect. 3), in the light of article 1 of the Covenant." *Fifth Concluding Observations*, p. 4, par. 17.

92. *Fifth Concluding Observations*, p. 4, par. 17, p. 2, par. 8; Individual communication No. 779/1997 (*Anni Äärelä and Jouni Näkkäläjärvi v. Finland*).

93. The Committee highlights how Sámi issues remain unresolved in Finland with a continued lack of understanding by public authorities over the Sámi way of life, as well as "a lack of legal clarity on the use of land in areas traditionally inhabited by the Sámi people (arts. 1, 26 and 27)." *Sixth Concluding Observations*, p. 4, par 16.

94. Ibid. Simultaneously, the Committee notes positive legislative initiatives, most significantly Finland's commitment to ratify the International Labour Organization Convention No. 169, to which Finland is not a party, in contrast to the other Nordic countries.

95. The Committee adopted the follow-up procedure in 2012 to improve the realization of the Concluding Observations as well as to bestow on the Committee a greater oversight into state action. In the procedure selected issues are graded on a scale from A, "satisfactory," to E, "contrary to the Covenant," on the basis of how they had complied with covenant obligations since the previous cycle. UN Human Rights Committee (2021), Note by the Human Rights Committee on the Procedure for Follow-up to Concluding Observations, 23 December 2021, CCPR/C/161.

96. Finland shared how a working group of the Ministry of Justice has proposed a revision of the Act on the Sámi Parliament (1974/1995), with a legislative proposal including sections on Sámi consultation and participation to be submitted to the national Parliament by Autumn 2014. UN Human Rights Committee (2014), *Concluding Observations on the Sixth Periodic Report of Finland, Addendum: Information Received from Finland on Follow-up to Concluding Observations*, CCPR/C/FIN/CO/6/Add.1, pp. 4–5.

97. UN Human Rights Committee (2014), *Concluding Observations on the Sixth Periodic Report of Finland, Addendum: Information Received from Finland on Follow-up to Concluding Observations*, CCPR/C/FIN/CO/6/Add.2, pp. 4–6, par. 14–18. In February 2015 the Constitutional Committee of Parliament delivered its report, which was not unanimous with the majority of Committee members voting against the proposed revision on the question of who is defined to be a Sámi, a highly contested and politically flammable issue. In March 2015 a vote in the Sámi Parliament showed that it did not support that government bill, specifically the included proposal on who is considered to be a Sámi. Subsequently, the government decided to withdraw the whole bill rather than let Parliament pass a bill that would not have the Sámi Parliament's consent.

98. UN Human Rights Committee (2016), Concluding Observations, information provided by the Government of Finland on its follow-up to recommendations contained in paragraphs 10, 11 and 16, 11 April 2016, document available at UN Treaty Bodies: CCPR—Civil and Political Rights, 108th session (8–26 July 2013), p. 5, par 16, https://tbinternet.ohchr.org/_layouts/15/treatybodyexternal/Download.aspx?symbolno=INT%2FCCPR%2FAST%2FFIN%2F25246&Lang=en. The new Act also resulted in the setting up of a new working group established by the Ministry of Agriculture and Forestry to "prepare an increase of the rights of the Sámi to participate in decision-making on the use of State-owned lands and waters in the Sámi Homeland." Ibid., p. 5.

99. This as was reflected in the overall outcome of the follow-up procedure on Finland's sixth state report. After the first round of replies the Committee granted Finland a grade of B2 on Sámi rights, meaning that Finland's reply/action was seen by the Committee as partially satisfactory. UN OHCHR, Reference: GH/fup-120, document available at UN Treaty Bodies: CCPR—Civil and Political Rights, 108th session (8–26 July 2013), p. 2, https://tbinternet.ohchr.org/_layouts/15/treatybodyexternal/Download.aspx?symbolno=INT%2FCCPR%2FFUT%2FFIN%2F28397&Lang=en. After the second round, when the new proposed Sámi act was withdrawn from the Parliament and the ratification of ILO 169 was pushed to the next session of Parliament, the assessment fell to C1, meaning that reply or action by Finland was not seen as satisfactory. After the third follow-up round with more information from Finland, the final evaluation became B, with an A awarded to Finland's realization of Sámi language rights. Ibid., p. 2.

100. *Seventh Concluding Observations*, p. 9, par. 42.

101. Ibid.; for summary on the status of ILO 169's ratification, see T. Joona (2020), "ILO Convention No. 169 and the Governance of Indigenous Identity in Finland: Recent Developments," *International Journal of Human Rights* 24(2–3), 241–256.

102. Act Amending the Act on the Sámi Parliament (Finland)—414/2025 (Laki saamelaiskäräjistä annetun lain muuttamisesta), promulgated 27 June 2025, entered into force 1 August 2025, official text on Finlex (Statute Book of Finland).

103. UN Committee on the Rights of the Child (2025), *Views Adopted by the Committee Under the Optional Protocol to the Convention on the Rights of the Child on a Communications Procedure, Concerning Communication No 172/2022*, UN Doc CRC/C/97/D/172/2022; UN Committee on Economic, Social and Cultural Rights (2024), Views Adopted by the Committee Under the Optional Protocol to the International Covenant on Economic, Social and Cultural Rights, Concerning Communications Nos. 251/2022 and 289/2022, 9 December 2024, UN Docs E/C.12/76/D/251/2022, E/C.12/76/D/289/2022.

104. In his analysis Krommendijk (2014) identifies thirty Concluding Observations from different treaty bodies that have been partially impactful according to the criteria he selected; for inconsistencies and contradictions between Finland's international human rights obligations and the treatment of conscientious objectors as well as the Sámi people, see also M. Lempinen (2008), *The Activity, Progressiveness and Consistency of the Human Rights Policy of Finland: Economic, Social and Cultural Rights* (Åbo: Åbo Akademi University).

105. See Krommendijk's (2015a) comparative analysis between Finland, the Netherlands, and New Zealand illustrating the Netherlands' performance to lag behind Finland.

106. See discussion in Chapter 3.

107. UN Web TV (2021), Consideration of Finland, 3,758th Meeting, 131st Session of the Human Rights Committee, 2 March 2021, https://webtv.un.org/en/asset/k10/k10wh64ybg.

108. Ulkoministeriö (2013), Lehdistötiedotteet, "YK:n ihmisoikeuskomitea antoi loppupäätelmänsä Suomelle," Tiedote 158/2013, 25 July 2013, https://valtioneuvosto.fi/-/un-human-rights-committee-submitted-its-concluding-observations-to-finland.

109. "YK huolissaan naisten asemasta Suomessa," *Helsingin Sanomat*, 26 July 2013, https://www.hs.fi/kotimaa/art-2000002663546.html; "YK moittii Suomea tasa-arvon puuttumisesta," YLE, 25 July 2013, http://yle.fi/uutiset/yk_moittii_suomea_tasa-arvon_puuttumisesta/6748783; "YK:n ihmisoikeuskomitealta Suomelle pyyhkeitä miesten ja naisten välisestä palkkaerosta," Verkkouutiset, 25 July 2013, http://www.verkkouutiset.fi/politiikka/Ihmisoikeuskomitean%20loppupäätelmät%20Suomelle-6055.

110. "Valtioneuvoston perus- ja ihmisoikeusverkosto," Oikeusministeriö (Ministry of Justice), https://oikeusministerio.fi/perus-ja-ihmisoikeusverkosto.

111. UN Web TV (2021).

Chapter 6

1. Bens (2002); Clark (2019).

2. Cowan (2020).

3. Mathur (2012), 2; see also Greenberg (2025).

4. Bear and Mathur (2015). On the role of state actors within human rights monitoring, see also S. Lagoutte (2019), "The Role of State Actors Within the National Human Rights System," *Nordic Journal of Human Rights* 37(3), 177–194.

5. O. A. Hathaway (2002), "Do Human Rights Treaties Make a Difference?," *Yale Law Journal* 111(8), 1935–2042; see also Simpson (2004).

6. Riles (1998), 388.

7. M. Strathern (2006), "Bullet-Proofing: A Tale from the United Kingdom," in *Documents: Artefacts of Modern Knowledge*, ed. A. Riles (Michigan: University of Michigan Press), 181–205, quotation on 196.

8. J. Comaroff and J. Comaroff (1992), *Ethnography and the Historical Imagination* (Boulder, CO: Westview).

9. Hull (2012a), 207.

10. Weber (1978), 975.

11. D. Graeber (2018), *Bullshit Jobs: A Theory* (New York: Simon & Schuster); see also Herzfeld (1992).

12. See Cowan (2021); Lagoutte (2019); Babül (2017).

13. The name "Sam" is a gender-neutral pseudonym to blur the person's identity. The exchange builds on several interviews with Sam over numerous years. The original language of the interviews was Finnish, and the English translations are my own.

14. Such groups do not exist in Finland.

15. This tenor connects with Krommendijk's (2014) analysis. He noted "the dedication and relative enthusiasm of current and former officials from the Ministry for Foreign Affairs," echoed by one interviewee's comment that it was their duty to defend and promote the treaty body system.

16. See discussion on transparency in the Committee's operations, as well as in international law and policy, in Chapter 2.

17. Merry (2006).

18. As Chapter 5 discussed, Sámi issues have remained a source of controversy, and national debates on the matter increasingly refer to UN human rights monitoring mechanisms, the Human Rights Committee's individual views in particular.

19. Cowan and Billaud have made similar observations regarding the UPR, where state delegates likewise may characterize it as an oral exam. Cowan and Billaud (2015).

20. These findings are replicated in Krommendijk's (2014) analysis. He notes how "Finnish government officials were generally motivated and interested in the [outcome of the] process and the COs. In contrast to officials in the other two countries, they did not question the necessity or relevance of reporting or the existence of treaty bodies. Even though almost all officials noted the labour and time intensity of the process, the burden of reporting seems to have affected fewer officials' willingness to report, at least of those interviewed. The majority of

officials perceived the reporting process as useful. Several officials held that reporting can actually be a vehicle or tool for improving the domestic human rights situation by raising attention and awareness about [new] challenges and issues at the domestic level"; see also Krommendijk 2015b.

21. Strathern (2006).

22. Billaud and Cowan (2020), 1.

23. For a general introduction into Finland's history, see M. Klinge (1987), *A Brief History of Finland* (Helsinki: Otava); T. Kinnunen and Markku Jokisipilä (2012), "Shifting Images of 'Our Wars': Finnish Memory Culture of World War II," in *Finland in World War II: History, Memory, Interpretations*, ed. T. Kinnunen and V. Kivimäki (Leiden: Brill), 435–482. For summary of Finland's relationship with the international human rights regime, see M. Halme-Tuomisaari (2010b), "From the Periphery to the Center: Emergence of the Human Rights Phenomenon in Finland," in *Finnish Yearbook of International Law*, ed. J. Klabbers and T. Tuori (Leiden: Brill), 257–281.

24. To avoid occupation, Finland allied itself with Germany, a matter that still causes discomfort for the Finnish population. See T. Polvinen (1986), *Between East and West: Finland in International Politics, 1944–1947* (Minneapolis: University of Minnesota Press). In the agreement Finland agreed to defend its territory against military invasion, if required, with Soviet assistance, and not to allow its area to be utilized in military action against the Soviet Union. See V. Rasila, E. Jutikkala, and K. Kulha (1980), *Suomen poliittinen historia 1905–1975* (Porvoo: Werner Söderström); Blomstedt et al. (1988), *Suomen Historia, osa 8: Paasikiven aika, Kekkosen aika, taloudellinen kasvu ja yhteiskuntamurros, massakulttuurin maihinnousu, taistelut kulttuurista* (Espoo: Weilin Göös); I. Saraviita (1989), *YYA-sopimus* (Helsinki: Lakimiesliiton kustannus); K. Joutsamo (1990), *Puolueettomuus ja EY* (Turku: Euro Consulting Oy).

25. T. Vihavainen (1991), *Kansakunta rähmällään: suomettumisen lyhyt historia* (Helsinki: Otava); J. Luoto (1997), *Ulkopolitiikka ja Ihmisoikeudet: Suomen kansainvälisen ihmisoikeuspolitiikan murroskausi 1985–1995* (Helsinki: Gaudeamus); K. Törnudd (2021), *Finland and the International Norms of Human Rights* (Leiden: Brill), 22–28, 276–285.

26. "Signatures and Ratifications," Council of Europe, https://www.coe.int/en/web/conventions/recent-changes.

27. M. Pellonpää (1998), *Euroopan neuvoston ihmisoikeussopimus Suomen näkökulmasta* (Helsinki: Oikeusministeriön lainvalmisteluosaston julkaisu), 21, 313–316; J. Tervo (1998), "Pintaremontti riittää," *Helsingin Sanomat, Kuukausiliite* 11, 36–38; M. Scheinin (1998), *Aseistakieltäytymisoikeus* (Helsinki: Hakapaino Oy). The status of Finnish conscientious objectors continues to provoke occasional controversy. See L. Ervo (2006), "Förhållandet mellan Europadomstolen och nationella domstolar—Findländska perspektiv," in *Juridisk Tidskrift* 4, 411–422.

28. See, for example, J. Luoto (1996), "Suomi varovainen ihmisoikeussaralla," *Kumppani*, 10 March 1996; M. Pellonpää (1984), *Expulsion in International Law: A Study in International Aliens Law and Human Rights with Special Reference to Finland* (Helsinki: Suomalainen tiedeakatemia).

29. Halme-Tuomisaari (2010b), 273; *Amnesty International Report 2006—Finland*, UNHCR, https://www.refworld.org/docid/447ff7a72.html; J. Relander (1997), "Ulkoinen totuus ja sisäinen kokemus taistolaisliikkeessä," *Tieteessä tapahtuu* 4, 31–37.

30. M. Hidén and I. Saraviita (1994), *Valtiosääntöoikeuden pääpiirteet*, 6th rev. ed. (Helsinki: Lakimiesliiton kustannus), 272; M. Scheinin (1991), *Ihmisoikeudet Suomen oikeudessa* (Jyväskylä: Suomalainen Lakimiesyhdistys); T. Ojanen (2003), *Perusoikeudet ja ihmisoikeudet*

Suomessa (Helsinki: Forum Iuris); T. Ojanen and A. Haapea, eds. (2006), *EU-oikeuden perusteita* (Helsinki: Edita); V.-P. Viljanen (1996), "Perusoikeusuudistus ja kansainväliset ihmisoikeussopimukset," *Lakimies* 5–6, 788–815; Ojanen and Salminen (2019); M. Scheinin (1990), "The Status of Human Rights Conventions in Finnish Domestic Law," in *International Human Rights Norms in Domestic Law: Finnish and Polish Perspectives*, ed. A. Rosas (Helsinki: Finnish Lawyers Publishing), 25–43.

31. See T. Ojanen (2009), "From Constitutional Periphery Toward the Center—Transformations of Judicial Review in Finland," *Nordic Journal of Human Rights* 27(2), 194–207; Halme-Tuomisaari (2010b).

32. Finland's Ministry of Education (2006), "Opetusministeriön ja opetushallituksen välinen tulosopimus vuosille 2006–2008."

33. See *United Nation Human Rights Report 2022*, UN OHCHR, 95, https://www.ohchr.org/sites/default/files/documents/publications/ohchr-reports/ohchr-report-2022.pdf; *Report 2024*, UN OHCHR, https://www.ohchr.org/sites/default/files/documents/publications/ohchr-reports/ohchr-report-2024.pdf.

34. Since summer 2023 Finland's adherence to human rights values has faced a new phase via the government of Prime Minister Orpo, which has, among others, introduced a new deportation law that numerous Finnish international law experts view as being against Finland's international human rights obligations. The law has resulted in numerous complaints to the European Court of Human Rights, which were still pending at the start of 2026.

35. Babul (2017), 3.

36. Thanks to Elif Babül for this discussion.

37. K. Bjorkdahl and A. de Bengy Puyvallee (2021), *Do-Gooders at the End of Aid: Scandinavian Humanitarianism in the Twenty-First Century* (Cambridge: Cambridge University Press); L. P. Andersen, F. Lindberg, and J. Ostberg (2021), "Unpacking Nordic Branding: The Value Regimes of Nordicness," *Journal of Place Management and Development* 14(3), 362–378; D. Brommesson (2018), "'Nordicness' in Swedish Foreign Policy—from Mid Power Internationalism to Small State Balancing?," *Global Affairs* 4(4–5), 391–404; A. Hyde-Price (2018), "Epilogue: 'Nordicness'—Theory and Practice," *Global Affairs* 4(4–5), 435–443.

38. Simpson (2005).

39. Cowan (2013), 118, 120.

40. For comparison from the ECHR, see J. Greenberg (2020), "Law, Politics, and Efficacy at the European Court of Human Rights," *American Ethnologist* 47(4), 417–431.

41. Finland's state report was discussed in the following sessions: UN Human Rights Committee, Constructive Dialogue on Finland, 108th session, 2,987th & 2,988th sessions, 12 July 2013, 10:00 a.m.–1:00 p.m. and 3:00–6:00 p.m., Palais Wilson.

42. When a state becomes a party to a treaty, it may issue reservations on certain covenant provisions, yet these reservations cannot be against the intent of the treaty. On reservations, see UN Treaty Collection: ICCPR, https://treaties.un.org/Pages/ViewDetails.aspx?src=TREATY&mtdsg_no=IV-4&chapter=4&clang=_en.

43. Cowan (2021).

44. For discussion on continuity of issues and recommendations between different reporting cycles, see Chapter 5.

45. Bens (2022), 4.

46. Of reporting fatigue, see also Krommendijk (2015).

47. Brown et al. (2017).

48. These comments resemble Graeber's (2018) work on "bullshit jobs."

49. C. Creamer and B. Simmons (2020), "The Proof Is in the Process: Self-Reporting Under International Human Rights Treaties," *American Journal of International Law* 114(1), 1–50.

Chapter 7

1. LGBT was the acronym utilized in Committee parlance at the time. Today the equivalent acronym might be LGBTIQ+, referring to lesbian, gay, bisexual, transsexual, intersexual, or questioning/queer +.

2. See discussion on translation processes in Chapter 5.

3. Feldman (2011).

4. Korey (2004).

5. Reiners (2021); see also Keck and Sikkink (1998); Riles (2000).

6. F. McGaughey (2018), "From Gatekeepers to Gongos: Taxonomy of Non-governmental Organisations Engaging with United Nations Human Rights Mechanisms," *Netherlands Quarterly of Human Rights* 36(2), 111–132.

7. Ibid., 128, 129. See also K. Tsutsui and C. M. Wotipka (2004), "Global Civil Society and the International Human Rights Movement: Citizen Participation in Human Rights International Nongovernmental Organizations," *Social Forces* 83(2), 587–620; Halme-Tuomisaari (2017).

8. D. Lewis, N. Kanji, and N. Themudo, eds. (2020), *Non-Governmental Organizations and Development* (London: Routledge).

9. N. C. Biraben (2020), "Book Review: *Cultures of Doing Good: Anthropologists and NGOs* edited by Amanda Lashaw, Christian Vannier and Steven Sampson," *LSE Review of Books*, 25 February 2020, https://blogs.lse.ac.uk/lsereviewofbooks/2020/02/25/book-review-cultures-of-doing-good-anthropologists-and-ngos-edited-by-amanda-lashaw-christian-vannier-and-steven-sampson/.

10. A. Lashaw, C. Vannier, and S. Sampson, eds. (2017), *Cultures of Doing Good: Anthropologists and NGOs* (Tuscaloosa: University of Alabama Press).

11. Lewis et al. (2020); see also W. Wong (2012), *Internal Affairs: How the Structure of NGOs Transforms Human Rights* (Ithaca, NY: Cornell University Press); T. Davies (2014), *NGOs: A New History of Transnational Civil Society* (Oxford: Oxford University Press); McGaughey (2018), 2.

12. Charter of the United Nations (adopted 26 June 1945, entered into force 24 October 1945), 1 UNTS XVI, Chapter X: The Economic and Social Council, Article 71, https://www.un.org/en/about-us/un-charter/chapter-10. Article 71 continues, "Such arrangements may be made with international organizations and, where appropriate, with national organizations after consultation with the Member of the United Nations concerned."

13. "The UN and Civil Society," United Nations, https://www.un.org/en/get-involved/un-and-civil-society.

14. See UN Human Rights Treaty Bodies: Sessions for CCPR—Covenant on International and Political Rights, https://tbinternet.ohchr.org/_layouts/15/TreatyBodyExternal/SessionsList.aspx?Treaty=CCPR.

15. K. O'Sullivan (2021), *The NGO Moment: The Globalisation of Compassion from Biafra to Live Aid* (Cambridge: Cambridge University Press), 3–4; see also Davies (2014); Lewis et al. (2021).

16. Claeys assesses that socialist rights experiments created unexpected precedents for later human rights advocacy, whereas Ceadel concludes that the connections of peace movements to

human rights were more complex. See discussions in M. Ceadel (2015), "The Peace Movement and Human Rights," in Slotte and Halme-Tuomisaari, *Revisiting the Origins of Human Rights*, 189–205; G. Claeys (2015), "Socialism and the Language of Rights: The Origins and Implications of Economic Rights," in Slotte and Halme-Tuomisaari, *Revisiting the Origins of Human Rights*, 206–236.

17. See discussion in E. Seidenfaden (2022), "The League of Nations' Collaboration with an 'International Public,' 1919–1939," *Contemporary European History* 31(3), 368–380; M. Herren (2017), "Geneva, 1919–1945: The Spatialities of Public Internationalism and Global Networks," in *Mobilities of Knowledge: Knowledge and Space*, ed. H. Jöns, P. Meusburger, and M. Heffernan (Cham, Switzerland: Springer); T. R. Davies (2012), "A 'Great Experiment' of the League of Nations Era: The Emerging Roles of NGOs in the UN System," *Global Governance* 18(3), 299–311.

18. S. Walker (1999), *In Defense of American Liberties: A History of the ACLU*, rev. ed. (Oxford: Oxford University Press).

19. C. Moores (2017), *Civil Liberties and Human Rights in Twentieth-Century Britain* (Cambridge: Cambridge University Press).

20. Eckel (2013); Halme-Tuomisaari (2017).

21. Moyn (2010).

22. Amnesty's exponential growth continued into the early 1980s, with its membership reaching 570,000 in 1983. Eckel (2013), 193. The shifting status of human rights NGOs in the fields of international politics and collaboration were sealed by the awarding of the Nobel Peace Prize to Amnesty in 1977. "History: 64 Years Protecting Human Rights," Amnesty International, https://www.amnestyusa.org/about-us/history/; see also Hopgood (2013).

23. See, for example, Korey (2004).

24. Borgwardt (2007); Mazower (2004); Halme-Tuomisaari (2015).

25. In legal terms Amnesty International Charity is a company registered in England and Wales limited by guarantee (no. 02007475) and a registered charity (no. 294230), with registered office at 1 Easton Street, London WC1X 0DW. "Who We Are," Amnesty International, https://www.amnesty.org/en/who-we-are/.

26. Human Rights Watch was founded in 1978 as Helsinki Watch to investigate human rights abuses particularly in countries within the Soviet bloc. "About Us," Human Rights Watch, https://www.hrw.org/about/about-us.

27. "Our History," Save the Children, https://www.savethechildren.org/us/about-us/why-save-the-children/history.

28. "Our History," Plan International, https://plan-international.org/organisation/history/.

29. Oxfam was founded in 1942 in the UK as the Oxford Committee for Famine Relief. The organization today has its headquarters in Nairobi, Kenya. "History of Oxfam," https://www.oxfam.org.uk/about-us/history-oxfam/.

30. See O'Sullivan (2021).

31. On the civilizing mission of international law, see Koskenniemi (2001); Obregón (2012).

32. J. Whyte (2017), *Morals of the Market: Human Rights and the Rise of Neoliberalism* (New York: Verso); Hopgood (2013); Lashaw et al. (2017); O'Sullivan (2021), 113.

33. O'Sullivan (2021), 113.

34. Lewis et al. (2020), 42.

35. Ibid., 172; see also Hopgood (2013); O'Sullivan (2021).

36. "UN Paris Principles and Accreditation," European Network of National Human Rights Institutions, https://ennhri.org/about-nhris/un-paris-principles-and-accreditation/.

37. Lewis et al (2020), 4.

38. Ibid., 174.

39. Lashaw et al (2017).

40. Ibid.

41. See Englund (2006).

42. Lewis et al. (2020), 166–167.

43. Hopgood (2013); see also D. Joyce (2022), *Informed Publics, Media and International Law* (London: Bloomsbury).

44. Lewis et al. (2020).

45. Biraben (2020); see also A. Mbembe (1992), "The Banality of Power and the Aesthetics of Vulgarity in the Postcolony," *Public Culture* 4(2), 1–30.

46. See A. Clapham (2000), "Defining the Role of Non-Governmental Organizations with Regard to the UN Human Rights Treaty Bodies," in *The UN Human Rights System in the 21st Century*, ed. A. Bayefsky (The Hague: Kluwer), 183–194.

47. See McGaughey (2021).

48. UN Human Rights Council (2016), *Annual Report of the United Nations High Commissioner for Human Rights and Reports of the Office of the High Commissioner and the Secretary General*, 11 April 2016, UN Doc A/HRC/32/20, agenda items 2 and 3, par. 53; see also McGaughey (2021), 112.

49. United Nations Conference on the Human Environment, 5–16 June 1972, https://www.un.org/en/conferences/environment/stockholm1972.

50. United Nations World Population Conference, 19–30 August 1974, Bucharest. See discussion in Lewis et al. (2020), 35–36.

51. Lewis et al. (2020), 35–36.

52. See "Nigel Rodley 1941–2017," Amnesty International, 26 January 2017, https://www.amnesty.org/en/latest/news/2017/01/nigel-rodley-1941-2017/; Kelly (2011).

53. K. Martens (2006), "Professionalised Representation of Human Rights NGOs to the United Nations," *International Journal of Human Rights* 10(1), 19–30, esp. 21–23.

54. J. Ron, H. Ramos, and K. Rodgers (2005), "Transnational Information Politics: NGO Human Rights Reporting, 1986–2000," *International Studies Quarterly* 49(3), 557–587.

55. O'Sullivan (2021), 3; see also Ron et al. (2005). During the same time frame the CERD Committee also discussed the reliability of NGO reports. Thanks to Joshua Clark for this discussion.

56. Martens (2006), 24.

57. For example, Nigel Rodley was characterized in his obituary as a "member of the Amnesty Community, having had decades long association with the NGO among many others." See discussion in Chapter 3.

58. UN Human Rights Committee (2004), Third Informal Meeting with States Parties to the Covenant, Eighty-Second Session; Summary Record of the 2,242nd Meeting, 28 October 2004, CCPR/C/SR.2242, par. 30.

59. See discussion in Chapter 3.

60. UN Human Rights Committee (2004), par. 31.

61. Ibid., par. 32.

62. Warm thanks to Walter Kälin for this discussion.

63. For example, in early 2010 the NGO briefings organized by the CERD Committee monitoring state compliance with the Convention on the Elimination of All Forms of Racial Discrimination were called "Informal Meetings." Thanks to Joshua Clark for this discussion.

64. The Committee's minutes from sessions in 2004 and 2005 include mentions of meetings with representatives of non-governmental and intergovernmental organizations during the Committee's sessions. Yet no minutes are available on these meetings. For example, UN Human Rights Committee (2005a), Eighty-Third Session, 14 March–1 April 2005, Provisional Agenda CCPR/C/15528 January, https://tbinternet.ohchr.org/_layouts/15/treatybodyexternal/Download.aspx?symbolno=CCPR%2FC%2F155&Lang=en; UN Human Rights Committee (2005b), 11–29 July 2005, https://tbinternet.ohchr.org/_layouts/15/treatybodyexternal/Download.aspx?symbolno=INT%2FCCPR%2FPOW%2F84%2F15003&Lang=en.

65. UN Human Rights Committee (2012), The Relationship of the Human Rights Committee with Non- governmental Organizations, 4 June 2012, CCPR/C/104/3, par. 3, https://documents-dds-ny.un.org/doc/UNDOC/GEN/G12/431/82/PDF/G1243182.pdf?OpenElement.

66. Ibid., par. 4, 5, italics added.

67. Ibid., par. 9, 17.

68. UN OHCHR (2023), "Human Rights Committee: Information for Civil Society, NGOs and National Human Rights Institutions; https://www.ohchr.org/en/treaty-bodies/ccpr/information-civil-society-ngos-and-national-human-rights-institutions; see also Halme-Tuomisaari (2013).

69. The very first shadow report posted to the Human Rights Committee's website was from the committee's eighty-sixth session in March 2006. The state in question was Saint Vincent and the Grenadines, and more specifically, instead of a Constructive Dialogue, the session was called a "Country Situation" because the state had not submitted a report. The session was accompanied by submissions from two civil society organizations, namely Global Initiative to End All Corporal Punishment on Children NGO and World Coalition Against the Death Penalty. UN Human Rights Treaty Bodies (2006), CCPR—International Covenant on Civil and Political Rights, Eighty-Sixth Session, 13–31 March (2006), https://tbinternet.ohchr.org/_layouts/15/treatybodyexternal/SessionDetails1.aspx?SessionID=439&Lang=en. The Committee has since adopted the practice of considering state situations in the absence of a report.

70. UN Human Rights Treaty Bodies (2007), CCPR—International Covenant on Civil and Political Rights, Ninetieth Session (9–27 Jul 2007), https://tbinternet.ohchr.org/_layouts/15/treatybodyexternal/SessionDetails1.aspx?SessionID=435&Lang=en.

71. Halme-Tuomisaari (2013).

72. Ron et al. (2005); Moon (2012).

73. Moon (2012), 876, 878; see also Halme-Tuomisaari (2013).

74. Moon (2012), 881.

75. Merry (2016).

76. Moon (2012), 883; see also Lewis et al. (2020).

77. Joyce (2020), 37; see also A. Orford (2003), *Reading Humanitarian Intervention: Human Rights and the Use of Force in International Law* (Cambridge: Cambridge University Press), 66; L. Malkki (1996), "Speechless Emissaries: Refugees, Humanitarianism, and Dehistoricization," *Cultural Anthropology* 11(3), 377–404, esp. 378, 385–386, 388; M. Halme-Tuomisaari (2022), "Visibility, Impact and Relevance in International Law," *London Review of International Law* 10(2), 313–324, esp. 321.

78. A report submitted to accompany the state report of the Republic of Korea simply labeled "NGO Submission" exemplifies the matter: the report is an undated and unsigned document of sixty-four pages addressing general issues falling under the ICCPR with no clarification on what kind of changes or Committee recommendations the report supports. UN Human

Rights Treaty Bodies (2006), CCPR—International Covenant on Civil and Political Rights, Eighty-Eighth Session (16 October–3 November 2006), Republic of Korea, "NGO Submission," https://tbinternet.ohchr.org/_layouts/15/treatybodyexternal/Download.aspx?symbolno=INT%2FCCPR%2FNGO%2FKOR%2F88%2F9441&Lang=en,

79. McGaughey (2018), 119.

80. CCPR—Centre for Civil and Political Rights; http://www.ccprcentre.org/about-us/board-and-staff/; the first annual report available is for 2015 (earlier links are inactive; https://ccprcentre.org/about-ccpr).

81. Merry (2006).

82. McGaughey (2018), 120 (quotation), 121.

83. Ibid., 124.

84. CCPR Centre (2015), *Annual Report 2015*, https://ccprcentre.org/files/media/Annual_Report_Final_web_2.pdf.

85. Lewis et al. (2020), 179.

86. In 2019–2020, the Centre received grants from the Open Society Foundation, the Confédération Suisse, Ville de Genève, National Endowment for Democracy, Foreign & Commonwealth Office, East-West Management Institute, République et Canton de Genève, Organisation internationale de Francophone, Loterie Romande, and the Taiwan Foundation for Democracy. See "CCPR Centre: How to Support CCPR Centre," https://ccprcentre.org/support-ccpr.

87. Charlesworth and Larkin (2015).

88. UN OHCHR (2023), "Information for Civil Society, NGOs and National Human Rights Institutes."

89. UN Human Rights Treaty Bodies (2013), International Covenant on Civil and Political Rights, 108th session (8–26 July 2013), https://tbinternet.ohchr.org/_layouts/15/treatybodyexternal/SessionDetails1.aspx?SessionID=623&Lang=en.

90. Amnesty International (2013), *Finland: Submission to the United Nations Human Rights Committee for the 108th Session of the Human Rights Committee*; Coalition of Finnish Women's Associations (NYTKIS) (2013), "Consideration of the Sixth Periodic Report of Finland Under the International Covenant on Civil and Political Rights—Comments," Submission to the UN Human Rights Committee, Helsinki, 10 June 2013; International Fellowship of Reconciliation (IFOR) and Conscience and Peace Tax International (CPTI) (2013), *Submission to the 108th Session of the Human Rights Committee: Finland (Military Service, Conscientious Objection and Related Issues)* (rev. June 2013); Saami Council (2013), *Observations with Regard to Finland's Sixth Periodic Report to the Human Rights Committee*, Submission to the Human Rights Committee, 2013; Finnish Disability Forum (Vammaisfoorumi ry / Handikappforum rf), European Disability Forum (EDF), and International Disability Alliance (IDA) (2013), *Joint DPO Submission on Finland to the Human Rights Committee (108th Session)*, Submission to the UN Human Rights Committee, 2013; Union of Conscientious Objectors (AKL) (2013), *Submission to the Human Rights Committee Concerning the Consideration of the Sixth Periodic Report of Finland: The Situation of Conscientious Objectors in Finland* (Helsinki: Union of Conscientious Objectors); Union of Freethinkers of Finland (Vapaa-ajattelijain Liitto ry) (2013), *Written Comments to Finland's Sixth Periodic Report and to the List of Issues Adopted by the Human Rights Committee*, Submission to the UN Human Rights Committee, 2013. All reports available at available at https://tbinternet.ohchr.org/_layouts/15/treatybodyexternal/SessionDetails1.aspx?SessionID=623&Lang=en.

91. Amnesty International (2013), *Finland*; ibid.

92. Sámi Council (2013), *Observations by the Saami Council with Regard to Finland's Sixth Report to the Committee.*

93. Halme-Tuomisaari (2017).

94. This emphasis has since intensified with Amnesty submitting fewer reports on UN treaty bodies. Thanks to Heather McGill for this discussion.

95. Finnish League for Human Rights, https://ihmisoikeusliitto.fi/english/.

Chapter 8

1. See J. Krommendijk (2012); Cole (2015); Connors (2000); Heyns and Viljoen (2002); Simmons (2009), *Mobilizing for Human Rights: International Law in Domestic Politics* (Cambridge: Cambridge University Press). Carraro suggests that the treaty bodies' significance lies in their ability to offer states learning opportunities and an overview of their human rights situation. V. Carraro (2019b), "Promoting Compliance with Human Rights: The Performance of the United Nations' Universal Periodic Review and Treaty Bodies," *International Studies Quarterly* 63(4), 1079–1093.

2. See J. Krommendijk (2015b), "The (In)effectiveness of UN Human Rights Treaty Body Recommendations," *Netherlands Quarterly of Human Rights* 33(2), 194–223; Crawford (2013).

3. See, for example, Niezen and Sapignoli (2017), "Introduction," 1; Klabbers and Sinclair (2020), 490.

4. UN Human Rights Committee (2013), *Seventh Report of the Ukraine* (CCPR/C/UKR/7), 9 July 2013 (public), 108th session, 2,981st session, italics added.

5. Finland's Constructive Dialogue with the Committee on Economic, Social and Cultural Rights on 13 November 2014, Committee on Economic, Cultural and Social Rights, 53rd Session, 10–28 November 2014, Palais Wilson, Geneva. Krommendijk (2014) also discovered mention of a "spiral continuum" in his research among Finnish civil servants participating in UN treaty body proceedings.

6. G. Robertson with I. Crewe, "Sir Nigel Rodley Obituary," *Guardian*, 2 February 2017, https://www.theguardian.com/law/2017/feb/02/sir-nigel-rodley-obituary. Carraro quotes in her interview study an interviewee summarizing how "you cannot come and talk of promoting human rights for women in a country where a woman still doesn't have an ID, so you have to come *step by step, movement by movement*." Carraro (2019a), italics added.

7. Carraro (2019a), italics added.

8. See N. Lacey (1988), *State Punishment: Political Principles and Community Values* (London: Routledge).

9. See Riles (1998); Halme-Tuomisaari (2013).

10. The graph initially appeared in *Reporting to the United Nations Human Rights Treaty Bodies Training Guide Part I*, but this guidebook is no longer available online. It has been reproduced at https://academy.ishr.ch/upload/resources_and_tools/Treaty_Body_Reporting_cycle.pdf.

11. Ingold (2011). On movement, see also J. M. Smith (2021), *In the Eyes of the World: Mining the Digital Age in the Eastern DR Congo* (Chicago: University of Chicago Press).

12. Ingold (2011), 3–4, 1.

13. Ibid., 150.

14. For discussion on the "forward-looking progressiveness" of the contemporary human rights phenomenon, see also Halme-Tuomisaari and Slotte (2015).

15. Feldman discusses similar findings in EU migration policy where many of the policymakers appeared not to believe that the policy really mattered in terms of on-the-ground

improvements in peoples' lives. See G. Feldman (2012), *The Migration Apparatus: Security, Labor, and Policymaking in the European Union* (Stanford, CA: Stanford University Press).

16. The idea that human rights form a secular religion, or are based on belief, has generated voluminous scholarship. See, for example, M. Perry (2000), *The Idea of Human Rights: Four Inquiries* (New York: Oxford University Press); H. Féron (2014), "Human Rights and Faith: A 'World-Wide Secular Religion'?," *Ethics and Global Politics* 7(4), 181–200. See also discussion in Dembour (2006).

17. H. Miyazaki (2004), *The Method of Hope: Anthropology, Philosophy and Fijian Knowledge* (Stanford, CA: University of Stanford Press); Ingold (2011), 142. See also discussion on hope in L. Berlant (2011), *Cruel Optimism* (Durham, NC: Duke University Press).

18. G. Urban (2001), *Metaculture: How Culture Moves Through the World* (Minneapolis: University of Minnesota Press), 104.

19. Krommendijk (2014).

20. See Allen (2013).

21. Human Rights Committee: Constructive Dialogue on Belize, 107th Session, 15 March 2013, 3:00 p.m.

22. UN Human Rights Committee, *Rules of Procedure.*

23. Council of Europe (n.d.), *Your Application to the ECHR*, https://www.echr.coe.int/documents/d/echr/your_application_eng.

24. "Human Rights Committee Opens One-Hundred and Thirty-Fifth Session," UN OHCHR, 27 June 2022, https://www.ohchr.org/en/press-releases/2022/06/human-rights-Committee-opens-one-hundred-and-thirty-fifth-session.

25. Latour (1987), 227–228.

26. Eriksen (2016).

27. See, for example, Krommendijk (2015).

28. Latour (1987), 227–228.

29. Graeber (2018).

30. See discussion in Chapter 5.

31. Mazower (2004).

32. See discussion in Chapter 4.

33. See Billaud (2014); see also Moon (2012).

34. Tsing (2005), 6; see also Appadurai (1996).

35. Latour (1978), 227.

36. M. Halme-Tuomisaari (2025), "Standards for a Better World: Anthropological Approaches to the Study of International Organizations," in *Ways of Seeing International Organizations*, eds. N. Mansouri and D. Quigoral-Villamarin (Cambridge: Cambridge University Press), 208–226; Tzouvala notes how the standard of civilization is increasingly seen as synonymous with "metrics, indexes and 'best practices' that give contemporary iterations." N. Tzouvala (2020), *Capitalism as Civilisation: A History of International Law* (Cambridge: Cambridge University Press), 79. This finding connects with Feldman's (2012) analysis on the "migration apparatus."

37. For discussions on the universalist value basis of human rights, see, for example, Donnelly (2003); M. K. Addo (2010), "Practice of United Nations Human Rights Treaty Bodies in the Reconciliation of Cultural Diversity with Universal Respect for Human Rights," *Human Rights Quarterly* 32(3), 601–664.

38. Riles (2015), 258.

39. See discussion in Donnelly (2003).

40. See Barreto (2013); Madhok (2021); Tsing (2005), 214.

41. Appadurai (1996), 43.

42. Riles (2015); Englund (2006).

43. Obregón (2012), 917. Obregón connects this assertion to Kant's *Perpetual Peace*, in which he states that the difference between "savage" and "civilised" rests on insistence on a constitution and a preference for "rational liberty" as opposed to a "savage state of lawlessness." See Kant (1795/1991).

44. A. Mbembe (2002), "African Modes of Self-Writing," *Public Culture* 14(1), 239–273.

45. See examples in R. I. Rotberg (2016), *Failed States, Collapsed States, Weak States: Causes and Indicators* (Washington, DC: Brookings Institution); N. A. Englehart (2009), "State Capacity, State Failure, and Human Rights," *Journal of Peace Research* 46(2), 163–180; D. G. Evans (2009), "Human Rights and State Fragility: Conceptual Foundations and Strategic Directions for State-Building," *Journal of Human Rights Practice* 1(2), 181–207.

46. See J. Bentham (1790/2002), "Anarchical Fallacies: Being an Examination of the Declarations of Rights Issued During the French Revolution," in *Rights, Representation, and Reform: Nonsense upon Stilts and Other Writings on the French Revolution*, ed. P. Schofield, C. Pease-Watkin, and C. Blamires (Oxford: Oxford University Press); see also J. A. Rawls (1971), *Theory of Justice* (Cambridge, MA: Harvard University Press).

47. S. Marks (2011), "Human Rights and Root Causes," *Modern Law Review* 74(1), 57–78, quotation on 75; see also J. Linarelli, M. E. Salomon, and M. Sornarajah (2018), *The Misery of International Law: Confrontations with Injustice in the Global Economy* (Oxford: Oxford University Press).

48. See Moyn (2018).

49. P. Alston (2016), "Phantom Rights: The Systemic Marginalization of Economic and Social Rights," Open Global Rights, 4 August 2016, 6, 7, https://www.openglobalrights.org/phantom-rights-systemic-marginalization-of-economic-and-social-rights/; P. Alston (2015), "Extreme Inequality as the Antithesis of Human Rights," Open Global Rights, 27 August 2015, https://www.openglobalrights.org/extreme-inequality-as-the-antithesis-of-human-rights/; see also Whyte (2017); P. Alston (2015), *Report of the Special Rapporteur on Extreme Poverty and Human Rights*, UN Doc A/HRC/29/31, 8.

50. For attempts to change this, see initiatives within human rights and business: J. G. Ruggie (2007), "Business and Human Rights: The Evolving International Agenda," *American Journal of International Law* 101(4), 819–840; S. Aaronson and I. Higham (2013), "Re-Righting Business: John Ruggie and the Struggle to Develop International Human Rights Standards for Transnational Firms," *Human Rights Quarterly* 35(2), 333–264; P. Feng and C. Sing-bik Ngai (2020), "Doing More on the Corporate Sustainability Front: A Longitudinal Analysis of CSR Reporting of Global Fashion Companies," *Sustainability* 12(6), 1–18.

51. See discussion, for example, in Anghie (2005).

52. Whyte (2017).

53. J. Whyte (2025), "Economic Coercion and the Crises of the (Neo)Liberal International Order," Keynote Address, "Crises Redux: Europe in a Global Context," Centre of Excellence in Law, Identity and the European Narratives, University of Helsinki, 1 October 2025.

54. "Human Rights Committee Holds Emergency Meeting with States Parties as the United Nations' Financial Crisis Threatens Its Survival," UN OHCHR, 10 July 2025, https://

www.ohchr.org/en/meeting-summaries/2025/07/human-rights-committee-holds-emergency-meeting-states-parties-united.

55. I analyze LGBTIQ+ advocacy in my ongoing book project "Looping for Human Rights." See M. Halme-Tuomisaari, "Looping for Human Rights: An Ethnographic Theory of Expansion," Riksbankens Jubileumsfond: Grants 2022, https://www.rj.se/en/grants/2022/looping-for-human-rights-an-ethnographic-theory-of-expansion/.

BIBLIOGRAPHY

Aaronson, S., and I. Higham (2013). "'Re-Righting Business': John Ruggie and the Struggle to Develop International Human Rights Standards for Transnational Firms." *Human Rights Quarterly* 35(2), 333–364.

Abélès, M. (2011). *Des anthropologues à l'OMC: scènes de la gouvernance mondiale*. Paris: CNRS Editions.

Adams, R. (2020). *Transparency: New Trajectories in Law*. London: Routledge.

Addo, M. K. (2010). "Practice of United Nations Human Rights Treaty Bodies in the Reconciliation of Cultural Diversity with Universal Respect for Human Rights." *Human Rights Quarterly* 32(3), 601–664.

Afshari, R. (2007). "On Historiography of Human Rights: Reflections on Paul Gordon Lauren's *The Evolution of International Human Rights*: Visions Seen." *Human Rights Quarterly* 29(1), 1–67.

Alfredsson, G., J. Grimheden, B. Ramcharan, and A. Zayas, eds. (2009). *International Human Rights Monitoring Mechanisms: Essays in Honour of Jakob Th. Möller*. Leiden: Brill.

Allen, L. (2013). *The Rise and Fall of Human Rights Cynicism and Politics in Occupied Palestine*. Stanford, CA: Stanford University Press.

Alloa, E., and D. Thomä, eds. (2018). *Transparency, Society and Subjectivity: Critical Perspectives*. Cham, Switzerland: Springer.

Alston, P. (1988). "Making Space for New Human Rights: The Case of the Right to Development." *Harvard Human Rights Yearbook* 1(3), 3–40.

Alston, P. (2014). "Against a World Court of Human Rights." *Ethics and International Affairs* 28(4), 197–212.

Alston, P. (2015). "Extreme Inequality as the Antithesis of Human Rights." Open Global Rights, 27 August 2015, https://www.openglobalrights.org/extreme-inequality-as-the-antithesis-of-human-rights/.

Alston, P. (2016). "Phantom Rights: The Systemic Marginalization of Economic and Social Rights." Open Global Rights, 4 August 2016. https://www.openglobalrights.org/phantom-rights-systemic-marginalization-of-economic-and-social-rights/.

Alston, P., and J. Crawford, eds. (2000). *The Future of UN Human Rights Treaty Monitoring*. Cambridge: Cambridge University Press.

Amahazion, F. (2016). "Epistemic Communities, Human Rights, and the Global Diffusion of Legislation against the Organ Trade." *Social Sciences* 5(4), 69.

American Law Institute (1998). *Statement of Essential Human Rights*. Philadelphia: American Law Institute.

Andersen, L. P., F. Lindberg, and J. Ostberg (2021). "Unpacking Nordic Branding: The Value Regimes of Nordicness." *Journal of Place Management and Development* 14(3), 362–378.

Anghie, A. (2005). *Imperialism, Sovereignty, and the Making of International Law*. Cambridge: Cambridge University Press.

Appadurai, A. (1996). *Modernity at Large: Cultural Dimension of Globalization*. Minneapolis: University of Minnesota Press.

Avikainen, P., Y. Blomstedt, and I. Hetemäki, eds. (1988). *Suomen Historia, osa 8: Paasikiven aika, Kekkosen aika, taloudellinen kasvu ja yhteiskuntamurros, massakulttuurin maihinnousu, taistelut kulttuurista*. Espoo: Weilin Göös.

Babül, E. (2017). *Bureaucratic Intimacies: Translating Human Rights in Turkey*. Stanford, CA: Stanford University Press.

Ballestro, A. (2014). "What Is in a Percentage? Calculations as the Poetic Translation of Human Rights." *Indiana Journal of Global Legal Studies* 24(1), 27–53.

Ballestro, A. (2018). "Transparency." In *The International Encyclopedia of Anthropology*. Wiley Online Library, https://onlinelibrary.wiley.com/doi/abs/10.1002/9781118924396.wbiea1505.

Barreto, J.-M., ed. (2013). *Human Rights from a Third World Perspective*. Cambridge: Cambridge Scholars Publishing.

Bassiouni, M. C., and W. A. Schabas, eds. (2011). *New Challenges for the UN Human Rights Machinery: What Future for the UN Treaty Body System and the Human Rights Council Procedures?* Portland, OR: Intersentia.

Bayefsky, A. (2000). *The UN Human Rights Treaty System in the 21st Century*. Leiden: Kluwer Law International.

Bear, L., and N. Mathur, eds. (2015). Special issue, "Remaking the Public Good: A New Anthropology of Bureaucracy." *Cambridge Journal of Anthropology* 33(1).

Beckett, J. (2022). "The Divisible College: A Day in the Lives of Public International Lawyers." *German Law Journal* 23(9), 1159–1192.

Bens, J. (2022). *The Sentimental Court: The Affective Life of International Criminal Justice*. Cambridge: Cambridge University Press.

Bentham, J. (1790/2002). *Anarchical Fallacies: Being an Examination of the Declarations of Rights Issued During the French Revolution*. In *Rights, Representation, and Reform: Nonsense upon Stilts and Other Writings on the French Revolution*, edited by P. Schofield, C. Pease-Watkin, and C. Blamires. Oxford: Oxford University Press, 317–401.

Berlant, L. (2011). *Cruel Optimism*. Durham, NC: Duke University Press.

Berliner, D. (2014). "The Political Origins of Transparency." *Journal of Politics* 76(2), 479–491.

Bianchi, A. (2013). "On Power and Illusion: The Concept of Transparency in International Law." In *Transparency in International Law*, edited by A. Bianchi and A. Peters. Cambridge: Cambridge University Press, 1–20.

Bianchi, A. (2018). "The Unbearable Lightness of International Law." *London Review of International Law* 6(3), 335–359.

Bianchi, A. (2019). "Epistemic Communities." In *Concepts for International Law*, edited by J. d'Aspremont and S. Sing. Cheltenham, UK: Edward Elgar, 251–266.

Billaud, J. (2014). "Keepers of the 'Truth': Producing 'Transparent' Documents for the Universal Periodic Review." In *Human Rights and the Universal Periodic Review: Ritual and Ritualism*, edited by H. Charlesworth and E. Larkin. Cambridge: Cambridge University Press, 63–84.

Billaud, J., and J. Cowan (2020). "The Bureaucratisation of Utopia: Ethics, Affects and Subjectivities in International Governance Processes." *Social Anthropology / Anthropologie Sociale* 28(1), 6–16.

Biltoft, C. (2021). *A Violent Peace: Media, Truth, and Power at the League of Nations*. Chicago: University of Chicago Press.

Biraben, N. C. (2020). "Book Review: *Cultures of Doing Good: Anthropologists and NGOs* edited by A. Lashaw, C. Vannier, and S. Sampson." *LSE Review of Books*, 25 February 2020. https://blogs.lse.ac.uk/lsereviewofbooks/2020/02/25/book-review-cultures-of-doing-good-anthropologists-and-ngos-edited-by-amanda-lashaw-christian-vannier-and-steven-sampson/.

Björk, A., J.-M. Paavola, T. Strik, I. Tanhua, and A. Vainio (2019). *Finland in the International Human Rights System*. Helsinki: Publications of the Government's Analysis, Assessment and Research Activities.

Bjorkdahl, K., and A. de Bengy Puyvallee (2021). *Do-Gooders at the End of Aid: Scandinavian Humanitarianism in the Twenty-First Century*. Cambridge: Cambridge University Press.

Bódig, M. (2017). "Soft Law, Doctrinal Development, and the General Comments of the UN Committee on Economic, Social and Cultural Rights." In *Tracing the Roles of Soft Law in Human Rights*, edited by S. Lagoutte, T. Gammeltoft-Hansen, and J. Cerone. Oxford: Oxford University Press, 69–88.

Borgwardt, E. (2007). *A New Deal for the World: America's Vision for Human Rights*. Cambridge, MA: Belknap Press.

Bourdieu, P. (1977). *Outline of a Theory of Practice*. Cambridge: Cambridge University Press.

Bourdieu, P. (1990). *In Other Words: Essays Toward a Reflexive Sociology*. Stanford, CA: Stanford University Press.

Boyle, A., and K. McCall-Smith (2013). "Transparency in International Law-making." In *Transparency in International Law*, edited by A. Bianchi and A. Peters. Cambridge: Cambridge University Press, 419–435.

Boyle, J. (1985). "Ideals and Things: International Legal Scholarship and the Prison-House Language." *Harvard International Law Journal* 26(1), 327–359.

Brommesson, D. (2018). "'Nordicness' in Swedish Foreign Policy—from Mid Power Internationalism to Small State Balancing?" *Global Affairs* 4(4–5), 391–404.

Brown, H., A. Reed, and T. Yarrow (2017). "Introduction: Towards an Ethnography of Meeting." *Journal of the Royal Anthropological Institute* 23(1), 10–27.

Bruno-van Vijfeijken, T. (2019). "'Culture Is What You See When Compliance Is Not in the Room': Organizational Culture as an Explanatory Factor in Analyzing Recent INGO Scandals." *Notprofit Policy Forum*, 8 November 2019. https://www.degruyter.com/document/doi/10.1515/npf-2019-0031/html.

Çali, B. (2017). "In Memoriam: Professor Sir Nigel Rodley." *EJIL* TALK! 2 February 2017, https://www.ejiltalk.org/in-memoriam-professor-sir-nigel-rodley/.

Carraro, V. (2019a). "Electing the Experts: Expertise and Independence in the UN Human Rights Treaty Bodies." *European Journal of International Relations* 25(3), 826–851.

Carraro, V. (2019b). "Promoting Compliance with Human Rights: The Performance of the United Nations' Universal Periodic Review and Treaty Bodies." *International Studies Quarterly* 63(4), 1079–1093.

Cassese, A., ed. (2012). *Realizing Utopia: The Future of International Law*. Oxford: Oxford University Press.

Ceadel, M. (2015). "The Peace Movement and Human Rights." In *Revisiting the Origins of Human Rights*, edited by P. Slotte and M. Halme-Tuomisaari. Cambridge: Cambridge University Press, 189–205.

Celermajer, D., and A. Lefebre, eds. (2020). *The Subject of Human Rights*. Stanford, CA: Stanford University Press.

Charlesworth, H., and E. Larking, eds. (2014). *Human Rights and the Universal Periodic Review: Rituals and Ritualism*. Cambridge: Cambridge University Press.

Chimney, B. S. (1999). "Marxism and International Law: A Contemporary Analysis." *Economic and Political Weekly* 34(6), 337–349.

Chipaike, R., N. Tshuma, and S. Hofisi (2019). "African Move to Withdraw from the ICC: Assessment of Issues and Implications." *India Quarterly* 75(3), 334–350.

Claeys, G. (2015). "Socialism and the Language of Rights: The Origins and Implications of Economic Rights." In *Revisiting the Origins of Human Rights*, edited by P. Slotte and M. Halme-Tuomisaari. Cambridge: Cambridge University Press, 206–236.

Clapham, A. (2000). "Defining the Role of Non-Governmental Organizations with Regard to the UN Human Rights Treaty Bodies." In *The UN Human Rights System in the 21st Century*, edited by A. Bayefsky. The Hague: Kluwer, 183–194.

Clark, J. (2016). "The Global Fight Against Racial Discrimination: Human Rights Assessment and the Making of Obligation in Costa Rica and at the United Nations." PhD diss., University of California, Irvine.

Clark, J., and M. Halme-Tuomisaari, eds. (2016). "Virtual Edition: Human Rights." *PoLAR: Political and Legal Anthropology Review*. https://polarjournal.org/2016-virtual-edition-human-rights/.

Clark, K. (2019). *Affective Justice: The International Criminal Court and the Pan-Africanist Pushback*. Durham, NC: Duke University Press.

Clarke, L. (1999). *Mission Improbable: Using Fantasy Documents to Tame Disaster*. Chicago: University of Chicago Press.

Cohen, A. (2017). "ADR and Some Thoughts on 'the Social' in Contemporary Legal Thought." In *Searching for Contemporary Legal Thought*, edited by J. Desautels-Stein and C. Tomlins. Cambridge: Cambridge University Press, 454–464.

Cohen, D. W., and E. S. Atieno Odhiambo (1989). *Siaya: The Historical Anthropology of an African Landscape*. London: James Currey.

Cole, W. M. (2015). "Mind the Gap: State Capacity and the Implementation of Human Rights Treaties." *International Organization* 69(2), 405–441.

Comaroff, J., and J. Comaroff, eds. (1992). *Ethnography and the Historical Imagination*. Boulder, CO: Westview Press.

Comaroff, J., and J. Comaroff, eds. (2006). *Law and Disorder in the Postcolony*. Chicago: University of Chicago Press.

Connors, J. (2000). "An Analysis and Evaluation of the System of State Reporting." In *The UN Human Rights System in the 21st Century*, edited by A. F. Bayefsky. The Hague: Kluwer Law International, 4–21.

Cowan, J. K. (2007). "The Success of Failure? Minority Supervision at the League of Nations." In *Paths to International Justice: Social and Legal Perspectives*, edited by M.-B. Dembour and T. Kelly. Cambridge: Cambridge University Press, 29–56.

Cowan, J. K. (2013). "Before Audit Culture: Towards a Genealogy of International Oversight of Rights." In *The Gloss of Harmony: The Politics of Policy Making in Multilateral Organisations*, edited by B. Muller. London: Pluto Press, 103–133.

Cowan, J. K. (2014). "The Universal Periodic Review as Public Audit Ritual: An Anthropological Perspective on Emerging Practices in the Global Governance of Human Rights." In *Human Rights and the Universal Periodic Review: Rituals and Ritualism*, edited by H. Charlesworth and E. Larkin. Cambridge: Cambridge University Press, 42–62.

Cowan, J. K. (2020). "The Feeling of Pursuing an Ideal': A League of Nations Civil Servant Reflects on His Work." *Social Anthropology / Anthropologie Sociale* 28(1), 17–34.

Cowan, J. K. (2021). "Modes of Acting Virtuously at the Universal Periodic Review." In *Ethical Leadership in International Organizations: Concepts, Narratives, Judgment, and Assessment*, edited by G. Vilaça and M. Varaki. Cambridge: Cambridge University Press, 176–202.

Cowan, J. K. (2024). "Recommendations in Words and Numbers: Thinking with Sally Engle Merry at the Universal Periodic Review." In *The Complexity of Human Rights: From Vernacularization to Quantification*, edited by P. Alston. Oxford: Hart, 203–228.

Cowan, J. K., and J. Billaud (2015). "Between Learning and Schooling: The Politics of Human Rights Monitoring at the Universal Periodic Review." *Third World Quarterly* 36(6), 1175–1190.

Cowan, J. K., and J. Billaud (2017). "The 'Public' Character of the Universal Periodic Review: Contested Concept and Methodological Challenge." In *Palaces of Hope: Anthropology of the United Nations*, edited by Ronald Niezen and Maria Sapignoli. Cambridge: Cambridge University Press, 106–126.

Cowan, J. K., M.-B. Dembour, and R. Wilson, eds. (2001). *Culture and Rights: Anthropological Perspectives*. Cambridge: Cambridge University Press.

Crane, D. M. (2020). "The Wrong Side of History: The United States and the International Criminal Court." *Jurist*, 13 June 2020. https://www.jurist.org/commentary/2020/06/david-crane-wrong-history-icc/.

Crawford, J. (2000). "The UN Human Rights Treaty System: A System in Crisis?" In *The Future of UN Human Rights Treaty Monitoring*, edited by P. Alston and J. Crawford. Cambridge: Cambridge University Press, 1–13.

Crawford, J. (2013). "The 'Compliance Gap' and the Efficacy of International Human Rights Institutions." In *The Persistent Power of Human Rights: From Commitment to Compliance*, edited by T. Risse, S. Ropp, and K. Sikkink. Cambridge: Cambridge University Press, 85–102.

Creamer, C., and B. Simmons (2020). "The Proof Is in the Process: Self-Reporting Under International Human Rights Treaties." *American Journal of International Law* 114(1), 1–50.

Cross, M. (2013). "Rethinking Epistemic Communities Twenty Years Later." *Review of International Studies* 39(1), 137–160.

Cubucku, A. (2018). *For the Love of Humanity: The World Tribunal on Iraq*. Philadelphia: University of Pennsylvania Press.

Dancy, G., and C. J. Fariss (2017). "Rescuing Human Rights Law from International Legalism and Its Critics." *Human Rights Quarterly* 39(1), 1–36.

Davies, T. (2012). "A 'Great Experiment' of the League of Nations Era: The Emerging Roles of NGOs in the UN System." *Global Governance* 18(3), 299–311.

Davies, T. (2014). *NGOs: A New History of Transnational Civil Society*. Oxford: Oxford University Press.

Deeb, H., and G. Marcus (2011). "In the Green Room: An Experiment in Ethnographic Method at the WTO." *PoLAR: Political and Legal Anthropology Review* 34(1), 51–76.

de la Rasilla, I. (2019). "The World Court of Human Rights: Rise, Fall and Revival?" *Human Rights Law Review* 19, 585–603.

Dembour, M.-B. (2006). *Who Believes in Human Rights? Reflections on the European Convention*. Cambridge: Cambridge University Press.

Di Nunzio, M. (2018). "Anthropology of Infrastructure." *LSE Cities, Governing Infrastructure Interfaces—Research Note* 1, 1–4.

Domínguez-Redondo, E. (2012). "The Universal Periodic Review—Is There Life Beyond Naming and Shaming in Human Rights Implementation?" *New Zealand Law Review* 4, 673–706.

Donnelly, J. (1998). "Human Rights: A New Standard of Civilization?" *International Affairs* 74(1), 1–23.

Donnelly, J. (2003). *Universal Human Rights in Theory and Practice*. 2nd ed. Ithaca, NY: Cornell University Press.

Dunoff, J., and J. Trachtman (2009). "A Functional Approach to International Constitutionalization." In *Ruling the World?: Constitutionalism, International Law, and Global Governance*, edited by J. Dunoff and J. Trachtman. Cambridge: Cambridge University Press, 3–35.

Duranti, M. (2017). *The Conservative Human Rights Revolution: European Identity, Transnational Politics and the Origins of the European Convention*. Oxford: Oxford University Press.

Eckel, J. (2013). "The International League for the Rights of Man, Amnesty International, and the Changing Fate of Human Rights Activism from the 1940s through the 1970s." *Humanity: An International Journal of Human Rights, Humanitarianism, and Development* 4(2), 183–214.

Eckel, J., and S. Moyn (2014). *The Breakthrough: Human Rights in the 1970s*. Philadelphia: University of Pennsylvania Press.

Egan, S. (2011). *The UN Human Rights Treaty System: Law and Procedure*. New York: Bloomsbury Professional.

Egan, S. (2020). "Transforming the UN Human Rights Treaty System: A Realistic Appraisal." *Human Rights Quarterly* 42(4), 762–789.

Ellis, J. (2012). "Shades of Grey: Soft Law and the Validity of Public International Law." *Leiden Journal of International Law* 25(2), 313–334.

Englehart, N. A. (2009). "State Capacity, State Failure, and Human Rights." *Journal of Peace Research* 46(2), 163–180.

Englund, H. (2006). *Prisoners of Freedom: Human Rights and the African Poor*. Berkeley: University of California Press.

Eriksen, T. H. (2016). *Overheating: An Anthropology of Accelerated Change*. New York: Pluto Press.

Ervo, L. (2006). "Förhållandet mellan Europadomstolen och nationella domstolar—Findländska perspektiv." *Juridisk Tidskrift* 4, 411–422.

Eslava, L. (2015). *Local Space, Global Life: The Everyday Operations of International Law and Development*. Cambridge: Cambridge University Press.

Evans, D. G. (2009). "Human Rights and State Fragility: Conceptual Foundations and Strategic Directions for State-Building." *Journal of Human Rights Practice* 1(2), 181–207.

Feldman, G. (2011). "If Ethnography Is More Than Participant-Observation, Then Relations Are More Than Connections: The Case for Nonlocal Ethnography in a World of Apparatuses." *Anthropological Theory* 11(4), 375–395.

Feldman, G. (2012). *The Migration Apparatus: Security, Labor, and Policymaking in the European Union*. Stanford, CA: Stanford University Press.

Feng, P., and C. Sing-bik Ngai (2020). "Doing More on the Corporate Sustainability Front: A Longitudinal Analysis of CSR Reporting of Global Fashion Companies." *Sustainability* 12(6), 1–18.

Ferguson, J., and A. Gupta (2002). "Spatializing States: Toward an Ethnography of Neoliberal Governmentality." *American Ethnologist* 29(4), 981–1002.

Féron, H. (2014). "Human Rights and Faith: A 'World-Wide Secular Religion'?" *Ethics and Global Politics* 7(4), 181–200.

Fidler, D. P. (2001). "Return of the Standard of Civilization: The International Human Rights Law in Practice." *Chicago Journal of International Law* 2, 137–157.

Fischer-Lescano, A. (2020). "Sociological Aesthetics of Law." *Law, Culture and the Humanities* 16(2), 268–293.

Foucault, M. (1972). *The Archaelogy of Knowledge and the Discourse on Language*. New York: Pantheon Books.

Foucault, M. (1980 [1977]). "The Confessions of the Flesh." In *Power/Knowledge: Selected Interviews and Other Writings*, edited by C. Gordon. New York: Pantheon Books, 194–228.

Fox, J. (2007). "The Uncertain Relationship Between Transparency and Accountability." *Development in Practice* 17(4–5), 663–671.

Frankenberg, G. (2014). "Human Rights and the Belief in a Just World." *International Journal of Constitutional Law* (12)1, 35–60.

Frohmann, B. (2008). "Documentary Ethics, Ontology, and Politics." *Archival Science* 8(3), 165–180.

Fukuyama, F. (1992). *The End of History and the Last Man*. New York: Free Press.

Gal, S. (2015). "Politics of Translation." *Annual Review of Anthropology* 44, 225–240.

Galbreath, D. J., and J. McEvoy (2013). "How Epistemic Communities Drive International Regimes: The Case of Minority Rights in Europe." *Journal of European Integration* 35(2), 169–186.

Garsten, C., and M. Lindh de Montoya (2008). "Introduction: Examining the Politics of Transparency." In *Transparency in a New Global Order: Unveiling Organizational Visions*, edited by C. Garsten and M. Lindh de Montoya. Cheltenham, UK: Edward Elgar, 1–21.

Gearty, C., and C. Douzinas, eds. (2012). *The Cambridge Companion to Human Rights Law*. Cambridge: Cambridge University Press.

Giauque, D., S. Anderfuhren-Biget, and F. Varone (2019). "Stress and Turnover Intents in International Organizations: Social Support and Work-Life Balance as Resources." *International Journal of Resource Management* 30(5), 879–901.

Goldmann, M. (2012). "We Need to Cut Off the Head of the King: Past, Present, and Future Approaches to International Soft Law." *Leiden Journal of International Law* 25(2), 335–368.

Goodale, M., and S. Merry, eds. (2007). *The Practice of Human Rights: Tracking the Law Between the Local and the Global*. Cambridge: Cambridge University Press.

Goodrich, P. (2008). "On the Relational Aesthetics of International Law: Philosophy of International Law." *Journal of the History of International Law* 10, 321–341.

Graeber, D. (2018). *Bullshit Jobs: A Theory*. New York: Simon & Schuster.

Grear, A. (2018). "Human Rights and New Horizons? Thoughts Toward a New Juridical Ontology." *Science, Technology, and Human Values* 43(1), 129–145.

Grear, A. (2021). "International Law, Legal Anthropocentrism and Facing the Planetary." In *The Handbook of International Law and Anthropocentrism*, edited by V. Chapaux, F. Mégret, and N. Usha. New York: Routledge, 165–182.

Greenberg, J. (2020). "Law, Politics, and Efficacy at the European Court of Human Rights." *American Ethnologist* 47(4), 417–431.

Greenberg, J. (2025). *Justice in the Balance: Democracy, Rule of Law, and the European Court of Human Rights*. Stanford, CA: Stanford University Press.

Guilfoyle, D. (2019). "The Future of International Law in an Authoritarian World." *European Journal of International Law* TALK! 3, June 2019, https://www.ejiltalk.org/the-future-of-international-law-in-an-authoritarian-world/.

Gusterson, H. (1997). "Studying Up Revisited." *Political and Legal Anthropological Review* 20(1), 114–119.

Guzman, A. T., and T. L. Meyer (2010). "International Soft Law." *Journal of Legal Analysis* 2(1), 171–225.

Haas, P. (1992). "Introduction: Epistemic Communities and International Policy Coordination." *International Organization* 46(1), 1–35.

Haas, P. (2012). "Epistemic Communities." In *The Oxford Handbook of International Environmental Law*, edited by D. Bodansky, J. Brunnée, and H. Hey. Oxford: Oxford University Press, 791–806.

Haas, P. (2014). "Ideas, Experts and Governance." In *The Role of "Experts" in International and European Decision-Making Processes: Advisors, Decision Makers or Irrelevant Actors?*, edited by M. Ambrus, K. Arts, E. Hey, and H. Raulus. Cambridge: Cambridge University Press, 19–43.

Halme-Tuomisaari, M. (2010a). *Human Rights in Action: Learning Expert Knowledge*. Leiden: Brill.

Halme-Tuomisaari, M. (2010b). "From the Periphery to the Center: Emergence of the Human Rights Phenomenon in Finland." In *Finnish Yearbook of International Law*, edited by J. Klabbers and T. Tuori. Leiden: Brill, 257–281.

Halme-Tuomisaari, M. (2012). "'The State Is One': Examining What 'Fact' Means in the Compilation of a Human Rights Report." *Suomen Antropologi: Journal of the Finnish Anthropological Society* 37(1), 22–30.

Halme-Tuomisaari, M. (2013). "Contested Representation: Exploring China's State Report." *Journal of Legal Anthropology* 1(3), 333–359.

Halme-Tuomisaari, M. (2015). "Lobbying for Relevance: US Internationalists, French Civil Libertarians and the UDHR." In *Revisiting the Origins of Human Rights*, edited by P. Slotte and M. Halme-Tuomisaari. Cambridge: Cambridge University Press, 330–361.

Halme-Tuomisaari, M. (2017). "Meeting 'the World' at the Palais Wilson: Embodied Universalism at the UN Human Rights Committee." In *Palaces of Hope: Anthropology of the United Nations*, edited by R. Niezen and M. Sapignoli. Cambridge: Cambridge University Press, 127–151.

Halme-Tuomisaari, M. (2018). "Methodologically Blonde at the UN in a Tactical Quest for Inclusion." *Social Anthropology / Anthropologie Sociale* 26(4), 456–470.

Halme-Tuomisaari, M. (2019). "Consultancy, Confidentiality and Scholarly Responsibility: Glimpses from the UN OHCHR." *Humanity Journal's Blog*, 5 September 2019. http://humanityjournal.org/blog/consultancy-confidentiality/.

Halme-Tuomisaari, M. (2020). "Guarding Utopia: Law, Vulnerability and Frustration at the UN Human Rights Committee." *Social Anthropology / Anthropologie Sociale* 28(1), 35–49.

Halme-Tuomisaari, M. (2021). "Between Organizational Narratives and Individual Stories: Pseudonyms Revisited." In *Rethinking Pseudonyms in Ethnography*, edited by C. McGranahan and E. Weiss, 13 December 2021. https://americanethnologist.org/online-content/collections/rethinking-pseudonyms-in-ethnography/between-organizational-narratives-and-individual-stories-pseudonyms-revisited/.

Halme-Tuomisaari, M. (2022). "Visibility, Impact and Relevance in International Law." *London Review of International Law* 10(2), 313–324.

M. Halme-Tuomisaari (2025), "Standards for a Better World: Anthropological Approaches to the Study of International Organizations." In *Ways of Seeing International Organizations*, edited by N. Mansouri & D. Quigoral-Villamarin. Cambridge: Cambridge University Press, 208–226.

Halme-Tuomisaari, M. and P. Slotte (2015). "Revisiting the History of Human Rights: Introduction." In *Revisiting the Origins of Human Rights*, edited by P. Slotte and M. Halme-Tuomisaari. Cambridge: Cambridge University Press, 1–36.

Halme-Tuomisaari, M., and R. Toivanen (forthcoming). "The Dangers of Distant Evidence: The UN Human Rights Committee's Individual Communications, 512,000 Potential New Sámi Voters and Other 'Objective' Facts." In *UN Evidentiary Regimes*, edited by D. Casalin, M.-B. Dembour, and C. Klocker. Cambridge: Cambridge University Press.

Hannerz, U. (1992). *Cultural Complexity: Studies in the Social Organization of Meaning*. New York: Columbia University Press.

Harris, O., ed. (1996). *Inside and Outside the Law*. London: Routledge.

Hathaway, O. A. (2002). "Do Human Rights Treaties Make a Difference?" *Yale Law Journal* 111(8), 1935–2042.

Heritier, P. (2014). "Legal Liturgies: The Aesthetic Foundation of Positive Law." *Pólemos* 8(1), 137–152.

Heritier, P. (2023). "Aesthetics of Law as 'Iconic Legal Theology': Legendre, Schmitt and Vico." *International Journal for the Semiotics of Law* 36, 477–508.

Herren, M. (2017). "Geneva, 1919–1945: The Spatialities of Public Internationalism and Global Networks." In *Mobilities of Knowledge: Knowledge and Space*, edited by H. Jöns, P. Meusburger, and M. Heffernan. Cham, Switzerland: Springer.

Herzfeld, M. (1992). *The Social Production of Indifference: Exploring the Symbolic Roots of Western Bureaucracy*. London: Routledge.

Hetherington, G. (2011). *Guerrilla Auditors: The Politics of Transparency in Neoliberal Paraguay*. Durham, NC: Duke University Press.

Heyns, C., and F. Viljoen (2002). *The Impact of the United Nations Human Rights Treaties on the Domestic Level*. The Hague: Kluwer Law International.

Hidén, M., and I. Saraviita (1994). *Valtiosääntöoikeuden pääpiirteet*. 6th rev. ed. Helsinki: Lakimiesliiton kustannus.

Higgins, R. (2009). *Themes and Theories: Selected Essays, Speeches, and Writings in International Law*. Oxford: Oxford University Press.

Hoag, C. (2010). "The Magic of the Populace: An Ethnography of Illegibility in the South African Immigration Bureaucracy." *Political and Legal Anthropology Review* 33(1), 6–25.

Hobbes, T. (1651/1996). *Leviathan*. Edited by R. Tuck. Cambridge: Cambridge University Press.

Hobbins, A. J. (2001). "Humphrey and the High Commissioner: The Genesis of the Office of the UN High Commissioner for Human Rights." *Journal of the History of International Law* 3(1), 38–74.

Hoffmann, S.-L., ed. (2010). *Human Rights in the Twentieth Century*. Cambridge: Cambridge University Press.

Holmes, D., and G. Marcus (2005). "Cultures of Expertise and the Management of Globalization: Toward the Re-functioning of Ethnography." In *Global Assemblages*, edited by A. Ong and S. J. Collier. Oxford: Blackwell, 235–252.

Hood, C. (2006). "Transparency in Historical Perspective." In *Transparency: The Key to Better Governance?*, edited by C. Hood and D. Heald. Oxford: Oxford University Press, 3–23.

Hoopes, T., and D. Brinkley (2000). *FDR and the Creation of the UN*. New Haven, CT: Yale University Press.

Hopgood, S. (2013). *The Endtimes of Human Rights*. Ithaca, NY: Cornell University Press.

Hopgood, S. (2016). "Law and Lawyers in a World After Virtue." *London Review of International Law* 4(3), 451–466.

Hull, M. S. (2012a). *Government of Paper: The Materiality of Bureaucracy in Urban Pakistan*. Berkeley: University of California Press.

Hull, M. S. (2012b). "Documents and Bureaucracy." *Annual Review of Anthropology* 41, 251–267.

Humphrey, J. P. (1976). "The International Bill of Rights: Scope and Implementation." *William and Mary Law Review* 17(3), 527–541.

Humphrey, J. P. (1983). "The Memoirs of John P. Humphrey, the First Director of the United Nations Division of Human Rights." *Human Rights Quarterly* 5(4), 387–439.

Humphrey, J. P. (1984). *The Great Adventure: Human Rights and the United Nations*. New York: Transnational.

Hurd, I. (2015). "The International Rule of Law and the Domestic Analogy." *Global Constitutionalism* 4(3), 365–395.

Hyde-Price, A. (2018). "Epilogue: 'Nordicness'—Theory and Practice." *Global Affairs* 4(4–5), 435–443.

Ingold, T. (2011). *Being Alive: Essays on Movement, Knowledge and Description*. London: Routledge.

Iriye, A., P. Goedde, and W. I. Hitchcock, eds. (2012). *The Human Rights Revolution: An International History*. New York: Oxford University Press.

Jean-Klein, I., and A. Riles (2005). "Introducing Discipline: Anthropology and Human Rights Administrations." *PoLAR: Political and Legal Anthropology Review* 28(2), 173–202.

Jensen, S. (2016). *The Making of International Human Rights: The 1960s, Decolonization, and the Reconstruction of Global Values*. Cambridge: Cambridge University Press.

Joona, T. (2020). "ILO Convention No. 169 and the Governance of Indigenous Identity in Finland: Recent Developments." *International Journal of Human Rights* 24(2–3), 241–256.

Joutsamo, K. (1990). *Puolueettomuus ja EY*. Turku: Euro Consulting Oy.

Kälin, W. (2012). "Examination of State Reports." In *UN Human Rights Treaty Bodies*, edited by H. Keller and G. Ulfstein. Cambridge: Cambridge University Press, 16–72.

Kamminga, M. T., and M. Scheinin, eds. (2009). *The Impact of Human Rights Law on General International Law*. Oxford: Oxford University Press.

Kang, H. Y., and S. Kendall (2019). "Legal Materiality." *Oxford Handbooks Online*. https://www.oxfordhandbooks.com/view/10.1093/oxfordhb/9780190695620.001.0001/oxfordhb-9780190695620-e-9#oxfordhb-9780190695620-e-9-bibliography-2.

Kant, I. (1795/1991). "Perpetual Peace: A Philosophical Sketch." In *Kant: Political Writings*, edited by H. S. Reiss. Cambridge: Cambridge University Press, 93–115.

Kasa, T., M. Rautiainen, M. Malama, and A. Kallioniemi (2021). "'Human Rights and Democracy Are Not Self-Evident': Finnish Student Teachers' Perceptions on Democracy and Human Rights Education." *Human Rights Education Review* 4(2), 69–84.

Keck, M. E., and K. Sikkink (1998). *Activists Beyond Borders: Advocacy Networks in International Politics*. Ithaca, NY: Cornell University Press.

Keller, H., and L. Grover (2012). "General Comments of the Human Rights Committee and Their Legitimacy." In *UN Human Rights Treaty Bodies*, edited by H. Keller and G. Ulfstein. Cambridge: Cambridge University Press, 116–198.

Keller, H., and G. Ulfstein, eds. (2012). *UN Human Rights Treaty Bodies: Law and Legitimacy.* Cambridge: Cambridge University Press.

Kelly, T. (2009). "The UN Committee Against Torture: Human Rights Monitoring and the Legal Recognition of Cruelty." *Human Rights Quarterly* 31(3), 777–800.

Kelly, T. (2011). *This Side of Silence: Human Rights, Torture, and the Recognition of Cruelty.* Philadelphia: University of Pennsylvania Press.

Kennedy, D. (2002a). "The Critique of Rights." In *Left Legalism / Left Critique*, edited by W. Brown and J. Halley. Durham, NC: Duke University Press, 178–228.

Kennedy, D. (2002b). "International Human Rights Movement: Part of the Problem?" *Harvard Human Rights Journal* 15, 101–126.

Kinnunen, T., and M. Jokisipilä (2012). "Shifting Images of 'Our Wars': Finnish Memory Culture of World War II." In *Finland in World War II: History, Memory, Interpretations*, edited by T. Kinnunen and V. Kivimäki. Leiden: Brill, 435–482.

Kirby, M. (2020). "Multilateralism, Pushback, and Prospects for Global Engagement?" *Indiana Journal of Global Legal Studies* 27(2), 1–32.

Klabbers, J. (1996). "The Redundancy of Soft Law." *Nordic Journal of International Law* 65(2), 167–182.

Klabbers, J. (1998). "The Undesirability of Soft Law." *Nordic Journal of International Law* 67(4), 381–391.

Klabbers, J., A. Peters, and G. Ulfstein (2011). *The Constitutionalization of International Law.* New York: Oxford University Press.

Klabbers, J., and G. F. Sinclair (2020). "On Theorizing International Organizations Law: Editors' Introduction." *European Journal of International Law* 31(2), 489–496.

Klinge, M. (1987). *A Brief History of Finland.* Helsinki: Otava.

Koivisto, I. (2022). *The Transparency Paradox.* Oxford: Oxford University Press.

Korey, W. (2004). *The UDHR and NGOs: A Curious Grapevine.* New York: Palgrave Macmillan.

Koskenniemi, M. (1989/2009). *From Apology to Utopia: The Structure of International Legal Argument.* Cambridge: Cambridge University Press.

Koskenniemi, M. (2001). *The Gentle Civilizer of Nations: The Rise and Fall of International Law, 1870–1960.* Cambridge: Cambridge University Press.

Koskenniemi, M. (2006). *Fragmentation of International Law: Difficulties Arising from the Diversification and Expansion of International Law.* Report of the Study Group of the International Law Commission, A/CN.4/L.682.

Krisch, N., ed. (2021). *Entangled Legalities Beyond the State.* Cambridge: Cambridge University Press.

Krommendijk, J. (2012). "The (Non) Implementation of Recommendations of the Committee on the Elimination of Racial Discrimination in the Netherlands Explained." *Perspectives on European Politics and Society* 13(4), 462–479.

Krommendijk, J. (2014). "Finnish Exceptionalism at Play? The Effectiveness of the Recommendations of UN Human Rights Treaty Bodies in Finland." *Nordic Journal of Human Rights* 32(1), 18–43.

Krommendijk, J. (2015a). "The Domestic Effectiveness of International Human Rights Monitoring in Established Democracies. The Case of the UN Human Rights Treaty Bodies." *Review of International Organizations* 10(4), 489–512.

Krommendijk, J. (2015b). "The (In)effectiveness of UN Human Rights Treaty Body Recommendations." *Netherlands Quarterly of Human Rights* 33(2), 194–223.

Krommendijk, J. (2020). "Less Is More: Proposals for How UN Human Rights Treaty Bodies Can Be More Selective." *Netherlands Quarterly of Human Rights* 38(1), 5–11.

Kuntz, J. (2016). *International Geneva: 100 Years of Architecture.* Translated by V. Lowe. Genève internationale, 19 May. https://www.geneve-int.ch/chapter-2-palais-wilson-memory-and-hostage-geneva.

Lacey, N. (1988). *State Punishment: Political Principles and Community Values.* London: Routledge.

Lagoutte, S. (2019). "The Role of State Actors Within the National Human Rights System." *Nordic Journal of Human Rights* 37(3), 177–194.

Lagoutte, S., T. Gammeltoft-Hansen, and J. Cerone, eds. (2016). *Tracing the Roles of Soft Law in Human Rights.* Oxford: Oxford University Press.

Larkin, B. (2013). "The Politics and Poetics of Infrastructure." *Annual Review of Anthropology* 42, 327–343.

Lashaw, A., C. Vannier, and S. Sampson, eds. (2017). *Cultures of Doing Good: Anthropologists and NGOs.* Tuscaloosa: University of Alabama Press.

Latour, B. (1987). *Science in Action: How to Follow Scientists and Engineers Through Society.* Cambridge, MA: Harvard University Press.

Latour, B. (1999). *Pandora's Hope: Essays on the Reality of Science Studies.* Cambridge: Cambridge University Press.

Latour, B. (2009). "Scientific Objects and Legal Objectivity." In *Law, Anthropology, and the Constitution of the Social: Making Persons and Things*, edited by A. Pottage and M. Mundy. Cambridge: Cambridge University Press, 73–114.

Lauren, P. (2003). *The Evolution of International Human Rights: Visions Seen.* Philadelphia: University of Pennsylvania Press.

Lavapuro, J., T. Ojanen, and M. Scheinin (2016). "Intermediate Constitutional Review in Finland: Promising in Theory, Problematic in Practice." In *Rights-Based Constitutional Review: Constitutional Courts in a Changing Landscape*, edited by J. Bell and M.-L. Paris. London: Edward Elgar, 218–244.

Lave, J., and E. Wenger (1991). *Situated Learning: Legitimate Peripheral Participant.* Cambridge: Cambridge University Press.

Leino-Sandberg, P. (2021). *The Politics of Legal Expertise in EU Policy-Making.* Cambridge: Cambridge University Press.

Lempinen, M. (2008). *The Activity, Progressiveness and Consistency of the Human Rights Policy of Finland: Economic, Social and Cultural Rights.* Åbo: Åbo Akademi University.

Lewis, D., N. Kanji, and N. Themudo, eds. (2020). *Non-Governmental Organizations and Development.* London: Routledge.

Linarelli, J., M. E. Salomon, and M. Sornarajah (2018). *The Misery of International Law: Confrontations with Injustice in the Global Economy.* Oxford: Oxford University Press.

Littoz-Monet, A. (2021). *Governing Through Expertise.* Cambridge: Cambridge University Press.

Luoto, J. (1997). *Ulkopolitiikka ja Ihmisoikeudet: Suomen kansainvälisen ihmisoikeuspolitiikan murroskausi 1985–1995.* Helsinki: Gaudeamus.

Madhok, S. (2021). *Vernacular Rights Cultures: The Politics of Origins, Human Rights and Gendered Struggles for Justice.* Cambridge: Cambridge University Press.

Malkki, L. (1996). "Speechless Emissaries: Refugees, Humanitarianism, and Dehistoricization." *Cultural Anthropology* 11(3), 377–404.

Marcus, G. (1995). "Ethnography in/of the World System: The Emergence of Multi-sited Ethnography." *Annual Review of Anthropology* 24, 95–117.

Marks, S. (2011). "Human Rights and Root Causes." *Modern Law Review* 74(1), 57–78.

Martens, K. (2006). "Professionalised Representation of Human Rights NGOs to the United Nations." *International Journal of Human Rights* 10(1), 19–30.

Mathur, N. (2012). *Paper Tiger: Law, Bureaucracy and the Developmental State*. Cambridge: Cambridge University Press.

Mazower, M. (2004). "The Strange Triumph of Human Rights, 1933–1950." *Historical Journal* 47(2), 379–398.

Mbembe, A. (1992). "The Banality of Power and the Aesthetics of Vulgarity in the Postcolony." *Public Culture* 4(2), 1–30.

Mbembe, A. (2002). "African Modes of Self-Writing." *Public Culture* 14(1), 239–273.

McCall-Smith, K. (2017). "Interpreting International Human Rights Standards: Treaty Body General Comments as a Chisel or a Hammer." In *Tracing the Roles of Soft Law in Human Rights*, edited by S. Lagoutte, T. Gammeltoft-Hansen, and J. Cerone. Oxford: Oxford University Press, 27–46.

McGaughey, F. (2018). "From Gatekeepers to Gongos: Taxonomy of Non-governmental Organisations Engaging with United Nations Human Rights Mechanisms." *Netherlands Quarterly of Human Rights* 36(2), 111–132.

Meckled-Garcia, S., and B. Çali, eds. (2007). *The Legalization of Human Rights: Multidisciplinary Perspectives on Human Rights and Human Rights Law*. London: Routledge.

Mégret, F., and P. Alston (2020). *The United Nations and Human Rights: A Critical Appraisal*. Oxford: Oxford University Press.

Merry, S. (2006). *Human Rights and Gender Violence: Translating International Law into Local Justice*. Chicago: University of Chicago Press.

Merry, S. (2016). *Seduction of Quantification*. Chicago: University of Chicago Press.

Miyazaki, H. (2004). *The Method of Hope: Anthropology, Philosophy and Fijian Knowledge*. Stanford, CA: University of Stanford Press.

Moon, C. (2012). "What One Sees and How One Files Seeing: Human Rights Reporting, Representation and Action." *Sociology* 46(5), 876–890.

Moore, H. (2004). "Global Anxieties: Concept-Metaphors and Pre-Theoretical Commitments in Anthropology." *Anthropological Theory* 4(1), 71–88.

Moores, C. (2017). *Civil Liberties and Human Rights in Twentieth-Century Britain*. Cambridge: Cambridge University Press.

Morsink, J. (2000). *The Universal Declaration of Human Rights: Origins, Drafting, and Intent*. Philadelphia: University of Pennsylvania Press.

Moses, A. D., M. Duranti, and R. Burke, eds. (2020). *Decolonization, Self-Determination, and the Rise of Global Human Rights Politics*. Cambridge: Cambridge University Press.

Moyn, S. (2010). *The Last Utopia: Human Rights in History*. Cambridge, MA: Harvard University Press.

Moyn, S. (2018). *Not Enough: Human Rights in an Unequal World*. Cambridge, MA: Harvard University Press.

Müller, B., ed. (2013). *Gloss of Harmony: The Politics of Policy Making in Multilateral Organizations*. London: Pluto Press.

Mutua, M. (2002). *Human Rights: A Political and Cultural Critique*. Philadelphia: University of Pennsylvania Press.

Nader, L. (1974). "Up the Anthropologist--Perspectives Gained from Studying Up." In *Reinventing Anthropology*, edited by Dell Hymes. New York: Vintage Books, 284–311.

Näre, L. (2020). "'Finland Kills with a Pen'—Asylum Seekers' Protest Against Bureaucratic Violence as Politics of Human Rights." *Citizenship Studies* 24(8), 979–993.

Neier, A. (2013). *The International Human Rights Movement: A History*. Princeton, NJ: Princeton University Press.

Neuman, G. L. (2018a). "Human Rights, Treaties, and International Legitimacy." In *Human Rights, Democracy, and Legitimacy in a World of Disorder*, edited by S. Voeneky and G. L. Neuman. Cambridge: Cambridge University Press, 51–72.

Neuman, G. L. (2018b). "Giving Meaning and Effect to Human Rights: The Contributions of Human Rights Committee Members." In *The Human Rights Covenants at 50: Their Past, Present, and Future*, edited by D. Moeckli, H. Keller, and C. Heri. Cambridge: Cambridge University Press, 31–47.

Niezen, R., and M. Sapignoli (2016). "Introduction." In *Palaces of Hope: The Anthropology of Global Organizations*, edited by R. Niezen and M. Sapignoli. Cambridge: Cambridge University Press, 1–57.

Nowak, M. (2018). "A World Court of Human Rights." In *International Human Rights Institutions, Tribunals, and Courts*, edited by Gerd Obertleinter. The Hague: Springer Link, 271–290.

Obregon, L. (2012). "The Civilized and the Uncivilized." In *The Oxford Handbook of the History of International Law*, edited by B. Fassbender and A. Peters. Oxford: Oxford University Press, 917–940.

Oette, L. (2018). "The UN Human Rights Treaty Bodies: Impact and Future." In *International Human Rights Institutions, Tribunals, and Courts*, edited by G. Oberleitner. Leiden: Springer, 95–116.

O'Flaherty, M. (2006). "The Concluding Observations of United Nations Human Rights Treaty Bodies." *Human Rights Law Review* 6(1), 27–52.

O'Flaherty, M. (2010). "The Professionalization of Human Rights Field Work." *Journal of Human Rights Practice* 2(1), 1–27.

O'Flaherty, M., and G. Ulrich, eds. (2010). *The Professional Identity of the Human Rights Field Officer*. London: Ashgate.

O'Flaherty, M., and P. Tsai (2011). "Periodic Reporting: The Backbone of the UN Treaty Body Review Procedures." In *New Challenges for the UN Human Rights Machinery*, edited by M. C. Bassiouni and W. A. Schabas. Antwerp: Intersentia, 37–56.

Ojanen, T. (2003). *Perusoikeudet ja ihmisoikeudet Suomessa*. Helsinki: Forum Iuris.

Ojanen, T. (2009). "From Constitutional Periphery toward the Center—Transformations of Judicial Review in Finland." *Nordic Journal of Human Rights* 27(2), 194–207.

Ojanen, T., and J. Salminen (2019). "Finland: European Integration and International Human Rights Treaties as Source of Domestic Constitution Change and Dynamism." In *National Constitutions in European and Global Governance: Democracy, Rights, the Rule of Law*, edited by A. Albi and S. Bardutzky. The Hague: Asser Press, 359–404.

Ong, A., and S. J. Collier, eds. (2007). *Global Assemblages: Technology, Politics, and Ethics as Anthropological Problems*. Hoboken, NJ: Blackwell.

Onuf, N. (1985). "Do Rules Say What They Do? From Ordinary Language to International Law." *Harvard International Law Journal* 26(2), 385–410.

Orange, J. A. (2016). "Translating Law into Practice: Museums and a Human Rights Community of Practice." *Human Rights Quarterly* 38(3), 706–735.

Orford, A. (2003). *Reading Humanitarian Intervention: Human Rights and the Use of Force in International Law*. Cambridge: Cambridge University Press.

Ortner, S. (2006). *Anthropology and Social Theory: Culture, Power, and the Acting Subject*. Durham, NC: Duke University Press.

Osborne, T. (1994). "Bureaucracy as a Vocation: Governmentality and Administration in Nineteenth-Century Britain." *Sociology Lens* 7(3), 289–313.

O'Sullivan, K. (2021). *The NGO Moment: The Globalisation of Compassion from Biafra to Live Aid*. Cambridge: Cambridge University Press.

Parfitt, R. (2019). *The Process of International Legal Reproduction: Inequality, Historiography, Resistance*. Cambridge: Cambridge University Press.

Partonen, T., O. Kiviruusu, M. Grainger, J. Suvisaari, A. Eklin, A. Virtanen, and R. Kauppila (2022). "Suicides from 2016 to 2020 in Finland and the Effect of the COVID-19 Pandemic." *British Journal of Psychiatry* 220(1), 38–40.

Pauwelyn, J., R. Wessel, and J. Wouters, eds. (2012). *Informal International Lawmaking*. Oxford: Oxford University Press.

Pedersen, S. (2015). *The Guardians: The League of Nations and the Crisis of Empire*. Oxford: Oxford University Press.

Pellonpää, M. (1984). *Expulsion in International Law: A Study in International Aliens Law and Human Rights with Special Reference to Finland*. Helsinki: Suomalainen tiedeakatemia.

Pellonpää, M. (1998). *Euroopan neuvoston ihmisoikeussopimus Suomen näkökulmasta*. Helsinki: Oikeusministeriön lainvalmisteluosaston julkaisu 21.

Perry, M. (2000). *The Idea of Human Rights: Four Inquiries*. New York: Oxford University Press.

Peters, A. (2013). "Towards Transparency as a Global Norm." In *Transparency in International Law*, edited by A. Bianchi and A. Peters. Cambridge: Cambridge University Press, 534–607.

Peters, A. (2015). "The Transparency Turn of International Law." *Chinese Journal of Global Governance* 1(1), 3–15.

Philippopoulos-Mihalopoulos, A. (2019). "Law Is a Stage: From Aesthetics to Affective Aestheses." In *Research Handbook on Critical Legal Theory*, edited by E. Christodoulidis, R. Dukes, and M. Goldoni. London: Routledge, 201–222.

Piccone, T. (2012). *Catalysts for Change: How the U.N.'s Independent Experts Promote Human Rights*. Washington, DC: Brookings Institution Press.

Pillay, N. (2012). *Strengthening the United Nations Human Rights Treaty Body System: A Report by the United Nations High Commissioner for Human Rights*. Report A/66/86, 26 June 2012.

Polvinen, T. (1986). *Between East and West: Finland in International Politics, 1944–1947*. Minneapolis: University of Minnesota Press.

Prost, A., and J. M. Winter (2013). *René Cassin and Human Rights: From the Great War to the Universal Declaration*. Cambridge: Cambridge University Press.

Rabinow, P., G. E. Marcus, and J. D. Faubion (2008). *Designs for an Anthropology of the Contemporary*. Durham, NC: Duke University Press.

Rasila, V., E. Jutikkala, and K. Kulha (1980). *Suomen poliittinen historia 1905–1975*. Porvoo: Werner Söderström.

Rawls, J. A. (1971). *Theory of Justice*. Cambridge, MA: Harvard University Press.

Reiners, N. (2021). *Transnational Law-making Coalitions for Human Rights.* Cambridge: Cambridge University Press.

Relander, J. (1997). "Ulkoinen totuus ja sisäinen kokemus taistolaisliikkeessä." *Tieteessä tapahtuu* 4, 31–37.

Riedel, E., G. Giacca, and C. Golay, eds. (2014). *Economic, Social, and Cultural Rights in International Law: Contemporary Issues and Challenges.* Oxford: Oxford University Press.

Riles, A. (1998). "Infinity Within the Brackets." *American Ethnologist* 25(3), 378–398.

Riles, A. (2000). *The Network Inside Out.* Ann Arbor: University of Michigan Press.

Riles, A. (2004). "Real Time: Unwinding Technocratic and Anthropological Knowledge." *American Ethnologist* 31(3), 392–405.

Riles, A., ed. (2005). *Documents: Artefacts of Modern Knowledge.* Ann Arbor: University of Michigan Press.

Riles, A. (2015). "Afterword: A Method More Than a Subject." In *Exploring the "Legal" in Socio-legal Studies*, edited by D. Cowan and D. Wincott. London: Palgrave Macmillan, 249–256.

Riles, A. (2017). "Outputs: The Promises and Perils of Ethnographic Engagement After the Loss of Faith in Transnational Dialogue." *Journal of the Royal Anthropological Society* 23 (S1), 182–197.

Riles, A. (2021). "Introduction to the Symposium on the Anthropology of International Law." *AJIL Unbound* 115, 268–271.

Ron, J., H. Ramos, and K. Rodgers (2005). "Transnational Information Politics: NGO Human Rights Reporting, 1986–2000." *International Studies Quarterly* 49(3), 557–587.

Rotberg, R. I. (2016). *Failed States, Collapsed States, Weak States: Causes and Indicators.* Washington, DC: Brookings Institution.

Ruggie, J. G. (2007). "Business and Human Rights: The Evolving International Agenda." *American Journal of International Law* 101(4), 819–840.

Saez, M. (2019). "In the Right Direction: Family Diversity in the Inter-American System of Human Rights." *North Carolina Journal of International Law* 44(2), 317–352.

Sapignoli, M. (2017). "A Kaleidoscopic Institutional Form: Expertise and Transformation in the UN Permanent Forum on Indigenous Issues." In *Palaces of Hope: Anthropology of the United Nations*, edited by Ronald Niezen and Maria Sapignoli. Cambridge: Cambridge University Press, 78–105.

Sapignoli, M. (2018). *Hunting Justice: Displacement, Law and Activism in the Kalahari.* Cambridge: Cambridge University Press.

Sarat, A., and W. Felstiner (1995). *Divorce Lawyers and Their Clients: Power and Meaning in the Legal Process.* Oxford: Oxford University Press.

Saraviita, I. (1989). *YYA-sopimus.* Helsinki: Lakimiesliiton kustannus.

Sarfaty, G. (2012). *Values in Translation: Human Rights and the Culture of the World Bank.* Stanford, CA: Stanford University Press.

Schabas, W., ed. (2013). *The Universal Declaration of Human Rights: The Travaux Préparatoires.* Cambridge: Cambridge University Press.

Schachter, O. (1977). "The Invisible College of International Lawyers." *Northwestern University Law Review* 72(2), 217–226.

Scheinin, M. (1990). "The Status of Human Rights Conventions in Finnish Domestic Law." In *International Human Rights Norms in Domestic Law: Finnish and Polish Perspectives* (ed. A. Rosas). Helsinki: Finnish Lawyers Publishing Company, 25–43.

Scheinin, M. (1991). *Ihmisoikeudet Suomen oikeudessa.* Jyväskylä: Suomalainen Lakimiesyhdistys.

Scheinin, M. (1998). *Aseistakieltäytymisoikeus.* Helsinki: Hakapaino Oy.

Scheinin, M. (2009). "Toward a World Court of Human Rights." Agenda for Human Rights, June 2009. https://enlazandoalternativas.org/IMG/pdf/hrCourt_scheinin0609.pdf.

Schulte-Tenckhoff, I., and A. H. Khan (2011). "The Permanent Quest for a Mandate: Assessing the UN Permanent Forum on Indigenous Issues." *Griffith Law Review* 20(3), 673–701.

Scott, J. (1998). *Seeing Like a State: How Certain Schemes to Improve the Human Condition Have Failed.* New Haven, CT: Yale University Press.

Scott, S. V. (2018). "The Decline of International Law as a Normative Ideal." *Victoria University of Wellington Law Review* 49(4), 627–644.

Seibert-Fohr, A. (2018). "The UN Human Rights Committee." In *International Human Rights Institutions, Tribunals, and Courts,* edited by G. Oberleitner. Leiden: Springer, 1–25.

Seidenfaden, E. (2022). "The League of Nations' Collaboration with an 'International Public,' 1919–1939." *Contemporary European History* 31(3), 405–421.

Seiderman, I. (2019). "The UN High Commissioner for Human Rights in the Age of Global Backlash." *Netherlands Quarterly of Human Rights* 37(1), 5–13.

Sellars, K. (2002). *The Rise and Rise of Human Rights.* Phoenix Mill, UK: Sutton.

Seo, S. A. (2007). "A Shattered Dream: The American Law Institute and the Drafting of the International Bill of Rights." *Thomas Jefferson Law Review* 30, 179–196.

Shelton, D., ed. (2011). *International Law and Domestic Legal Systems: Incorporation, Transformation, and Persuasion.* Oxford: Oxford University Press.

Shikhelman. V. (2019). "Implementing Decisions of International Human Rights Institutions—Evidence from the United Nations Human Rights Committee." *European Journal of International Law* 30(3), 753–777.

Shipton, P. (2003). "Legalism and Loyalism: European, African, and Human 'Rights.'" In *At the Risk of Being Heard: Identity, Indigenous Rights, and Postcolonial States,* edited by B. Dean and J. Levi. Ann Arbor: University of Michigan Press, 45–79.

Shore, C., and S. Wright (2015). "Audit Culture Revisited: Rankings, Ratings, and the Reassembling of Society." *Current Anthropology* 56, 421–444.

Simmons, B. (2009). *Mobilizing for Human Rights: International Law in Domestic Politics.* Cambridge: Cambridge University Press.

Simpson, A. W. B. (2001). *Human Rights and the End of Empire: Britain and the Genesis of the European Convention.* Oxford: Oxford University Press.

Simpson, G. (2004). *Great Powers and Outlaw States: Unequal Sovereigns in the International Legal Order.* Cambridge: Cambridge University Press.

Simpson, G. (2015). "The Sentimental Life of International Law." *London Review of International Law* 3(3), 3–29.

Slotte, P., and M. Scheinin (2011). "Captain, Fire Brigade or Icebreaker? Political Legitimacy as a Rationale in Human Rights Adjudication." In *Legitimacy: The Treasure of Politics,* edited by T. Kurtén and L. Hertzberg. Lausanne: Peter Lang, 89–128.

Smith, J. M. (2021). *In the Eyes of the World: Mining the Digital Age in the Eastern DR Congo.* Chicago: University of Chicago Press.

Soave, T. (2022). *The Everyday Makers of International Law: From Great Halls to Back Rooms.* Cambridge: Cambridge University Press.

Soirila, U. (2021). *The Law of Humanity: A Story of International Law Reform and State Making.* London: Hart.

Steiner, H. J., and P. Alston (2002). *International Human Rights in Context: Law, Politics, Morals.* Oxford: Oxford University Press.

Strathern, M. (2000a). *Audit Cultures: Anthropological Studies in Accountability, Ethics and the Academy*. London: Routledge.

Strathern, M. (2000b). "The Tyranny of Transparency." *British Educational Research Journal* 26(3), 309–321.

Strathern, M. (2006). "Bullet-Proofing: A Tale from the United Kingdom." In *Documents: Artefacts of Modern Knowledge*, edited by A. Riles. Ann Arbor: University of Michigan Press, 181–205.

Taylor, P. M. (2020). *A Commentary on the International Covenant on Civil and Political Rights: The UN Human Rights Committee's Monitoring of ICCPR Rights*. Cambridge: Cambridge University Press.

Tervo, J. (1998). "Pintaremontti riittää." *Helsingin Sanomat, Kuukausiliite* 11, 36–38.

Tilden, S. J. (2018). "Africa's Conflict with the International Criminal Court: The African Court of Justice and Human and Peoples' Right as an Alternative to the ICC." *Tulane Journal of International and Comparative Law* 27, 201.

Tistounet, E. (2020). *The UN Human Rights Council: A Practical Anatomy*. Cheltenham, UK: Edward Elgar.

Toivanen, R. (2003). "Saami People and the Nordic Civil Societies." In *Civil Society in the Baltic Sea Region*, edited by N. Götz and J. Heckmann. Aldershot, UK: Ashgate, 205–216.

Toivanen, R. (2019). "European Fantasy of the Arctic Region and the Rise of Indigenous Sámi Voices in the Global Arena." In *Arctic Triumph*, edited by N. Sellheim, Y. Zaika, and I. Kelman. Cham, Switzerland: Springer Polar Sciences.

Tomkins, A. (2001). "Introduction: On Being Sceptical About Human Rights." In *Sceptical Essays on Human Rights*, edited by K. D. Ewing and A. Tomkins. Oxford: Oxford University Press, 1–11.

Törnudd, K. (2021). *Finland and the International Norms of Human Rights*. Leiden: Brill.

Trouillot, M.-R. (2001). "The Anthropology of the State in the Age of Globalization." *Current Anthropology* 42(1): 125–138.

Tsing, A. (2005). *Friction: An Ethnography of Global Connection*. Princeton, NJ: Princeton University Press.

Tsutsui, K., and C. M. Wotipka (2004). "Global Civil Society and the International Human Rights Movement: Citizen Participation in Human Rights International Nongovernmental Organizations." *Social Forces* 83(2), 587–620.

Tushnet, M. (1984). "An Essay on Rights." *Texas Law Review* 62(8), 1363–1403.

Tyagi, Y. (2011). *The UN Human Rights Committee: Practice and Procedure*. Cambridge: Cambridge University Press.

Tzouvala, N. (2020). *Capitalism as Civilisation: A History of International Law*. Cambridge: Cambridge University Press.

Urban, G. (2001). *Metaculture: How Culture Moves Through the World.* Minneapolis: University of Minnesota Press.

van Bueren, G. (2016). "Obituary: Professor Sir Nigel Rodley." *Queen Mary Human Rights Review* 3(1), 1–3. https://www.qmul.ac.uk/law/humanrights/media/humanrights/news/hrlr/2016/Professor-Sir-Nigel-Rodley--Obituary-FINAL-(1).pdf.

Vihavainen, T. (1991). *Kansakunta rähmällään: suomettumisen lyhyt historia*. Helsinki: Otava.

Viljanen, V.-P. (1996). "Perusoikeusuudistus ja kansainväliset ihmisoikeussopimukset." *Lakimies* 5–6, 788–815.

Walker, S. (1999). *In Defense of American Liberties: A History of the ACLU*. Rev. ed. Oxford: Oxford University Press.

Wallerstein, I. (2004). *World-Systems Analysis: An Introduction*. Durham, NC: Duke University Press.

Webb, K. (1997). *Signs of Recognition: Powers and Hazards of Representation in an Indonesian Society*. Chicago: University of Chicago Press.

Weber, M. (1978). "Bureaucracy." In *Economy and Society*, vol. 2, edited by G. Roth and C. Wittich. Berkeley: University of California Press, 956–1005.

Weiss, E., and C. McGranahan (2021). "Rethinking Pseudonyms in Ethnography: An Introduction." In *Rethinking Pseudonyms in Ethnography*, edited by C. McGranahan and E. Weiss, 13 December 2021, https://americanethnologist.org/features/collections/rethinking-pseudonyms-in-ethnography/rethinking-pseudonyms-in-ethnography-an-introduction.

Wenger, E. (1998). *Communities of Practice: Learning, Meaning, and Identity*. Cambridge: Cambridge University Press.

Werner, W. G. (2014). "The Politics of Expertise: Applying Paradoxes of Scientific Expertise to International Law." In *The Role of 'Experts' in International and European Decision-Making Processes: Advisors, Decision Makers or Irrelevant Actors?*, edited by M. Ambrus, K. Arts, E. Hey, and H. Raulus. Cambridge: Cambridge University Press.

Whyte, J. (2017). *Morals of the Market: Human Rights and the Rise of Neoliberalism*. New York: Verso.

Whyte, J. (2025). "Economic Coercion and the Crises of the (Neo)Liberal International Order." Keynote Address, "Crises Redux: Europe in a Global Context," Centre of Excellence in Law, Identity and the European Narratives, University of Helsinki, 1 October 2025.

Wilson, R. (2001). *The Politics of Truth and Reconciliation in South Africa*. Cambridge: Cambridge University Press.

Wong, W. (2012). *Internal Affairs: How the Structure of NGOs Transforms Human Rights*. Ithaca, NY: Cornell University Press.

Young, K. (2002). *The Law and Process of the UN Human Rights Committee*. Leiden: Brill.

INDEX